First World War

and Army of Occupation

War Diary

France, Belgium and Germany

14 DIVISION
Headquarters, Branches and Services
Royal Army Medical Corps
Assistant Director Medical Services
1 March 1915 - 30 November 1918

WO95/1884/1

The Naval & Military Press Ltd
www.nmarchive.com
Published in association with The National Archives

Published by

The Naval & Military Press Ltd

Unit 10 Ridgewood Industrial Park,

Uckfield, East Sussex,

TN22 5QE England

Tel: +44 (0) 1825 749494

www.naval-military-press.com

www.nmarchive.com

This diary has been reprinted in facsimile from the original. Any imperfections are inevitably reproduced and the quality may fall short of modern type and cartographic standards.

© Crown Copyright
Images reproduced by permission of The National Archives, London, England, 2015.

Contents

Document type	Place/Title	Date From	Date To
Heading	1884/1 14th Division 1915 Assistant Director 1919 Mar Medical Service		
Heading	14th Division Asst Dir. Med. Services Mar 1915 1919 Mar		
Heading	14th Division Hd. Qrs 14th Div (A.D.M.S.) Vol I From March to Aug 15 Dec 18		
War Diary	Aldershot	01/03/1915	01/03/1915
War Diary	Mobilization	19/05/1915	19/05/1915
War Diary	Boulougne	19/05/1915	20/05/1915
War Diary	Saint Omer	20/05/1915	20/05/1915
War Diary	Watten	21/05/1915	27/05/1915
War Diary	Steenvoorde	27/05/1915	30/05/1915
War Diary	Belgium	30/05/1915	30/05/1915
War Diary	Westoutre	30/05/1915	31/05/1915
War Diary	Visit of DMS II Corps	31/05/1915	31/05/1915
War Diary	Medical Arrangements	31/05/1915	31/05/1915
War Diary	Westoutre	31/05/1915	31/05/1915
War Diary	B. Rest Station	31/05/1915	31/05/1915
Heading	June 1915		
War Diary	Westoutre (Belgium)	01/06/1915	02/06/1915
War Diary	Westoutre	02/06/1915	13/06/1915
War Diary	Square L 13 (d) West of Poperinghe	14/06/1915	14/06/1915
War Diary	Square L 13/14	14/06/1915	21/06/1915
War Diary	Vlamertinghe S.W. Of	22/06/1915	27/08/1915
Heading	14th Division H.Q. 14th Division A.D.M.S Vol 2 Sept 15		
War Diary	H7.c7.7. Sheet 28 N.W. Belgium B Serves	01/09/1915	01/09/1915
War Diary	H7c77 Sheet 28 1/20,000	08/09/1915	20/09/1915
War Diary	See Proceding Pages 1 & 2	20/09/1915	27/09/1915
War Diary	See 1.2 & 3 Pages	27/09/1915	27/09/1915
War Diary	See Previous Pages	29/09/1915	30/09/1915
Miscellaneous	R.A.M.C. Operation Order No.4 By Colonel S. Guise Moores C.B. A.M.S. Commanding R.A.M. Corps, 14th Division	23/09/1915	23/09/1915
Miscellaneous	Appendix 2	30/09/1915	30/09/1915
Miscellaneous	Report On Aid Post At Bois Cross Road	27/09/1915	27/09/1915
Miscellaneous	2nd Attack On Bellewaarde (Battle Of Loos) 14th Division-6th Corps	26/09/1915	26/09/1915
Heading	H.Q. 14th Div A.D.M.S. Vol 3 Oct 15		
War Diary	Brandhoek	01/10/1915	31/10/1915
Map	Map		
Heading	H.Q. 14th Division A.D.M.S Vol 4 Nov 15		
War Diary	Brandhoek H.Q.14 Div	17/11/1915	17/11/1915
War Diary	Brandhoek	18/11/1915	18/11/1915
War Diary	Brandhoek H 7 C.8.5 H.Q	18/11/1915	18/11/1915
War Diary	Brandhoek HQ 14th Div	18/11/1915	19/11/1915
War Diary	Brandhoek	19/11/1915	21/11/1915
War Diary	Brandhoek H 7 C 8.5	22/11/1915	24/11/1915
War Diary	Brandhoek	24/11/1915	30/11/1915
Heading	A.D.M.S 14th Division Vol 5 Dec 1915		

War Diary	Brandhoek	01/12/1915	27/12/1915
War Diary	Brandhoek H 7 C 77	27/12/1915	27/12/1915
War Diary	Brandhoek	27/12/1915	31/12/1915
Heading	A.D.M.S. 14th Div. Vol 6 14 Div Jan 1916		
War Diary	Brandhoek	02/01/1916	30/01/1916
Miscellaneous	Defence Scheme Emergency Arrangements (Medical)	18/01/1916	18/01/1916
Heading	A.D.M.S. 14th Div Feb 1916		
War Diary	Brandhoek	01/02/1916	12/02/1916
War Diary	Esquelbecq	12/02/1916	18/02/1916
War Diary	Ref Map Lens 1/10000	18/02/1916	20/02/1916
War Diary	Flesselles	22/02/1916	23/02/1916
War Diary	Ref Sheets Lens 1/100000	24/02/1916	24/02/1916
War Diary	Flesselles	24/02/1916	24/02/1916
War Diary	Doullens	25/02/1916	25/02/1916
War Diary	Sus St Leger	26/03/1916	26/03/1916
War Diary	Barly	29/03/1916	29/03/1916
Heading	War Diaries Of A.D.M.S 14th Division For March April 1916		
Heading	ADMS 14 Div Vol 8		
War Diary	Barly	03/03/1916	03/03/1916
War Diary	Berneville	04/03/1916	15/03/1916
War Diary	Warlus	16/03/1916	30/03/1916
Heading	A.D.M.S. 14th Div April 1916		
War Diary	Warlus	01/04/1916	30/04/1916
Heading	A.D.M.S 14th Division May 1916		
War Diary	Warlus	01/05/1916	31/05/1916
Heading	A.D.M.S 14th Division June 1916		
War Diary	Warlus	01/06/1916	30/06/1916
Heading	A.D.M.S 14th Division July 1916		
War Diary	Warlus	01/07/1916	29/07/1916
War Diary	Sus-St-Leger	30/07/1916	30/07/1916
War Diary	Frohen Le Grand	31/07/1916	31/07/1916
Heading	A.D.M.S 14th Division August 1916		
War Diary	Bernaville	01/08/1916	12/08/1916
War Diary	Belle Vue Farm E 5 C 5.5	13/08/1916	31/08/1916
Miscellaneous	A.D.M.S Operation Order No.38 By Colonel M.G.	17/08/1916	17/08/1916
Miscellaneous	R.A.M.C. Operation Order No.39 Colonel H.V. Prynne A.M.S. Commanding R.A.M. Corps 14th Division	23/08/1916	23/08/1916
Heading	War Diary of A.D.M.S 14th (Light) Division For Month Of September 1916		
War Diary	Belloy	01/09/1916	01/09/1916
War Diary	St Leonard	02/09/1916	11/09/1916
War Diary	Buire Sur Ancre	12/09/1916	12/09/1916
War Diary	Fricourt Chateau F.36	13/09/1916	17/09/1916
War Diary	Buire Camp D 29.a.30	18/09/1916	22/09/1916
War Diary	Le Cauroy	23/09/1916	26/09/1916
War Diary	Gouy	27/09/1916	28/09/1916
War Diary	Warlus	29/09/1916	30/09/1916
Operation(al) Order(s)	R.A.M.C. Operation Order No.44 By Colonel H.V. Prynne A.M.S. Commanding R.A.M. Corps 14th Light Division	14/09/1916	14/09/1916
Heading	War Diary of Colonel H.V. Prynne A.M.S A.D.M.S 14th (Light) Division For Month Of October 1916		
War Diary	Warlus	02/10/1916	26/10/1916
War Diary	Le Cauroy	27/10/1916	31/10/1916

Operation(al) Order(s)	R.A.M.C. Operation Order No.47 By Colonel H.V. Prynne Commanding R.A.M. Corps 14th Division	17/10/1916	17/10/1916
Heading	War Diary of ADMS 14th Division For Month November 1916		
War Diary	Le Cauroy	01/11/1916	30/11/1916
Heading	A.D.M.S. 14th (Light) Division War Diary for Period- December 1 to 31 1916		
War Diary	Le Cauroy	01/12/1916	19/12/1916
War Diary	Warlus	20/12/1916	31/12/1916
Heading	War Diary of Colonel H.V. Prynne D.S.O. ADMS 14th Division January 1917		
War Diary	Warlus	01/01/1917	31/01/1917
Heading	War Diary of Colonel H.V. Prynne D.S.O. ADMS 14th Division For Month February 1917		
War Diary	Warlus	01/02/1917	28/02/1917
Heading	War Diary of Colonel H.V. Prynne D.S.O. ADMS 14th (Light) Division For Month Of March 1917		
War Diary	Warlus	01/03/1917	31/03/1917
Heading	War Diary of Colonel H.V. Prynne D.S.O. ADMS 14th (Light) Division For Month Of April 1917		
War Diary	Warlus	01/04/1917	23/04/1917
War Diary	Bailleulmont	24/04/1917	25/04/1917
War Diary	Arras	26/04/1917	30/04/1917
Miscellaneous	B.E.F. Summary Of Medical War Diaries For 14th Divn. 7th Corps 3rd Army		
Miscellaneous	B.E.F. 14th Divn. 7th Corps 3rd Army A.D.M.S Col. H.V. Prynne		
Heading	War Diary of Colonel H. V. Prynne D.S.O. A.M.S A.D.M.S 14th Division For Month Of May 1917		
War Diary	Arras	01/05/1917	18/05/1917
War Diary	M.25 A 60.5a	19/05/1917	31/05/1917
Miscellaneous	B.E.F. Summary Of Medical War Diaries For 14th Divn. 7th Corps 3rd Army		
Miscellaneous	B.E.F. 14th Divn. 7th Corps 3rd Army A.D.M.S. Col. H.V. Prynne		
Heading	War Diary A.D.M.S 14th (Light) Division June 1917		
War Diary	M 23.a 6.5	01/06/1917	09/06/1917
War Diary	Marieux	10/06/1917	30/06/1917
Heading	War Diary of ADMS 14th Division For July 1917		
War Diary	Marieux	01/07/1917	12/07/1917
War Diary	St Jans Cappel	13/07/1917	31/07/1917
Miscellaneous	B.E.F. Summary Of Medical War Diaries For 14th Divn. 9th Corps, 2nd Army. 2nd Corps, 5th Army From 15/8/17.		
Miscellaneous	B.E.F. 14th Divn. 9th Corps 2nd Army. A.D.M.S Lt. Col. H.V. Prynne	15/08/1917	15/08/1917
Heading	War Diary of ADMS 14th Division For Month Of August 1917		
War Diary	St. Jans Cappel	01/08/1917	05/08/1917
War Diary	Caestre	06/08/1917	14/08/1917
War Diary	Reninghelst	15/08/1917	17/08/1917
War Diary	H.27.b.6.8	18/08/1917	23/08/1917
War Diary	28 H 27 B6.8	24/08/1917	25/08/1917
War Diary	Reninghelst	26/08/1917	28/08/1917
War Diary	Berthen	29/08/1917	31/08/1917

Miscellaneous	B.E.F. Summary Of Medical War Diaries For 14th Divn. 9th Corps, 2nd Army. 2nd Corps, 5th Army From 15/8/17.		
Miscellaneous	B.E.F. Summary Of Medical War Diaries Of 14th Division		
Miscellaneous	B.E.F. 14th Division 2nd Corps 5th Army. 2nd Anzac Corps, 2nd Army	29/08/1917	29/08/1917
Miscellaneous	B.E.F. Summary Of Medical War Diaries Of 14th Division		
Miscellaneous	B.E.F. 14th Division 2nd Corps, 5th Army	29/08/1917	29/08/1917
Heading	War Diary of A.D.M.S 14th Division For Month Of September 1917		
War Diary	28.S.17 B.5.2	01/09/1917	30/09/1917
Miscellaneous	B.E.F. Summary Of Medical War Diaries Of 14th Division		
Miscellaneous	B.E.F. 14th Division 2nd Anzac Corps 2nd Army	02/09/1917	02/09/1917
Miscellaneous	B.E.F. Summary Of Medical War Diaries Of 14th Division		
Miscellaneous	B.E.F. 14th Division 2nd Anzac Corps 2nd Army Till 8th Corps	02/09/1917	02/09/1917
Heading	War Diary of A.D.M.S 14th Division For Month Of October 1917		
War Diary	28.S.17 B.2.2	01/10/1917	08/10/1917
War Diary	Westoutre	09/10/1917	10/10/1917
War Diary	28 M.6.d.5.8 Laclytte Camp	11/10/1917	18/10/1917
War Diary	28 M6.d.5.8	19/10/1917	23/10/1917
War Diary	Berthen	24/10/1917	31/10/1917
Miscellaneous	B.E.F. Summary of Medical War Diary For 14th Divn. 8th Corps 2nd Army		
Miscellaneous	B.E.F. 14th Divn. 8th Corps 2nd Army A.D.M.S 10th Corps	09/10/1917	09/10/1917
Miscellaneous	B.E.F. 14th Divn. 10th Corps 2nd Army A.D.M.S		
Miscellaneous	B.E.F. 14th Divn. 8th Corps 2nd Army A.D.M.S		
Miscellaneous	B.E.F. 14th Divn. 10th Corps 2nd Army A.D.M.S		
Heading	War Diary of Colonel H.V. Prynne D.S.O. A.M.S A.D.M.S 14th Division For Month Of November 1917		
War Diary	Berthen	01/11/1917	11/11/1917
War Diary	Wizernes	12/11/1917	30/11/1917
Miscellaneous	B.E.F. 14th Divn. 8th Corps 2nd Army A.D.M.S		
Heading	War Diary of A.D.M.S. 14th (Light) Division For December 1917		
War Diary	Wizernes	01/12/1917	02/12/1917
War Diary	Canal Bank Ypres I 1.b.7.8.	03/12/1917	26/12/1917
War Diary	Wizernes	27/12/1917	31/12/1917
Miscellaneous	B.E.F. Summary Of Medical War Diary For 14th Divn. 8th Corps, 2nd Army		
Miscellaneous	B.E.F. 14th Divn. 8th Corps 4th Army A.D.M.S		
Heading	War Diary of A.D.M.S 14th Division For Month Of January 1918		
War Diary	Wizernes	01/01/1918	03/01/1918
War Diary	Mericourt Sur Somme	04/01/1918	23/01/1918
War Diary	Guiscard	24/01/1918	27/01/1918
War Diary	Jussy M9.d.7.1	28/01/1918	31/01/1918
Heading	War Diary of A.D.M.S 14th Division For Month Of February 1918		
War Diary	Jussy M9.d.7.1	01/02/1918	16/02/1918

War Diary	Jussy	17/02/1918	28/02/1918
Heading	A.D.M.S 14 Divn From March 21st 1918		
War Diary	Jussy	21/03/1918	21/03/1918
War Diary	Beaumont En Beine	22/03/1918	23/03/1918
War Diary	Guivry	24/03/1918	24/03/1918
War Diary	Lassigny	25/03/1918	25/03/1918
War Diary	Chiry	26/03/1918	26/03/1918
War Diary	Villers Sur Coudon	27/03/1918	27/03/1918
War Diary	Estrees St Denis	28/03/1918	28/03/1918
War Diary	Sarron	29/03/1918	30/03/1918
War Diary	Hebecourt	31/03/1918	31/03/1918
Heading	War Diary of A.D.M.S 14th (Light) Division Form 1/4/18 To 30/4/18		
War Diary	Hebecourt	01/04/1918	01/04/1918
War Diary	Boves	02/04/1918	03/04/1918
War Diary	Aubigny	04/04/1918	04/04/1918
War Diary	Glisy	05/04/1918	07/04/1918
War Diary	St. Fuscien	08/04/1918	10/04/1918
War Diary	Feuquieres	11/04/1918	11/04/1918
War Diary	Hucqueliers	12/04/1918	15/04/1918
War Diary	Ecquerdecques	16/04/1918	21/04/1918
War Diary	Coyecque	22/04/1918	29/04/1918
War Diary	Torcy	30/04/1918	30/04/1918
Heading	A.D.M.S 14th (Light) Division War Diary from 1st May 1918 to 31st 1918		
War Diary	Torcy	01/05/1918	17/05/1918
War Diary	Moulin-le-Comte	12/05/1918	31/05/1918
Heading	14th Division A.D.M.S War Diary For Month Of June 1918		
War Diary	Moulin-le-Comte	01/06/1918	16/06/1918
War Diary	Boulogne	17/06/1918	17/06/1918
War Diary	Stoney Castle Camp	18/06/1918	30/06/1918
Heading	14th Division War Diary Period:- From 1st July 1918 to 31st July 1918		
War Diary	Brookwood (England)	01/07/1918	03/07/1918
War Diary	Folkestone	04/07/1918	04/07/1918
War Diary	Wierre Effroy	05/07/1918	12/07/1918
War Diary	Eperlecques	13/07/1918	31/07/1918
Heading	14th Division War Diary for A.D.M.S 14th Division from 1st August 1918 to 31st August 1918		
War Diary	Eperlecques	01/08/1918	19/08/1918
War Diary	Couthove (Chateau)	20/08/1918	31/08/1918
Heading	War Diary of A.D.M.S 14th Division From:- 1/9/18 To:- 30/9/18		
War Diary	Chateau	01/09/1918	01/09/1918
War Diary	Couthove	02/09/1918	20/09/1918
War Diary	Orwell Farm	21/09/1918	29/09/1918
War Diary	27/K.21c.23.	30/09/1918	30/09/1918
Operation(al) Order(s)	R.A.M.C. Operation Order No.14 By Colonel J. Hay Campbell D.S.O. A.D.M.S. Commanding R.A.M. Corps 14th Division		
Heading	14th Division War Diary of A.D.M.S 14th Division from:- 1st October 1918 to:- 31st October 1918		
War Diary	Waratah Camp 28/G 15a5.1	01/10/1918	09/10/1918
War Diary	Caestre	10/10/1918	17/10/1918
War Diary	Corps Farm	18/10/1918	19/10/1918

War Diary	Le Blanc Four	20/10/1918	21/10/1918
War Diary	Mouscron	22/10/1918	31/10/1918
Miscellaneous	Administrative Order No. 29 By Colonel J. Hay Campbell D.S.O. A.M.S. Commanding R.A.M. Corps 14th Division	01/10/1918	01/10/1918
Miscellaneous	Administrative Order No. 30 By Colonel J. Hay Campbell D.S.O. A.M.S. Commanding R.A.M. Corps 14th Division	03/10/1918	03/10/1918
Miscellaneous	Administrative Order No. 31 By Colonel J. Hay Campbell D.S.O. A.M.S. Commanding R.A.M. Corps 14th Division	04/10/1918	04/10/1918
Miscellaneous	Administrative Order No. 32 By Colonel J. Hay Campbell D.S.O. A.M.S. Commanding R.A.M. Corps 14th Division	12/10/1918	12/10/1918
Miscellaneous	R.A.M.C. Operation Order No.15 By Colonel J. Hay Campbell D.S.O. A.M.S Commanding R.A.M Corps 14th Division	13/10/1918	13/10/1918
Miscellaneous	R.A.M.C. Operation Order No.16 By Colonel J. Hay Campbell D.S.O. A.M.S Commanding R.A.M Corps 14th Division	15/10/1918	15/10/1918
Miscellaneous	Operation Order No.17 By Colonel J. Hay Campbell D.S.O. A.M.S Commanding R.A.M. Corps 14th Division	16/10/1918	16/10/1918
Miscellaneous	Operation Order No.18 By Colonel J. Hay Campbell D.S.O. A.M.S Commanding R.A.M. Corps 14th Division	17/10/1918	17/10/1918
Miscellaneous	Operation Order No.19 By Colonel J. Hay Campbell D.S.O. A.M.S Commanding R.A.M. Corps 14th Division	18/10/1918	18/10/1918
Miscellaneous	Administrative Order No. 34 By Colonel J. Hay Campbell D.S.O. A.M.S. Commanding R.A.M. Corps 14th Division	22/10/1918	22/10/1918
Miscellaneous	14th Division Medical Arrangements No. 17	31/10/1918	31/10/1918
Heading	14th Division War Diary of A.D.M.S 14th Division for Period 1st November 1918 to 30th November 1918		
War Diary	Mouscron	01/11/1918	04/11/1918
War Diary	Tourcoing	05/11/1918	30/11/1918
Operation(al) Order(s)	Operation Order No.20 By Colonel J. Hay. Campbell D.S.O. A.M.S., Commanding R.A.M. Corps 14th Division	08/11/1918	08/11/1918
Operation(al) Order(s)	Operation Order No.21 By Colonel J. Hay. Campbell D.S.O. A.M.S., Commanding R.A.M. Corps 14th Division	09/11/1918	09/11/1918
Operation(al) Order(s)	Operation Order No.22 By Colonel J. Hay. Campbell D.S.O. A.M.S., Commanding R.A.M. Corps 14th Division	13/11/1918	13/11/1918
Operation(al) Order(s)	Operation Order No.23 By Colonel J. Hay. Campbell D.S.O. A.M.S., Commanding R.A.M. Corps 14th Division	14/11/1918	14/11/1918
Heading	War Diary of A.D.M.S Office 14th Division 1st December 1918 To 31st December 1918		

1884/1

14th Division

1915 Mar Assistant Director
-1919 Mar Medical Services

14TH DIVISION

ASST DIR. MED. SERVICES

MAR 1915 - ~~DEC 1918~~ 1919 MAR

14th Division

121/6753

From March
To August 1915

S

Hd. Qrs: 14th Div: (A.D.M.S.)

Vol I

From March to Aug. 15

Dec '18

Summarised but not copied.

March — May/15

WAR DIARY
or
INTELLIGENCE SUMMARY.
(*Erase heading not required.*)

Army Form C. 2118.

Instructions regarding War Diaries and Intelligence Summaries are contained in F. S. Regs., Part II. and the Staff Manual respectively. Title pages will be prepared in manuscript.

Place	Date 1915	Hour	Summary of Events and Information	Remarks and references to Appendices
Aldershot	March		Joined the Division at Aldershot & reported arrival at H^d Qrs. MOORE LODGE. The Div^n is quartered mostly in the lines. (Stanhope lines.) Some units at BORDON, PANGBOURNE, & GUILDFORD	
Composition of 14th Light Division.			(A) H^d Qrs Staff.	
			G.O.C. Major Genl V. COUPER.	
			A.D.C. Lt. Fillson.	
			A.D.C. Lt. Mahoney.	
			1 G.S.O. Lt Col. Isacke	
			2 G.S.O. Major Dawe	
			3 G.S.O. Major Armitage	
			A.A. & Q.M.G. Lt Col Turner	
			D.A. & Q.M.G. Major Vivian	
			D.A.A. & Q.M.G. Major Conyers	
			A.D.M.S. Col Lane	
			D.A.D.M.S. Major Hartigan	
			A.D.V.S. Major Bartlett	
			D.A.D.O.S. Major Freeman	
			A.P.M. Major Cust.	

Instructions regarding War Diaries and Intelligence Summaries are contained in F. S. Regs., Part II. and the Staff Manual respectively. Title pages will be prepared in manuscript.

WAR DIARY
or
INTELLIGENCE SUMMARY.
(Erase heading not required.)

Army Form C. 2118.

2

Place	Date	Hour	Summary of Events and Information	Remarks and references to Appendices
Aldershot			(B) The following is the composition of the Division	
			41st Inf Brigade: 7th K.R. Rifles; 8th K.R. Rifles; 7th R. Brigade; 8th R. Brigade	
			42 Inf Brigade: 5th Shropshire Lt Inf; 5th Oxford & Bucks; 9th K.R. Rifles; 9th Rifle Brigade	
			43 Inf Brigade: 6th Somerset Lt Inf; 6 D. Cornwall Lt Inf; 6 K.O. York Lt Inf; 10 Durham Lt Inf	
			Divisional Artillery: 46 Brig. R.F.A.; 47th "; 48th "; 49th "; 14th Heavy Battery	
			Div. R.E.: 61 Fd Comp R.E.; 62 "; 89 "; Signal Comp R.E.	
			14th Cyclist Company	
			Pioneers. — 11th Liverpool Regt.	
			Divisional Train; Div. Amm. Column; Reserve Park; 42nd, 43rd, 44th Field Ambulance; 26 Sanitary Section; 17 Cas. Clearing Station *	[illegible]

Army Form C. 2118.

Instructions regarding War Diaries and Intelligence Summaries are contained in F. S. Regs., Part II. and the Staff Manual respectively. Title pages will be prepared in manuscript.

WAR DIARY
or
INTELLIGENCE SUMMARY.

(Erase heading not required.)

Place	Date	Hour	Summary of Events and Information	Remarks and references to Appendices
Aldershot	—		During the preliminary training men were trained in Sanitary duties, & some as Chiropodists. On receipt of Chemicals for purification of water the Special Water party men were put through a practical demonstration in the use of the Griffiths [?] water Carts. The Regtl. Officers showed good initiative & ability in their several charges. Camps inspected from time to time. Unfortunately an outbreak occurred in Bde. of measles & German measles with a few cases of Scarlet fever. Also some few cases of Cerebro Spinal fever. All precautions taken to isolate carriers by a systematic exam of the throats of all contacts, at the School of Army Sanitation. A Camp was formed at THESELDOWN, for the reception of contacts from measles. The health of the troops was on the whole good. Average from 3 to 6%. The measures for Anti Typhoid Inoculation were successfully carried out, the Bn. [?] units co-operating in promoting a high rate of percentage of Inoculated.	

1577 Wt. W10791/1773 500,000 1/15 D. D. & L. A.D.S.S./Forms/C. 2118.

Army Form C. 2118.

Instructions regarding War Diaries and Intelligence Summaries are contained in F. S. Regs., Part II. and the Staff Manual respectively. Title pages will be prepared in manuscript.

WAR DIARY
or
INTELLIGENCE SUMMARY.
(Erase heading not required.)

Place	Date	Hour	Summary of Events and Information	Remarks and references to Appendices
Other [illegible]			The Med. Equipment was [illegible] in Central, & was distributed to M.O. in charge of units. There was some delay in obtaining a thorough Equipment for the [illegible] & many of these showed signs of wear & tear after short period of use, due to faulty construction. Many parts found to be too weak to bear the strain. In the majority of cases only one set of [illegible] & Clothes was obtained from Field Stores prior to departure of the Division.	[illegible]
Mobilization.				
	19th May		The Division was ordered to proceed overseas, & various units left on 18 May for port of Embarkation according to W.O. Time Tables.	
BOULOGNE			I left with [illegible] Staff & C.R.A & [illegible] Staff & half Batt. of K.R. Rifles at 4.20 pm from ALDSHOT embarking at FOLKESTONE & crossing to BOULOGNE which port was reached at 10.40 pm	
	20th May		Left BOULOGNE by Motor Car for SAINT OMER at 10.20 Am, which place was reached at 12.30 pm	
SAINT OMER		12.30 pm	I reported to H^d Qrs, Office of D.G.M.S.	
			Inspected the [illegible] Ambulance [illegible] workshop, [illegible] in the Cattle Market, under Lieut BARTON.	

1577 Wt. W10791/1773 500,000 1/15 D. D. & L. A.D.S.S./Forms/C. 2118.

Army Form C. 2118.

Instructions regarding War Diaries and Intelligence Summaries are contained in F. S. Regs., Part II. and the Staff Manual respectively. Title pages will be prepared in manuscript.

WAR DIARY
or
INTELLIGENCE SUMMARY.
(*Erase heading not required.*)

Place	Date	Hour	Summary of Events and Information	Remarks and references to Appendices
St OMER	19th Aug	12 N	Found the Vehicles fairly complete & ready for use, 3 being under repair & some being painted.	
			The Officer i/c called attention to the weak design of the Springs of the SUNBEAM design heavy Ambulances	
			which are not capable of conveying more than 4 lying or 8 sitting — but are often asked to carry	
			more than this, with the result that the springs are strained.	
			This defect is capable of remedy by the artificers of the workshop.	
			Each Field Ambulance of the Div. will have 3 Heavy & 4 light (FORD) cars.	
	20th Aug	3 pm	— Proceeded the same afternoon to join the Division, in Hd Qrs group area, billetted at WATTEN	
			some 6 miles North West of SAINT OMER.	
			Water supply good, from pipe supply derived from Reservoir on the top of the hill.	
			Troops in barns & empty houses. Good sanitary conditions.	
			Report received that a case of Enteric fever had occurred in the area occupied by the 42 Inf Brigade	
			& some cases of Scarlet fever among civilian population. These houses are not occupied by troops	
			Portion of 46 Inf Brigade, & 41 Inf Brigade arrived during the afternoon.	
			42 Field Ambulance reported arrival at BOLZEELE.	
			Weather much warmer. Guns still [illegible] from [illegible] heavy [illegible].	

1577 Wt. W10791/1773 500,000 1/15 D. D. & L. A.D.S.S./Forms/C. 2118.

Instructions regarding War Diaries and Intelligence Summaries are contained in F. S. Regs., Part II. and the Staff Manual respectively. Title pages will be prepared in manuscript.

WAR DIARY
or
INTELLIGENCE SUMMARY.
(Erase heading not required.)

Army Form C. 2118.

Place	Date	Hour	Summary of Events and Information	Remarks and references to Appendices
WATTEN	21 May	—	Inspected billets & horse lines of 46 R.F.A. Brigade. Batteries arrived during the night. Also billets of 7th K.R. Rifles + No 2 Comp. Div. Train.	
WATTEN	22 May		Batt[eries] of 41st Inf Brigade arrived during the night & took up billets at MILLAIN. 2 Batteries of 46 Brigade R.F.A. arrived & billeted at WATTEN. Delay of movements of the Div. reported to be caused by fog in the Channel. Weather getting hot. Bright sunshine.	
"	23 May	1 pm	The Deputy D.G. Sanitary Officer passed through here on a tour of inspection.	
			During the night 8 pm 10 pm Somerset L.I. & Cornwall L.I. passed through railway St. en route for their Brigade area. Showing the resumption of the overseas traffic. HdQrs of 43 Brigade at LEDERZEELE.	
"	24 May	8 pm	44th Field Amb. passed through the station by foot march to billets at LE MONT (1 mile East of Town). 23rd Sanitary Section arrived with the above unit. Weather very hot + dusty.	

1577 Wt. W10791/1773 500,000 1/15 D. D. & L. A.D.S.S./Forms/C. 2118.

Army Form C. 2118.

Instructions regarding War Diaries and Intelligence Summaries are contained in F. S. Regs., Part II. and the Staff Manual respectively. Title pages will be prepared in manuscript.

WAR DIARY
or
INTELLIGENCE SUMMARY.
(Erase heading not required.)

Place	Date	Hour	Summary of Events and Information	Remarks and references to Appendices
WATTEN	25 May		Units keep arriving by train, so that the Division is now assuming its normal strength. Dispersed over a fairly large area some 8 miles x 8. Chiefly in Barns. Very clean. Water supply is suspicious, & all water for drinking treated by Chlorine. Inspected billets in 42 & 43 Brigade Area. Very hot day.	
WATTEN	26 May		Received instructions as to employment of Chemicals for keeping Respirators, Hypo & Soda Carb. As the Pioneer Batt (Liverpools) were to start early next morning – I took out a supply of the Chemicals, & personally spoke to O.C. & Adjutant & M.O. on the importance of the subject. From the M.O. was at that time instructing platoons. All Respirators to be Quilted. Quantities of Chemicals to be issued to this Batt. (Hypo – 70 lb, Soda Carb – 15 lb, Glycerine – 2 gals) for 500 men. All these Chemicals which are to scale, to be distributed under arrangement of O.C. to each Company entering the gas area. Carried by M.O. in Medicine Cart.	

1577 Wt. W10791/1773 500,000 1/15 D. D. & L. A.D.S.S./Forms/C. 2118.

Instructions regarding War Diaries and Intelligence Summaries are contained in F. S. Regs., Part II. and the Staff Manual respectively. Title pages will be prepared in manuscript.

WAR DIARY
or
INTELLIGENCE SUMMARY.
(Erase heading not required.)

Army Form C. 2118.

Place	Date	Hour	Summary of Events and Information	Remarks and references to Appendices
WATTEN	27 May.		The Division moved this day - Brigades by various routes all towards the front area. The 41st Inf Brigade starting at 5 pm yesterday 26th & 44 Field Ambulance to a position S.W of YPRES, are temporarily separated from the Division. Brigade Areas some 6 miles East of CASSEL, with Div Hd Qrs at STEENVOORDE. No 42 Field Ambulance at St SYLVESTRE CAPPEL, while 43 F Amb is on the right of the line at CAESTRE. Close billets, troops in farm houses & barns. Sanitary Section - distributed among Brigd Areas, 1 NCO & 4 men attached to each Field Ambulance: Hd Qrs at STEENVOORDE. The 4th NORTHUMBERLAND F. Amb. is billeted here, & capable of receiving light cases, & cases of Scabies. Town not very clean. Offensive smells & system of sewage into cesspools. Piped water supply. The only unit billeted being the 6th OXFORD & BUCKS L Inf. Divisional Cavalry Squadron has joined, & mobile Vet Section, making the Division complete. I motored via St OMER - & reported myself to DMS II Army at HAZEBROUCK. Saw the DADMS & received some information as to the methods of combating noxious gas. Reached Billeting Area at STEENVOORDE - at 3.30 pm. Strong cold North wind.	

Instructions regarding War Diaries and Intelligence Summaries are contained in F. S. Regs., Part II. and the Staff Manual respectively. Title pages will be prepared in manuscript.

Army Form C. 2118.

WAR DIARY
or
INTELLIGENCE SUMMARY.
(Erase heading not required.)

Place	Date	Hour	Summary of Events and Information	Remarks and references to Appendices
STEENVOORDE	7th May	3 pm	The Sanitary Officer 4 NORTHUMBERLAND Div. Army was superintending the evacuation of the cesspits in yard of MAIRIE, the building used as Div. H'Qrs, by means of large tanks & motor driven pumps = VIDAGES. Certain places in the town, at which British troops are billetted have been selected for this cleansing. Unfortunately the [illegible] & harness were taken back to HAZEBROUCK, causing great inconvenience as the English wagon harness will not fit the tank carts. However by borrowing spare parts, the RAMC & transport drivers succeeded in this service. It would be advisable for French harness to be always left with these wagons, as the absence of proper tools causes much delay. Men employed on this work should be provided with a working suit of canvas. [initials]	
"	8th May	10 am	The Officer i/c A. [illegible] WORKSHOP reported his arrival, & was directed to proceed to ST. SYLVESTRE CAPPEL to be attached for Rations to the 42 [illegible]. As there was some difficulty in obtaining rations when he was acting as an independent unit, & was with 2 different supply groups in as many days. It was thought that his services would be more useful if he were close to [illegible] Army.	
"	9	pm	The Artillery Brigades reached their new billeting areas along the line BORRÉ - PRADELLES — STRAZEELE. The Cyclists Company joined at this town. Weather cold & cloudy. Health of troops continues good.	

1577 Wt. W10791/1773 500,000 1/15 D. D. & L. A.D.S.S./Forms/C. 2118.

Army Form C. 2118.

WAR DIARY
or
INTELLIGENCE SUMMARY.
(Erase heading not required.)

Instructions regarding War Diaries and Intelligence Summaries are contained in F. S. Regs., Part II. and the Staff Manual respectively. Title pages will be prepared in manuscript.

Place	Date	Hour	Summary of Events and Information	Remarks and references to Appendices
STEENVOORDE	29th May	11.30 am	Inspected the [illegible] Oxford & Bucks L. Inf. ¾ mile south of the Town. Found that all men being in possession of respirators & arrangements made for the issue of Chemicals for replenishing these. Condition of Camp & arrangements satisfactory.	
		2.10 pm	Lt Col [illegible] RAMC [illegible] Infn 100 [illegible]	
STEENVOORDE	30th May	5 am	Sunday. The Division moved off early this morning & left HdQrs marching East to occupy the new Billeting area, between the POPERINGHE – YPRES Road on the north, BOESCHEPE – BAILLEUL on west, & DICKEBUSCH on Eastern extremity – in relief of the III Division. HdQrs Divn will be located at WESTOUTRE.	
		9.20 am	Motored to BAILLEUL at request of DDMS II Corps to have an interview at his Office. Accompanied by my DADMS & gathered information as to ordinary duties, & special attention directed to prevention of wastage in the fighting line. Also a discussion on the best methods of combating noxious gases. One case of Scarlet fever reported in "B" Company 9th [illegible] Rifles. Case transfd. to ST. OMER. Weather bright with cold wind.	[initials]
BELGIUM.				
WESTOUTRE		9.15 am	Arrived at new HdQrs in Belgium – the HdQrs of the 7th Division Field Ambulance, left for a 'point'	

1577 Wt. W10791/1773 500,000 1/15 D. D. & L. A.D.S.S./Forms/C. 2118.

WAR DIARY
or
INTELLIGENCE SUMMARY.
(Erase heading not required.)

Instructions regarding War Diaries and Intelligence Summaries are contained in F. S. Regs., Part II. and the Staff Manual respectively. Title pages will be prepared in manuscript.

Army Form C. 2118.

Place	Date	Hour	Summary of Events and Information	Remarks and references to Appendices
WESTOUTRE	31 May	9.15 a.m.	Left [illegible] BUSSEBOOM, some 2¼ mile S.E. of POPERINGHE.	
			The 42nd Field Ambulance had already taken over the building adapted as Office. Rest camps, Med. Inspection rooms in this town administered by the ADMS of 3rd Division, of whom I met in the Office.	
			This town is a mean little village & not particularly clean. Water is getting scarce. Drinking water from 2 pumps at a [illegible] farm some ¾ mile to the N.W., & this appears to be the sole supply for troops in the area. Scattered throughout the town are pumps, connected to shallow wells.	
BATH for troops			In a brewery in the town provision has been made for supplying hot baths to the troops. 50 men being accommodated at a time. Hot water admitted twice a day. Only 18" of water in the bath & no soap allowed. 500 kilos of coal allowed weekly for heating purposes.	
			Oxygen & Sulphur in bags is furnished for treating infected clothing. Cresol (about 1 pint) is added to the water in the bathing tank.	
			Patients have been prohibited from entering the main tank, but make use of tubs placed in a separate compartment. The effluent from the tank falls into a ditch. This method is not the best, as the water might find its way into the river.	
			The intake comes from springs in the hills, & is piped into the Brewery.	
			The supply is failing daily — & dries up annually from June to September, during which period	

Instructions regarding War Diaries and Intelligence Summaries are contained in F. S. Regs., Part II. and the Staff Manual respectively. Title pages will be prepared in manuscript.

WAR DIARY
or
INTELLIGENCE SUMMARY.
(Erase heading not required.)

Army Form C. 2118.

Place	Date	Hour	Summary of Events and Information	Remarks and references to Appendices
WESTOUTRE.	31 May		The water supply is obtained by manual labour (pumping) from a well fed by stream. The continuance of a supply to these baths is a problem to be solved.	
Visit of DMS II Army		1 pm	The DMS. II Army Surg General Porter paid a visit, & called attention to the necessity of best supervision by all med. officers to maintain the efficiency of our force at its fullest strength. Especially as to precautions to ensure that the troops understand the application of Respirators against gas, & need for alertness at all times in making use of preventative measures & constantly practising correct methods of using the Hypo preparations.	
Medical Arrangements		[illegible]	The 14th Division has entered the area in which of the 3rd Division II Corps, & the medical mobile units of the 14th Div are allotted to the area. The 42 F. Ambulance assuming the duties of the 7th F Ambulance, & taking over the Divisional Rest Camp & Officers Rest Hospital. The former at WESTOUTRE, the latter at MONT NOIR 1 1/2 miles to S.W. The 43 F Amb being stationed at LA CLYTTE & sending forward one section to DICKEBUSCH. This Unit is arranging for the training of junior officers & men of the RAMC in practical work of evacuating wounded from the trenches & This work has to be carried out by night.	

Instructions regarding War Diaries and Intelligence Summaries are contained in F. S. Regs., Part II. and the Staff Manual respectively. Title pages will be prepared in manuscript.

WAR DIARY
or
INTELLIGENCE SUMMARY.
(Erase heading not required.)

Army Form C. 2118.

Place	Date	Hour	Summary of Events and Information	Remarks and references to Appendices
WESTOUTRE	31 May. 1916		The 44th Field Ambulance is temporarily separated for instructional purposes, & is at LOCRE being instructed in practical work by the N. Midland Field Ambulance. Col. BEEVOR CMG	
Div. Rest Station			The Rest Station occupies 3 buildings in this village. One an Inspection Room with accommodation for Skin cases & Verminous patients; No. 2 a general reception for light ordinary cases, which No. 3 (a School) is at present not required.	
Water Supply in 14th Div. Area			The [illegible] supply is in a field in the centre of this village, & is conveniently central. No. 25 Sanitary Section have an office in the Town, & are working satisfactorily [illegible]. Water is scarce, & its provision in the area will require much care, & a certain amount of structural improvement to fully utilize the few sources available. A Committee reported upon the scheme & submitted proposals on 13th April. Col. Waite ADMS 3rd Division, an R.E. Officer & the DADMS (Sanitary) of the Corps — which I have this day received.	
			Chemical tests are made of all sources of supply — by Horrocks' method, Chlorine & KI, & Starch solution. These analyses are being carried out in the Office of the Sanitary Section.	

1577 Wt. W10791/1773 500,000 1/15 D. D. & L. A.D.S.S./Forms/C. 2118.

June/15

Instructions regarding War Diaries and Intelligence Summaries are contained in F. S. Regs., Part II. and the Staff Manual respectively. Title pages will be prepared in manuscript.

WAR DIARY
or
INTELLIGENCE SUMMARY.
(Erase heading not required.)

Army Form C. 2118.

Place	Date	Hour	Summary of Events and Information	Remarks and references to Appendices
			June 1915.	

1577 Wt. W10791/1773 500,000 1/15 D. D. & L. A.D.S.S./Forms/C. 2118.

Instructions regarding War Diaries and Intelligence Summaries are contained in F. S. Regs., Part II. and the Staff Manual respectively. Title pages will be prepared in manuscript.

WAR DIARY
or
INTELLIGENCE SUMMARY.
(Erase heading not required.)

Army Form C. 2118.

Place	Date	Hour	Summary of Events and Information	Remarks and references to Appendices
	June. 1915.			
WESTOUTRE (BELGIUM)	1st		44th Field Ambulance undergoing practical training the Bearers being pushed up into the trenches & motor ambulance visiting the Regimental aid posts each night. A few casualties occurred chiefly from "Snipers" - taken while approaching the trenches, or digging.	KEMMEL.
			In the same way the 43 Field Ambulance are assisting in evacuating wounded from the trenches to the S.E of DICKEBUSCH. Officers are taken in rotation to see the method of removal. One motor ambulance has proved sufficient. Only 4-6 casualties on an average per night.	
			The DADMS has been visiting most of the billets, & has spent last night in the trench with 43. Fd Ambulance.	
			The 7th F. Amb. III Div. removing all their equipment & apparatus for the baths. Referred the question to DDMS II Corps, who decided that the tubs etc were their property & to be removed.	
			They also are permitted to take away the Thresh Disinfector.	
			We shall now have to arrange for the supply of tubs / boilers to enable the baths at WESTOUTRE to be carried on. The DADOS 14th Div. has granted 500 francs to be spent in the purchase of boilers etc.	
			Water supply a great question, in all stations in the Div. area. No rain has fallen. Very hot.	
Do	2nd June		The 6th Sanitary Section is making analyses of the water supplies. Quality fair.	
			Have visited units round this town, & find sanitary arrangements satisfactorily carried out.	

1577 Wt. W10791/1773 500,000 1/15 D. D. & L. A.D.S.S./Forms/C. 2118.

Instructions regarding War Diaries and Intelligence Summaries are contained in F. S. Regs., Part II. and the Staff Manual respectively. Title pages will be prepared in manuscript.

WAR DIARY
or
INTELLIGENCE SUMMARY.
(Erase heading not required.)

Army Form C. 2118.

Place	Date	Hour	Summary of Events and Information	Remarks and references to Appendices
WESTOUTRE	June 2nd		One case of Measles reported in the Clerical Staff of Div! Train. The first case since leaving England. 3 contacts. Quarters (really Office) disinfected. Patient removed by Infectious Ambulance. Reported by Lt J. MORRISON. Weather very hot. Health of troops continues good. Owing to the fact that the troops of the 14th Div are widely scattered throughout other areas, it is not easy to gain a true estimate of the sick, as the cases pass through other Medical units. But we have adopted a system of mutual information	[illegible]
Do	June 3rd.		A few casualties occur nightly among the men in the trenches. The lightly wounded are treated locally, those severely wounded evacuated to the Casualty Clearing St! at BAILLEUL. Received a visit from ADMS 5th Div Col. [illegible] & met Col BEEVOR [illegible] 1st North Midland 46th DIVISION. We exchange views & gather much information from their experiences.	[illegible]
Ditto	4 June.		Very hot day. Water supply very scarce. This evening the 85th Brigade 3rd Div are joining the command, & will enter the trenches in the DICKEBUSCH fighting lines. These casualties will be evacuated by the 43 F. Amb. Col Ferguson ADMS of 3rd Div. came over to ascertain if arrangements were complete. This morning was notified to 43 Field Ambulance at DICKEBUSCH. Taken by hand by Lieut Stuart [illegible]	

1577 Wt. W10791/1773 500,000 1/15 D. D. & L. A.D.S.S./Forms/C. 2118.

Instructions regarding War Diaries and Intelligence Summaries are contained in F. S. Regs., Part II. and the Staff Manual respectively. Title pages will be prepared in manuscript.

WAR DIARY
or
INTELLIGENCE SUMMARY.
(Erase heading not required.)

Army Form C. 2118.

Place	Date	Hour	Summary of Events and Information	Remarks and references to Appendices
WESTOUTRE	June 4th.		The DADMS & D.A.D. Sanitary Section proceeded to BAILLEUL and on to HAZEBROUCK to purchase tubs & boilers for the baths. Two of the latter were obtained. It is proposed to modify the [illegible] arrangements by allowing more tubs of hot water & the use of soap soap to be issued free. The men's underclothing will then be disinfected by boiling with Cresol in the boilers & returned to them while still wet. & he will [illegible] them back to wash himself. The [illegible] tanks will be utilized for a plunge & splash after emerging from the hot water tubs. It is considered that no man can properly cleanse his skin without the use of soap.	
WESTOUTRE	5th June		The M.O. 1/10 Durham L.I. Inf. reports 20 men as suffering from SCURVY. In consultation with S.O.S. 14 Div. agreed to vary the [illegible] ration, & the following issues will be made: Vegetable Ration. (Fresh Vegetable — 3 days a week) (Preserved — 3 days a week) (Lime juice — 1 day a week) Some units are more favorably placed than others but the area is very crowded, & markets few, so that no facilities exist for the purchase of fruit & vegetables. Another problem is the supply of solution for [illegible] [illegible] gases. It has come to notice that	

1577 Wt. W10791/1773 500,000 1/15 D. D. & L. A.D.S.S./Forms/C. 2118.

Instructions regarding War Diaries and Intelligence Summaries are contained in F. S. Regs., Part II. and the Staff Manual respectively. Title pages will be prepared in manuscript.

WAR DIARY
or
INTELLIGENCE SUMMARY.
(Erase heading not required.)

Army Form C. 2118

Place	Date	Hour	Summary of Events and Information	Remarks and references to Appendices
WESTOUTRE.	1915. 5th June		Some units do not procure the crystals & glycerine as they should from the refilling point. The system adopted is that the Brigade Supply Officer should deliver in bulk, & Brigade Commanders arrange for the distribution to units. It is now contemplated to reduce the risk of accident by troops being found without an adequate supply – to establish depôts in area at which all the chemicals would be delivered & the solutions prepared by a special staff, & issued in tins. The units sending back empty tins, & drawing the solutions mixed in concentrated form. The most convenient spot for these depots being the Field Ambulances. At the same time it must be clearly understood that the supply of the service will remain under control of the Brigadiers & Staff & IS NOT MADE a medical service. The medical units exercising their knowledge in the mixing of the crystals only. A staff could be raised from men found unfit for the fighting line. Each depôt would require to be equipped with a boiler, coal, tubs for mixing, tanks for storing and the SOS has promised to deliver all empty petrol tins for the carriage to Regtl units. Since the solutions are different in composition, to avoid confusion I propose marking the tins by a band of paint. – Green for Respirators. Yellow for Knapsack Sprayers & Syringe pumps.	

1577 Wt. W10791/1773 500,000 1/15 D. D. & L. A.D.S.S./Forms/C. 2118.

Instructions regarding War Diaries and Intelligence Summaries are contained in F. S. Regs., Part II. and the Staff Manual respectively. Title pages will be prepared in manuscript.

WAR DIARY
or
INTELLIGENCE SUMMARY.
(Erase heading not required.)

Army Form C. 2118.

Place	Date	Hour	Summary of Events and Information	Remarks and references to Appendices
1915				
WESTOUTRE	6th June		The Brigades are this day ordered to move billeting areas the 41st moving North to take over trenches S.W. of St Eloi	
			The 42 entering the 46th N. Midland area for instruction in trenches round KEMMEL.	
			This involves a re-distribution of the Field Ambulances, i.e. a move round, occupying original sites.	
			The 44th F.A. — North to LA CLYTTE with an Inspection Room at DICKEBUSCH.	
			42nd Replacing 44th at LOCRE.	
			43rd " 42 at WESTOUTRE.	
			The period of training lasts 8 days.	
			The O.C. 42 F.Amb is anxious to retain the charge of the Officers Rest Hospital at MONT NOIR. This will be granted.	
			Some battalions Oxford & Bucks L.I. & 9th KRR & 7 KRR consequently pass out of the area, for this training.	
			The Durham Lt Inf & Yorkshire Lt Inf of 43 Brigade marching north East to occupy billets round DICKEBUSCH	
			The 8th KR Rifles are at CANADA HUTS.	
			Weather very hot. Water scarce. The chief source of supply being DICKEBUSCH ETANG	
			Regimental water carts have obtain water by the dams erected across the numerous small streams flowing North.	
			A few casualties occur daily. Troops are annoyed by snipers at night, while digging trenches.	
			Inspected Div. Cyclist Company at LA CLYTTE. Also the Laundry at this village.	

1577 Wt. W10791/1773 500,000 1/15 D. D. & L. A.D.S.S./Forms/C. 2118.

Instructions regarding War Diaries and Intelligence Summaries are contained in F. S. Regs., Part II. and the Staff Manual respectively. Title pages will be prepared in manuscript.

WAR DIARY
or
INTELLIGENCE SUMMARY.
(Erase heading not required.)

Army Form C. 2118.

Place	Date	Hour	Summary of Events and Information	Remarks and references to Appendices
WESTOUTRE.	1916 Jany.		Fresh orders received from GHQ in form of a circular giving the latest instructions as to methods of using Respirators & Smoke helmets. These are no longer to be moistened.	
			Great economy to be exercised in the use of Hypo which is difficult to procure.	
Respirators			This means drawing up fresh orders, & making fresh arrangements in the trenches. The majority of units in the Division are in possession of black gauze respirators. Others will be issued at once.	
			Visited the Officer R Hospl at MONT NOIR, as it was reported that the SADMS BAILLEUL had occupied one hut for the water guard.	
Mont Noir			The huts & their trench latrines are situated within the catchment area. Hear that the water supply of BAILLEUL is under control of Col Skinner DADMS - Sanitary Officer. The area is just outside our control. Matter referred to him, as it is proposed to abolish trench latrines & substitute buckets.	
			The manure at the farm should be burnt in an incinerator.	
			Reported that the automatic Ram pump is not delivering up to full capacity. Only 48 gallons a day received.	
			14 Officers under treatment. Prevailing disease - Influenza.	
			Cold very intense. This village lies in a hollow & is very trying. 57 cases in the Rest Station.	

1577 Wt. W10791/1773 500,000 1/15 D. D. & L. A.D.S.S./Forms/C. 2118.

Instructions regarding War Diaries and Intelligence Summaries are contained in F. S. Regs., Part II. and the Staff Manual respectively. Title pages will be prepared in manuscript.

WAR DIARY
or
INTELLIGENCE SUMMARY.

(Erase heading not required.)

Army Form C. 2118.

Place	Date	Hour	Summary of Events and Information	Remarks and references to Appendices
	1916.			
WESTOUTRE.	June 9th.		Accompanied the C.R.E. to various camps in the Area to decide on methods of improving water supplies, & the increase of water by sinking shallow wells. Inspected dam at the stream on LACLYTTE – KEMMEL Road. The C.R.E. found the earthen dam too weak. Leakage taking place at point where pipe pierces wall. Insufficient fall to filter tank. Proposed fresh dam by stream to the South to keep higher head of water, & lower intake pipe. Filter tank nearly completed. Suggested erection of a motor pump & storage tank from which water carts can fill direct. Visited LACLYTTE – water very scarce. Water may be obtained at depth of 8–12 feet. At ROSENHILL the stream was fair in capacity. Suggested cutting a trench in meadow to allow carts to fill more readily. In CANADA HUTS – water pumped to a trickling ditch. Drinking water brought by cart from DICKEBUSCH. The C.R.E. proposes to utilize the services of professional well sinkers. Wells to be lined with brick or stone.. Water carts are badly reported upon. Tyres buckled & special cloths shrunk. The water carts are not strong enough in construction to withstand these rough Belgian roads. The question of water for ablution purposes is being taken up. C.E. BAILLEUL requested to lend services of a specialist, but informed us by telegram to carry out temporary arrangements. Intense heat. Thunderstorm & slight shower.	
	June 10th.		Attended a practical demonstration at BAILLEUL on the protection afforded by Smoke helmets & Respirators. Representatives of all regiments in the Divn. & the Brigade Staffs witnessed the tests.	Th

1577 Wt. W10791/1773 500,000 1/15 D. D. & L. A.D.S.S./Forms/C. 2118.

Instructions regarding War Diaries and Intelligence Summaries are contained in F. S. Regs., Part II. and the Staff Manual respectively. Title pages will be prepared in manuscript.

WAR DIARY
or
INTELLIGENCE SUMMARY.

(Erase heading not required.)

Army Form C. 2118.

Place	Date	Hour	Summary of Events and Information	Remarks and references to Appendices
1915 WESTOUTRE	June 10th		The experiment was conducted in a trench, chlorine gas emitted from a cylinder. Everyone was unanimous as to the vast superiority of the Smoke Helmet. One was enabled to remain in the strongest gas with absolute comfort. The Helmet may be said to confer ABSOLUTE PROTECTION. It was not so with the Black Gauze Respirators. Even when carefully adjusted, one got occasional whiffs of gas, & coughing followed a short stay in the trench. In 3 cases men were quite distressed, cyanosed & in a condition that pointed to poisoning. One case was even admitted to Hospital. The use of the Respirators does not confer a sense of security & confidence. These will eventually be withdrawn & every man will be issued with 2 Helmets. Respirators should NOT be quitted. Management of the valve is not easy to acquire & practice without actual gas is useless, since one has not the moral effect of the presence of gas, & the actual discomfort attending faulty adjustment. Report upon this valuable demonstration was forwarded to the DDMS 2nd Corps, the same day. Heavy thunderstorm & rain during the night.	[initials]
	June 11th		Inspected the 3 wooden huts erected at LA CLYTTE forming a Laundry. All equipment has been removed, as being the property of the 3rd Division. Furnished report to AA & QMG as to what	

1577 Wt. W10791/1773 500,000 1/15 D. D. & L. A.D.S.S./Forms/C. 2118.

Instructions regarding War Diaries and Intelligence Summaries are contained in F. S. Regs., Part II. and the Staff Manual respectively. Title pages will be prepared in manuscript.

WAR DIARY
or
INTELLIGENCE SUMMARY.
(Erase heading not required.)

Army Form C. 2118.

Place	Date	Hour	Summary of Events and Information	Remarks and references to Appendices
WESTOUTRE	June 11th		Wringers [illegible] formally in use, & the general management of the institution. The DADMS & DADOS purchased a mangle & endeavoured to procure wooden tubs. Inspected well sunk 200 yds from LOCRE Road. This is the first constructed by Well Sinkers. Depth 17 feet reached. Heavy clay. Some rainfall	[illegible]
Do	June 12th		General redistribution these days of Battalions. Some Corps of [illegible] Division enter our area. Inspected Camps at CANADA Huts & Rosenhill. 102 Coy [illegible] — some artillery. Very hot day.	
Do	13 June		Inspected Laundry at LA CLYTTE with the AA & QMG. 42 Field Ambulance returns to WESTOUTRE and 43 move to 40 Divisional area at LOCRE. Visited water supply of area with CRE & Lieut Smith RE pointed out existing sources & selected sites for improving supply & spots at which shallow wells should be sunk. Officers Rest Hospital will be taken over by the 28th Division. Administration of 84th Field Ambulance. Orders issued for a general move to the north to a fresh area West of POPERINGHE. The 43 Field Amb & 43 Brigade remaining behind.	

1577 Wt. W10791/1773 500,000 1/15 D. D. & L. A.D.S.S./Forms/C. 2118.

Army Form C. 2118.

WAR DIARY
or
INTELLIGENCE SUMMARY.
(Erase heading not required.)

Instructions regarding War Diaries and Intelligence Summaries are contained in F. S. Regs., Part II. and the Staff Manual respectively. Title pages will be prepared in manuscript.

Place	Date	Hour	Summary of Events and Information	Remarks and references to Appendices
			Join V. Corps. II Army	
Reference Map of Belgium			Sheet 27. 1/40,000	
			The Division moved to a new area on joining the 5th Corps. Less 43 Brigade left in 46th Div Area	
Square L 13-(a) West of POPERINGHE.	June 14th		Hd Quarters in square named. 44 F. Ambulance in a field L 20 (c), while the 42 billeted in a brick field on Road to POPERINGHE. OK in place SCHOUDEMONTHOEK.	
			Divisional area = a parallelogram including the Squares K9 – 12 L 7–11 on the North; Squares K 21–24 — L 21. – 17. as a Southern boundary.	
			AREA • Poperinghe	
			The area has not been lately occupied by troops & farms is clean. Meadows & ploughs. Undulating & wooded. No running Streams. Water only in the wells in farms & few ponds for watering horses. This being a new area will require provision of a Div Rest Stn and Baths & Laundries.	
			The 5th Corps is Commanded by Lt. General Sir E H H Allenby K.C.B.	
			And Consists of the following Divisions (3rd Division, 14th ", 50th ")	
			DDMS = Col. E C Nicol. HdQrs at ABEELE.	

1577 Wt. W10791/1773 500,000 1/15 D. D. & L. A.D.S.S./Forms/C. 2118.

Army Form C. 2118.

WAR DIARY
or
INTELLIGENCE SUMMARY.
(Erase heading not required.)

Instructions regarding War Diaries and Intelligence Summaries are contained in F. S. Regs., Part II. and the Staff Manual respectively. Title pages will be prepared in manuscript.

Place	Date	Hour	Summary of Events and Information	Remarks and references to Appendices
1915				
Square L 13/14.	14 June		Farms [illegible] & officers very indifferent accommodation. Men bivouac in the open. Majority of officers of HQ Staff sleeping in bivouac shelters. Weather fine but hot. On rounds discovered that a death had taken place in farm occupied by [illegible] Rifle Brigade. Placed out of bounds. Cause of death reported as Typhus. Not yet verified. Report awaited from Civil M.O.H. at POPERINGHE. Went round billets of 41 Inf Brigade with AA & QMG. Troops had only just reached their farms	[initials]
Do. 15th	June		Reported myself to DDMS 5th Corps at his office ABEELE. = DADMS = Major Irvine	
			The 42 Field Ambulance ordered to move eastward to a point in H.7.c South East of VLAMERTINGHE. 41st Field Amb. in Brickfields off the POPERINGHE Road – SCHOUDEMONTHOEK – Square L. 17(a). Established a Div Rest Station. Accommodation found by removing bricks, & erecting protecting walls of sun dried bricks.	
Do. 16th	June		At 2.30 am this morning the 3rd DIV. made an assault on the German trenches, South of Bellewaarde Wood & Ridge. The 41st Brigade moving up in support to point East of YPRES. I 9 & 10. The 42 Brigade to be in readiness to move at ½ hours notice. 42 Field Amb. moved during the night of 15th & established Main Dressing Station	

1577 Wt. W10791/1773 500,000 1/15 D. D. & L. A.D.S.S./Forms/C. 2118.

Instructions regarding War Diaries and Intelligence Summaries are contained in F. S. Regs., Part II. and the Staff Manual respectively. Title pages will be prepared in manuscript.

WAR DIARY
or
INTELLIGENCE SUMMARY.
(Erase heading not required.)

Army Form C. 2118.

Place	Date	Hour	Summary of Events and Information	Remarks and references to Appendices
1915			Map of Belgium Sheet 27 1/40,000	
16 June			in a School house at East End of VLAMERTINGHE Square H.9.6. Sending forward personnel 2 officers & 40 men to establish advanced dressing station at H.12.c. ½ mile to the east of YPRES. No vehicles to pass further East than point H.13.C. Cross roads S.W. of YPRES. The bombardment was very severe & our troops succeeded in gaining the objective taking 3 lines of trenches. But failed to keep possession of the third. & were driven out of the first part of the 2nd line. At 3.30 pm the 92 Brigade moved up in support, & after meeting with some success, were compelled by shell fire to fall back on the first line, again along a front of ¾ mile. Casualties heavy. The main dressing station acting with some	
			The advanced dressing station at H.12.c was under shell fire & but few cases passed through, the greater number of wounded passing by motor ambulance direct to the main dressing station at square H.9.13d	
			All cases evacuated by convoy & motor ambulance wagons to C.C. Stations at BAILLEUL, by 7. a.m.	
			The work proceeded smoothly & may be regarded as most creditable	
			To assist in the work of evacuation the O.C. 91 F. Amb. sent forward a party of 6 stretcher squads & 3 motor ambulances, to the Rendezvous at H.13.C	
			Officers' comforts had been sent up – in anticipation of the engagement.	
			The following casualties occurred among the personnel of 92 F. Am.	
			NCOs & men. None – wounded 4. gassed 6. Evacuated wounded – 3 gassed – 4 } by bombs shells	
			Mech. Transport drivers – wounded 1. Evacuated.	

1577 Wt. W10791/1773 500,000 1/15 D. D. & L. A.D.S.S./Forms/C. 2118.

Instructions regarding War Diaries and Intelligence Summaries are contained in F. S. Regs., Part II. and the Staff Manual respectively. Title pages will be prepared in manuscript.

WAR DIARY
or
INTELLIGENCE SUMMARY.
(Erase heading not required.)

Army Form C. 2118.

Place	Date	Hour	Summary of Events and Information	Remarks and references to Appendices
1916			Ref. Map of Belgium Sheet 27.	
June 17th			Inspected area to be occupied by 47th Brigade as to the water supply. A few good farms but water scarce. No running streams. Well water suspicious. [illegible] 3 scoops to water cart	
June 18th			Visited VLAMERTINGHE with view of selecting the building for conversion into Div. Baths. A school close to west end of [illegible] the most suitable. But the town has lately received the attention of the Germans who threw heavy shells into the town. Went over the 6th Div. Baths. Very interesting & a similar [illegible] should be undertaken.	
June 19th			Inspected cyclist & cavalry camps found them most satisfactory. The D. 44 Field Ambulance moved from original site at [illegible] to field in Square L.20.B where the Div. Rest Station will be opened. Tents erected. Two good ponds & good well. All quiet in the trenches. A few casualties every night.	[illegible]
June 20th			The 48th Inf. Brigade will move tonight. The Div. Artillery arrived this morning. Distributed in Squares K.9. 10. 11 22. 28. The Div. Ammn Col in Square K.21.	

1577 Wt. W10791/1773 500,000 1/15 D. D. & L. A.D.S.S./Forms/C. 2118.

Instructions regarding War Diaries and Intelligence Summaries are contained in F. S. Regs., Part II. and the Staff Manual respectively. Title pages will be prepared in manuscript.

WAR DIARY
or
INTELLIGENCE SUMMARY.
(Erase heading not required.)

Army Form C. 2118.

Place	Date	Hour	Summary of Events and Information	Remarks and references to Appendices
1915				
	20 June	10 AM	Visited the DDMS 5th Corps & obtained some information as to routine duties based on the experience of previous months war.	
		3 pm	Paid a visit to No 7 Field Amb. III Division. Officer Commanding Major Fielding Ould who showed me the method of organization, & the special equipment. Method of handling supplies & stores	
			No 49 Field Amb is engaged in preparation of the new Div. Rest Station.	
			The DADMS proceeded to YPRES to inspect the sanitary condition of the portion of the town allotted to the Division. Found considerable accumulation of filth in rear of ramparts. 1 NCO & 3 men of Sanitary Section to assist in cleansing this area. 30 men of the Liverpool Regt (Pioneers) to work daily on this task.	
			Sanitation of New Area — Published in Routine Order No 177. details 1 NCO & 3 men per Battalion to assist the Sanitary Section in cleansing the area round huts A & B. Daily until the 25th inst. These are to be detailed from among the men least fitted for active service in the field. This party is in addition to the ordinary Regtl Sanitary police.	
			The Thresh Disinfector arrived on the 19th & is in the charge of 83 Sanitary Section.	

1577 Wt. W10791/1773 500,000 1/15 D. D. & L. A.D.S.S./Forms/C. 2118.

Army Form C. 2118.

WAR DIARY
or
INTELLIGENCE SUMMARY.
(Erase heading not required.)

Instructions regarding War Diaries and Intelligence Summaries are contained in F. S. Regs., Part II. and the Staff Manual respectively. Title pages will be prepared in manuscript.

Place	Date	Hour	Summary of Events and Information	Remarks and references to Appendices
			Ref. Map of Belgium Sheet 27. 1/40000	
	21st June		The Brigade Field Artillery rejoin from the South & are billeted in the area to the West. Squares K. 9.10.11.21. 22. 28	
		9 am	43 Inf Brigade also passed during early this morning & are in billets in Squares L. 8 & 9.10.11.	
			43 Field Ambulance in a farm Square L. 8. C 2/4.	
			44 F. Amb. are remaining 200 beds for evacuation in the Div Rest Station. Good field with 2 ponds & a large farm. L 20 b 7/7	
		2.30 pm	Went to VLAMERTINGHE to superintend some experiments with Stink bombs, conducted by C.R.E. in the brickfields.	
			Two bathing pigs were selected to test the effect of the gas. The experiment proved that this pattern of bomb was of little value. The area affected being very limited, & the gas too innocuous to distress or cause confusion.	
			The pigs were but slightly affected when 3 bombs were discharged simultaneously. Submitted a Report to H.Q. 14th Div. on the test. The C.R.E. also reported on the inadequacy of the gas used to have any value on the enemy. The gas was apparently SO_2.	
			Inspected proposed site for baths at VLAMERTINGHE – about 100 yds to the West of the Church.	
			Sanitary Section despatched 1 N.C.O. & 4 men to YPRES to clear up collection of filth in rear of the Corps at Ramparts.	
			30 men of the Pioneer Regt to be detailed daily to assist in this work.	
			Sentence of F.G. Court Martial was forwarded to Pte 44 Field Amb. – a sentence of 1 year IMPT with hard labour imposed on a Pte of the Reserve "for striking his Superior Officer, being in the execution of his Office"	

Instructions regarding War Diaries and Intelligence Summaries are contained in F. S. Regs., Part II. and the Staff Manual respectively. Title pages will be prepared in manuscript.

WAR DIARY
or
INTELLIGENCE SUMMARY.
(Erase heading not required.)

Army Form C. 2118.

Place 1915	Date	Hour	Summary of Events and Information	Remarks and references to Appendices
			Ref. map of Belgium Sheet 28. 1/40,000.	
VLAMERTINGHE S.W. of	22 June	8.30 am	H.Q. & [illegible] Staff. The Div. H.Qrs., [illegible] moved off this morning to occupy the new area 1¼ mile S.W. of VLAMERTINGHE. Squares H. 7, 8, & 14, to be nearer the advanced area. The 43 Field Amb. remaining in their position in Brigade Rest Area. The 44th being left as forming the Div. Rest Station.	
			The DADMS paid a tour of inspection with CRE to YPRES, to inspect the [illegible] & offer suggestions as to the disposal of refuse. A good deal of this work had to be carried out at night to avoid drawing fire by the smoke of burning [illegible] etc. This area is not in a good condition having been left with large accumulation of organic refuse. The Pioneers are furnishing 30 men for the improvement of the conditions. This officer also visited the "Ecole" – which is shared as an advanced Dressing Station by the 3rd Div.	
			Weather very fine. Scarcity of water being felt. The area is very densely occupied. The 42 Inf. Brigade are now holding our line of trenches. Drinking water from tanks, a piped supply laid on from the DICKEBUSCH ETANG.	
			This evening a second attack was arranged upon the German trenches. Preceded by a heavy bombardment. Assault timed for 8 pm. With the DADMS I motored up to the ASYLUM at YPRES, the Dressing Station of No. 4 Field Amb. 3rd Division. Wounded came through until midnight. The 42 Field Amb. at VLAMERTINGHE were also busy at that time. Returned to Camp at 1 A.M. Casualties estimated at 326. Heavy shelling & machine gun fire.	

1577 Wt. W10791/1773 500,000 1/15 D. D. & L. A.D.S.S./Forms/C. 2118.

Army Form C. 2118.

Instructions regarding War Diaries and Intelligence Summaries are contained in F. S. Regs., Part II. and the Staff Manual respectively. Title pages will be prepared in manuscript.

WAR DIARY
or
INTELLIGENCE SUMMARY.
(Erase heading not required.)

Place	Date	Hour	Summary of Events and Information	Remarks and references to Appendices
1915				
S.E. of VLAMERTINGHE.	June 23rd		The A.A. & Q.M.G. [illegible] has selected a site for Div. Baths & Laundry in a Convent at RUE BOESCHEPE – POPERINGHE.	
			Capt. Kay [illegible] has been detailed to act as Commandant, & took over this day. Women engaged at 2 francs per diem. About 800 men will be enabled to have baths during the day, & change of underclothing, the soiled articles being washed & stored for Re-issue. Soft Soap etc. being supplied free.	
			The Casualties of the attack on night of 22nd passed through the 42 Field Amb. amounted to 4 Officers & 85 other Ranks. No other details to hand. Wounds mostly due to Shrapnel.	
			The area taken over by this Division has been much occupied, & consequently found to be fouled with large accumulations of manure & litter. The previous occupants have not destroyed manure, & many heaps of tins & litter lying on the ground.	
			Inhabitants spreading manure on the fields & spraying crops with liquid manure.	
			Flies are beginning to be abundant. Troops are so occupied, that fatigue parties not procurable.	
			In addition to Sanitary Section 2 N.C.O.s & 10 men of K.R. Rifles detailed as special sanitary fatigue to clean H.Q. Divl. Camp. The ponds are very inferior, small & stagnant, & full of weed.	
			These have been walled off by [illegible] & small channels cut to pits the water being passed through coarse filter of bricks & shingle. Horses are not watered from troughs. Men will be provided with water on [illegible] by the R.E. Water may be found at a depth of 5-6 feet. Soil all coarse clay, so	

1577 Wt. W10791/1773 500,000 1/15 D. D. & L. A.D.S.S./Forms/C. 2118.

Instructions regarding War Diaries and Intelligence Summaries are contained in F. S. Regs., Part II. and the Staff Manual respectively. Title pages will be prepared in manuscript.

WAR DIARY

or

INTELLIGENCE SUMMARY.

(Erase heading not required.)

Army Form C. 2118.

Place	Date	Hour	Summary of Events and Information	Remarks and references to Appendices
	1915			
S.W. of VLAMERTINGHE	June 23rd		[illegible] precaution is slow, & the supply from the shallow wells likely to be very limited. There was a depth of 29" of water in a pit sunk in a marsh in the lines of Signal Company.	
			The case of suspected Enteric reported from No 2 C.C. Station, WHITTAKER 9th K.R. Rifles. (Inoculated) was notified to take all precautions. This camp is liable to be shelled, the German having large shells of high explosive, very close to the adjoining huts of 9th K.R.R. & Transport. So far no casualties have occurred.	[illegible]
Do	24th June		Rain fell last evening. Weather dull & cold last night. The Sanitary Section at YPRES, assisted by Pioneers, are making progress in removal of filth heaps in the Ramparts. Sanitary Section [illegible] by Regimental parties are cleansing this camp. The Regtl units Signal Company & 61st Co. R.E. are being instructed in Camp Sanitation. The ground is so neglected that many days must elapse before the required standard of cleanliness is attained.	
			[illegible] reported yesterday by Somerset L.I. [illegible] water proved very scarce. Only 1½ pint per man. Reported to D.A.D.M.S. & passed to C.R.E. for purpose of suggestions.	

1577 Wt. W10791/1773 500,000 1/15 D. D. & L. A.D.S.S./Forms/C. 2118.

Army Form C. 2118.

Instructions regarding War Diaries and Intelligence Summaries are contained in F. S. Regs., Part II. and the Staff Manual respectively. Title pages will be prepared in manuscript.

WAR DIARY
or
INTELLIGENCE SUMMARY.
(Erase heading not required.)

Place	Date	Hour	Summary of Events and Information	Remarks and references to Appendices
	24th June		I propose that water should be sent to farms in Artillery Area to the West, & farms visited in relation to wells, opportunity of filling. Agreed to suggestion of A.D. that an attempt should be made to find water by digging shallow wells in spot selected by him. The whole of this part of Belgium soil is apparently stiff yellow clay, & no water bearing area. The only alternative would be for the Brigade wishing to move their present billets down to lower ground. The D.M.S. reported having [illegible] [illegible] in POPERINGHE, & also at the [illegible] on WATOU Road.	
	25th June		This morning an exchange took place between 42 & 43 F. Amb. The 43rd F. Amb. moving up to the Advanced Area to carry out duties of [illegible] Dressing Station at the School VLAMERTINGHE, in which the 42nd Amb. go back to rest. The O.C.s handing & taking over all supplementary equipment, & med. stores. The Field Ambulance is found to be sufficient to remain open in this the Advanced Area. The 43rd Inf. Brigade are now in the trenches. Advanced [illegible] [illegible] [illegible] The D.A.D.M.S. Major [illegible] inspected the trenches occupied by [illegible] [illegible] Infy., & specially noted that arrangements are made for protection of wounded during the day time, & more suitable sites of Regtl. Aid Posts, & the position at which Regtl. Medical Officers should remain, so as to afford greatest assistance. The [illegible] [illegible] has dug out cavities in which wounded can be made comfortable until opportunity arises for removal. This area is most dangerous owing to the nature of the terrain & the dangerous angle of the German fire, owing to our position being at the apex of the Salient. Fire from 3 sides.	

Instructions regarding War Diaries and Intelligence Summaries are contained in F. S. Regs., Part II. and the Staff Manual respectively. Title pages will be prepared in manuscript.

WAR DIARY
or
INTELLIGENCE SUMMARY.
(Erase heading not required.)

Army Form C. 2118.

Place	Date	Hour	Summary of Events and Information	Remarks and references to Appendices
S.W VLAMERTINGHE.	1915		any movement behind the communicating trench drawing fire. & the wounded being compelled to traverse a long	
	23rd June		distance swept by shell & rifle fire. This area is admitted to be the most difficult for removal of wounded.	
		3.30 pm.	Visited the Div. Baths opened in Convent at POPERINGHE yesterday. Work was actively proceeding, & the building admirably	
			adapted to the purpose. Water is pumped from a stream passing outside the building. Staff of 7 men & 20 women	
Baths & Laundry			under Capt. Kaye R.A.M.C. Provision made for officers' baths. The men receive change of underclothing.	
			Clothes disinfected, washed & mangled on the premises. Thresh's Portable Disinfector — will be located at this laundry	
			to deal with lice infested clothing. The men to receive treatment by rubbing bodies over with paraffin.	
			There is some difficulty in disposal of sullage water which falls back into the stream.	
			At present this is allowed to pass into a series of 3 pits with coarse filtration through coarse brick rubble	
			But any cannot get rid of the soap in the water to any appreciable extent.	
Divisional Rest Stn		5 pm	Inspected Div Rest Station. — Progress being made. Ablution arrangements by tubs in the open air. Sullage	
			caught in sunken barrel, & spread by a pump over the grass.	
			30 circular [illegible] & 15 soil buckets to be indented for. The [illegible] in corner of camp	
			[illegible] in Rest Station = 130. Some [illegible] has been collected, & some R.E. [illegible] sent for their re-construction.	
Heavy Rain.			Heavy thunderstorm burst, with tropical downpour of rain. This is filling ponds & ditches.	
			These ditches are connected with ponds [illegible] & surface pollution is carried into the water.	
			Fields here are heavily manured, & also dressed with human excreta.	

Instructions regarding War Diaries and Intelligence Summaries are contained in F. S. Regs., Part II. and the Staff Manual respectively. Title pages will be prepared in manuscript.

WAR DIARY
or
INTELLIGENCE SUMMARY.
(Erase heading not required.)

Army Form C. 2118.

Place	Date	Hour	Summary of Events and Information	Remarks and references to Appendices
S.W. of VLAMERTINGHE	26 June		Arrangements being made for the trial of Method of [illegible] with [illegible] in prevention of [illegible] lice. [illegible] Also the application of Paraffin, then to be supplied at the Div. Baths.	
			Plan suggested for the accommodation of wounded in the Res. Trenches by digging out chambers for the use of Medical Service only. These dug outs to be handed over on relief of Battalions. These dug outs to be made under arrangement of Brigade Commanders. Approved by General Staff.	
		3 pm	Inspected Lines of R.E. & Brigade Transport in Square H.7.a. Few suggestions as to improvements in Sanitary condition. Insufficient pits. Incinerator not working. Latrine trenches of the [illegible] pattern. Not cut too wide & too deep. Progress being made in well being dug by 9 K.R.R. in the hop field. Good prospect of an ample supply. Sandy strata. Water rising up at a depth of about 8 feet.	[illegible]
	27th June	10.30 am	Accompanied the C.R.E. to Div. Baths at POPERINGHE. C.R.E. asked to make arrangement for raising water from the Stream & disposal of Sullage water. Pumps may be required for supplying water in the trenches. Work on the Div. Rest Station HILLHOEK as to purpose of erecting the wooden huts. Only 2 men of the R.E. available. More promised from [illegible]. Good progress being made in the Camp. 120 men in the camp.	
		5 pm	Examined & tested a VERMOREL SPRAYER. The apparatus yielded a fine, suitable spray. 4 of these sent up to the trenches.	
			Report forwarded for the better protection of water supply. Under order from [illegible] Corps a Board will be assembled immediately.	

Instructions regarding War Diaries and Intelligence Summaries are contained in F. S. Regs., Part II. and the Staff Manual respectively. Title pages will be prepared in manuscript.

WAR DIARY
or
INTELLIGENCE SUMMARY.
(*Erase heading not required.*)

Army Form C. 2118.

Place	Date	Hour	Summary of Events and Information	Remarks and references to Appendices
S.W. of VLAMERTINGHE			Lieut [illegible] [illegible] Ypres, will supervise the operations of the Board. Advised by C.E. 5th Corps a Representative of the C.R.E. of the Division, who will be responsible for the water supply of the Division & the A.D.M.S. or his Representative. A detailed reconnaissance of the water supply of the Div^l area is to be made	
Ditto	28th June		During the night of 27/28 the ECOLE was heavily shelled & ignited becoming untenable. The wounded having to be evacuated under a hot shell fire, & the risk of the work increased by reason of 3 unexploded shells remaining in the burning building. The fire was chiefly in central part & the cellars used as shelters for wounded. Lt McKenzie [illegible] worked with great gallantry & all ranks showed marked coolness under the conditions. The whole building has now been evacuated & is still burning.	
		11 AM	Brigade Head Qrs to be housed in the large magazine in the ramparts S of the MENIN Gate. Consequently the Ad. Dressing Station has been placed further to the rear, & fairly good shelter found in the cellars of the Prison. The building being a few hundred yards to the west of the [illegible]. I met [illegible] during the day. The Water Board is now making a reconnaissance of the supply in this area. The 6th Sanitary Section detailed as my representative, working in conjunction with the C.R.E.	
		12.30 pm	Visited the Div. Rest Station & was engaged in searching W. POPERINGHE for suitable building for the housing	

Instructions regarding War Diaries and Intelligence Summaries are contained in F. S. Regs., Part II. and the Staff Manual respectively. Title pages will be prepared in manuscript.

WAR DIARY
or
INTELLIGENCE SUMMARY.
(Erase heading not required.)

Army Form C. 2118.

Place	Date	Hour	Summary of Events and Information	Remarks and references to Appendices
Sh. 28 VLAMERTINGHE.	23rd June		of the Main Dr. Dressing Station. The present School at VLAMERTINGHE is too dangerous, being liable to bombardment by heavy guns every morning & evening, so as to be quite untenable. Found suitable accommodation in a Convent Rue Boeschepe. Occupied partly in Billets by the 14th Division	
"	24th June		Called on DDMS 5th Corps re the report. I was later taken to interview with the DA & QMG of the 5th Corps on the co-ordination of the work of the ADMS's of each Division in the Corps. The opinion of the ADMS's is to be sought before a Committee to be held from time to time. Such a Committee forming an advisory Board to the Corps Commander.	
5th Corps.			The ~~[illegible]~~ at present consists of the following Divisions (3rd Division, 14th ", 46th "	
			On pointing out to the DDMS 5th Corps the impossibility of longer holding the School at VLAMERTINGHE as a Main Dressing Station he issued verbal orders for me to take over the School at BRANDHOEK from the 3rd Division at present in charge of [illegible] [illegible] [illegible] to take over the Asylum outside YPRES. [illegible] to see the ADMS of 3rd Div. to arrange this movement of exchange. [illegible] referred for consideration of DDMS 5th Corps. No reply received this night.	

1577 Wt. W10791/1773 500,000 1/15 D. D. & L. A.D.S.S./Forms/C. 2118.

Instructions regarding War Diaries and Intelligence Summaries are contained in F. S. Regs., Part II. and the Staff Manual respectively. Title pages will be prepared in manuscript.

WAR DIARY
or
INTELLIGENCE SUMMARY.
(Erase heading not required.)

Army Form C. 2118.

Place	Date	Hour	Summary of Events and Information	Remarks and references to Appendices
Sh 1 VLAMERTINGHE	30 June	8.45 11 am	Received telegraphic instructions from DDMS 2nd Corps M/337. Cancelling previous arrangement. The 14th Div to take over the Asylum from 9th Field Ambulance. Instructed to hand over to O.C. 43 F Amb to inspect the building. Good accom. & spacious cellars. O.C. 43 F Amb to proceed there at 2 pm today. To which [illegible] 3 Med Offrs & the personnel [illegible] Division. The remaining personnel of Unit, with transport to be billeted in the fields, on the Poperinghe — ABEILLE Road. Sheet 27 – Square L 16.d.	
			The [illegible] personnel of Bearer Div. (& 1 Med Offr if necessary) to go up each night in 4 Daimler motor Ambulance wagons. Evacuation of wounded by motor amb. convoy to No. 10 C.C. Station.	
			1 Med Offr & [illegible] will remain at the Asylum YPRES until the 43 F Amb has become thoroughly established, which should be by 7 pm this evening.	
			The [illegible] at VLAMERTINGHE heavily shelled this morning. Shells falling in dangerous proximity in front & behind the building.	

1577 Wt. W10791/1773 500,000 1/15 D. D. & L. A.D.S.S./Forms/C. 2118.

Instructions regarding War Diaries and Intelligence Summaries are contained in F. S. Regs., Part II. and the Staff Manual respectively. Title pages will be prepared in manuscript.

WAR DIARY
or
INTELLIGENCE SUMMARY.
(Erase heading not required.)

Army Form C. 2118.

Place	Date	Hour	Summary of Events and Information	Remarks and references to Appendices
Sh VLAMERTINGHE	30	June	The 43 Field Amb. moved into the ASYLUM this afternoon. [?] Officers 18 men & 2 Heavy Motor Ambulances.	
			A.D.M.S. visited this Station at 10.30 pm & found all in satisfactory working order.	
		4 pm	Inspected the troops billeted in Square H.7 a & found arrangements good. Officers appreciate the necessity for strict sanitary measures. Area much crowded as the 41st Brigade Transport is parked here & a great number of horses. Two ponds of inferior water available.	
			The water supply by 8 K.R. Rifles a great success. A hose pipe to which pump from water cart, lifts the water into a trough.	
			A.D.M.S. & Sanitary Officer made a reconnaissance of the new Area, Squares G.17 & 18 (c & d) & reports good ponds. Farms are fairly numerous & available.	
Enteric Carriers			Steps are being taken to discover possible carriers by inspecting all men of the Division at the Baths. Any man who has previously contracted Enteric, to have a sample of his urine collected for testing. The test tubes will be collected & forwarded to Mobile Laboratory daily.	
			[illegible] Committee Representatives are making the reconnaissance of the water supply in the Div. area.	

1577 Wt. W10791/1773 500,000 1/15 D. D. & L. A.D.S.S./Forms/C. 2118.

July – August/15

Instructions regarding War Diaries and Intelligence Summaries are contained in F. S. Regs., Part II. and the Staff Manual respectively. Title pages will be prepared in manuscript.

WAR DIARY
or
INTELLIGENCE SUMMARY.
(Erase heading not required.)

Army Form C. 2118.

Place	Date	Hour	Summary of Events and Information	Remarks and references to Appendices
36 VLAMERTINGHE	1915. 1st July.		Inspected billets of 84th Brigade Transport Camp. The complaint of the camps being much fouled on their arrival. Accumulation of tins & litter unburnt. Empty tins thrown in water ponds etc. The same difficulty has occurred throughout our [illegible] areas. The camps are not properly cleaned by the outgoing units. The R.E. is particularly handicapped by shortage of men. [illegible] 4 horses.	
	2nd July.		Inspected 83 Inf Brigade area, & also sites for section of Horsfall Destructors. 15 of these have been allotted to the 5th Corps.	[initials]
	3rd July		DDMS 5th Corps inspected proposed sites for the 15 Horsfall destructors, & approved of the selected sites. Inspected lines of C.R.A. & some Field Companies of R.E.	
	5th July.		Visited 83 Inf Brigade area. Scarcity of water great problem. Well has been sunk by 5th DCLI but the sides have fallen in. The C.R.E. has this matter in hand. Water Board held a Committee meeting under order of 5th Corps yesterday. Attended by DADMS as representative of this Division. Weather extremely hot & oppressive. Two large shells were thrown into the Asylum building, tearing great holes in roof & walls but fortunately missing the block used as the M. Dressing Station.	

1577 Wt. W10791/1773 500,000 1/15 D. D. & L. A.D.S.S./Forms/C. 2118.

Instructions regarding War Diaries and Intelligence Summaries are contained in F. S. Regs., Part II. and the Staff Manual respectively. Title pages will be prepared in manuscript.

WAR DIARY
or
INTELLIGENCE SUMMARY.
(Erase heading not required.)

Army Form C. 2118.

Place	Date	Hour	Summary of Events and Information	Remarks and references to Appendices
3rd. VLAMERTINGHE.	5th July		Visited the College at POPERINGHE to be utilized as the Main Dressing Station. The building was formerly used as a Hosp. by the French & has good accomod. for wounded. Especially one large single ward, with tiled floor, on ground floor.	
			The O/43rd. Amb. visited the College & was pleased at the prospect of conversion	
			More large shells & shrapnel have been thrown into the buildings & yard of the Asylum at YPRES.	
			Heavy rain has fallen.	
			Lieut. Sheppard R.A.M.C. has assumed the Command of the Div. Baths at POPERINGHE.	
			Iron tank is now in place. Large Sedimentation tank being dug in the garden for disposal of sullage water.	
			The Sand bag Dam is working satisfactorily & holding up considerable head of water. 45 Women employed.	[initials]
	6th July		Accompanied AA.&QMG. & C.R.E. on a tour of inspection through Rest Area, to select site for erection of Winter	
Winter Hutments			huts for One Brigade. The Committee decided to place the camps on the high ground, along ridge running E–W. West of POPERINGHE, on those farms that are at present occupied by the Brigade of the 14th Divn. from L 10. A 7/9 – through L 9 B. 6/2 L 9 c. 8/0 L. 8 c 6/0 L 7 D. 7/2 L 7 a. 4/6 up to L 7 B. 2/8	
			And managed to find some good pasture land. Some of these farms possess fairly good ponds.	
Water supply			Some difficulty in obtaining water is found in Summer, but probably there will be an ample supply in Winter. Drinking water however must always be procured by water carts, from a distance.	
Change of M. D. Station			The 43 F. Amb. moved today into the new M. D. Station at the College, POPERINGHE.	[initials]

1577 Wt. W10791/1773 500,000 1/15 D. D. & L. A.D.S.S./Forms/C. 2118.

Instructions regarding War Diaries and Intelligence Summaries are contained in F. S. Regs., Part II. and the Staff Manual respectively. Title pages will be prepared in manuscript.

WAR DIARY
or
INTELLIGENCE SUMMARY.
(Erase heading not required.)

Army Form C. 2118.

Place	Date	Hour	Summary of Events and Information	Remarks and references to Appendices
[illegible] VLAMERTINGHE	1915. 10th July		[illegible] yesterday the 42 Inf Brigade reported having no water in the trenches, owing to the fact that the tanks were empty. It was ascertained that leakage had occurred in main pipe from the DICKEBUSCH ETANG to our tanks. The O.R.E. taking steps to locate & repair the damage. To supply 42 I. Brigade for the night water was [illegible] from our Reserve Supply - the well in Brickfields. No water available this morning. Troops dependent upon the pumps in farms throughout the area. Rainfall yesterday - which will add to yield of ponds. No timber available for the shoring up of wells.	
	11th July.		DADMS attended meeting of the Water Patrol Committee. Inspected the sites for erection of Hospital Destructor, with representative of the C.R.E. Lt [illegible] R.E.	
	12th July		The Med Officer of [illegible] reported that the [illegible] dug out aid post, have been shattered by shell fire during the night, & had become untenable. The wounded [illegible] being prepared along Communication Trench some 200 yards to the East. Weather dull & cold. Hospital destructor in process of erection.	[initials]
	13th July.		Attended weekly conference of ADMS of the 6th Corps at the Office of the DDMS ABEELE. Inspected the main dressing station [?] in the College POPERINGHE [illegible]. Heavy bombardment by 6th Division for 2 hours last night, N of YPRES.	

1577 Wt. W10791/1773 500,000 1/15 D. D. & L. A.D.S.S./Forms/C. 2118.

Army Form C. 2118.

Instructions regarding War Diaries and Intelligence Summaries are contained in F. S. Regs., Part II. and the Staff Manual respectively. Title pages will be prepared in manuscript.

WAR DIARY
or
INTELLIGENCE SUMMARY.
(Erase heading not required.)

Place	Date	Hour	Summary of Events and Information	Remarks and references to Appendices
FLAERTINGHE. 15 July			Inspected lines of 43 Inf Brigade. Some improvement noted in Sanitary measures, the use of [illegible] latrines being superseded by tins. The DLI have an [illegible] Incinerator in which faecal matter is destroyed. Several wells have been sunk by units & yielded fair amount of water for washing.	
			The Hospital Disinfector has been erected on parade ground of [illegible] Camp. That will be the central dumping ground for [illegible] of all units in this area.	
			Weather turned cold & rain in the evening.	
17th July			The DDMS inspected the water supply of YPRES with ADMS 5th Corps.	[illegible]
			A general move this day of the Field Ambulance units took place in [illegible] which as follows:-	
			42 Field Amb — To Div Rest Station — [illegible] — 44	
			43 F.A. — To Camp in Rest Area	
			44 F.A. — To Main Dressing Station POPERINGHE — & ADS at The Prison YPRES.	
			Very violent storm of wind & rain from 4 pm throughout the night 17/18.	
			[illegible] attached 6th D Cornwall L. Inf had been evacuated	
			The Field Amb. at 43 are now deficient of 6 Med Officers.	
18th July			The Hospital Disinfector was started this morning — 2 men [illegible] attached to H.Q. for this service.	[illegible]

1577 Wt. W10791/1773 500,000 1/15 D. D. & L. A.D.S.S./Forms/C. 2118.

Instructions regarding War Diaries and Intelligence Summaries are contained in F. S. Regs., Part II. and the Staff Manual respectively. Title pages will be prepared in manuscript.

WAR DIARY
or
INTELLIGENCE SUMMARY.
(Erase heading not required.)

Army Form C. 2118.

Place	Date	Hour	Summary of Events and Information	Remarks and references to Appendices
Sh'd VLAMERTINGHE	1915 20th July		Attended Conference at Office of DDMS. 6th Corps. Surg Gen. Porter DMS. 2nd Army happened to be present. Nothing of importance took place. A Change is impending in the transfer of the 14th (Light) Division to the 6th Corps.	[illegible]
"	21st July		Called on the DDMS. 6th Corps Col H. Thompson at the Chateau COUTHOVE. Inspected 43 & 45 [illegible] in the [illegible].	[illegible]
"	22 July		Heavy rain. The transfer of [illegible] & area of 14th Div postponed for 24 hours. Inspected 2 Battalions of 42 Inf Brigade in the Support Area. 3 [illegible] Men joined for duty from HAVRE – posted to the 43rd Field Ambulance	
	23rd July		Heavy rain again. The transfer of 14th Div & absorption into 6th Corps takes place today. The new area – is slightly to the north of existing area & extends in a narrow strip to north of Road POPERINGHE – VLAMERTINGHE. Squares G 2,3,4,5,6 (c & d) = lower half. Square 12 taken over from the 3rd Division. The boundary line follows the road through H. 1 c & d	

Army Form C. 2118.

Instructions regarding War Diaries and Intelligence Summaries are contained in F. S. Regs., Part II. and the Staff Manual respectively. Title pages will be prepared in manuscript.

WAR DIARY
or
INTELLIGENCE SUMMARY.
(Erase heading not required.)

Place	Date	Hour	Summary of Events and Information	Remarks and references to Appendices
23. July.			Northern [illegible] follows the railway line to the Canal, in Square I.7.c. [illegible] to the [illegible] of YPRES. The Southern Boundary follows the dividing line between the S.W. angle of Square G.12. and the S.E. of Square H.12. up to the Canal. The Rest Area also includes ground to the North of existing area to the [illegible] of POPERINGHE [illegible] area having WATOU as the [illegible] boundary from [illegible] junction F.28.d.5/3 – in NE direction to cross roads at F.21 a 2/6 thence S.E. along road to POPERINGHE in L.6.c Southern boundary a line drawn East from K.10 b 4/10 to L.12 a 6/10 The billets in this area have not yet been allotted.	[initials]
24th July			The School at BRANDHOEK used as an Advanced Dressing Station by [illegible] Field Amb. III Div. [illegible] allotted to the [illegible] Division by the [illegible] Corps. This took over the buildings in the afternoon [illegible] parties are looking at each of the farms selected for billets in the new area. The Sanitary Section are assisting in remedying defects in our new area The Field Amb. [illegible] will be [illegible] in a farm to [illegible] of Road to Proven. Square F.21.c. (Sheet 27)	

1577 Wt. W10791/1773 500,000 1/15 D. D. & L. A.D.S.S./Forms/C. 2118.

Instructions regarding War Diaries and Intelligence Summaries are contained in F. S. Regs., Part II. and the Staff Manual respectively. Title pages will be prepared in manuscript.

WAR DIARY

or

INTELLIGENCE SUMMARY.

(Erase heading not required.)

Army Form C. 2118.

Place	Date	Hour	Summary of Events and Information	Remarks and references to Appendices
	1915 24th July	pm	Attended a Conference at [illegible] for the Office of DDMS 6th Corps at which ADsMS & O.C. Field Ambulances, [illegible] of Sanitary Sections were present. The weekly Conference. Surg-Genl. PORTER. DMS II Army [illegible]. Nothing of importance brought forward. [illegible] of [illegible] in 14th Div. explained to the Conference.	[illegible]
	25th July		Nothing to note.	
	27th July		Preparations being made to cleanse & organize the new Camps. [illegible] have moved into Camps in the new area, to the north of the YPRES Road. The Corps Commander [illegible] that troops & vehicles be hidden from the sight of hostile aircraft. All bivouacs to be kept close to hedges. NOTHING allowed in centre of the fields. The state of the ground [illegible] fields will not permit of this since previous occupants have picketed horses, & dug latrines in these positions. Camps found far from satisfactory, much litter & manure left, which has had to be removed by our Division entailing much labour. Great improvement already effected, & sanitary arrangements placed on a good footing. It would appear that previous occupants did not [illegible] suitable & up to their [illegible]. The O.C. Sanitary Section has reported upon these Camp sites, & also upon the town of YPRES, & on the trenches. The Corps have much to learn as to the standard of cleanliness required. Great cleanliness has been shown in the town of YPRES, [illegible] the arrival of the Division [illegible] in a	

1577 Wt. W10791/1773 500,000 1/15 D. D. & L. A.D.S.S./Forms/C. 2118.

WAR DIARY
or
INTELLIGENCE SUMMARY.
(Erase heading not required.)

Army Form C. 2118.

Instructions regarding War Diaries and Intelligence Summaries are contained in F. S. Regs., Part II. and the Staff Manual respectively. Title pages will be prepared in manuscript.

Place	Date	Hour	Summary of Events and Information	Remarks and references to Appendices
[illegible] POPERINGHE			indescribable state: manure, animal & vegetable refuse & dead bodies. Great improvement has been made but much more is required. The task is a tremendous one. Streets are systematically cleansed, & buildings cleared of refuse. Owing to heavy shelling most of this work has been carried out at night.	
			The Sanitary Section is doing admirable work under the O.C. Lieut BROOKE-PIKE.	
			The DDMS 5th Corps visited YPRES in the morning with DADMS.	[illegible]
		Afternoon	accompanied the former on a tour of inspection. The following places were visited:-	
			1 Main Dressing Station POPERINGHE	
			2 Divisional Baths "	
			3 Div'l Rest Station HILLHOEK	
			Weather warmer. Cold. Strong wind from the N.W.	[illegible]
	28th June		Heavy gale accompanied by heavy rain storms.	

1577 Wt. W10791/1773 500,000 1/15 D. D. & L. A.D.S.S./Forms/C. 2118.

Army Form C. 2118.

WAR DIARY
or
INTELLIGENCE SUMMARY.
(Erase heading not required.)

Instructions regarding War Diaries and Intelligence Summaries are contained in F. S. Regs., Part II. and the Staff Manual respectively. Title pages will be prepared in manuscript.

Place	Date	Hour	Summary of Events and Information	Remarks and references to Appendices
E.B. VLAMERTINGHE	31 July		Owing to 14th Div. being engaged in vicinity of HOOGE, the 43 Field Ambulance ordered to assume the duties at the ASYLUM & take over the Collecting area from the O.A. 49 = Main Dressing Station. The change duly took place & during the night of 30/31 July the Germans directed heavy attack against our troops on the right of our Division in G. Sector. It was in this attack about 2.30 AM that use was made for the first time against this Div. of the so called Liquid fire. Casualties unusually heavy. A counter attack was organized entailing more losses. The heaviest losses falling on 41st Inf. Brigade. Our medical units received valuable assistance from the 46th N. Midland Division, on the right of our position. The M. A. Convoy performed splendid service, taking their motor cars well forward towards the scene of action. All ranks behaved splendidly. The evacuation was carried out rapidly & smoothly in face of heavy shell fire. Unfortunately trenches were lost & the fate of many men is still unknown. Fighting in Zouave & Sanctuary Woods — [illegible] & the continued bombardment prevents [illegible]. The Bearer Div & Regt. Stretcher bearers cannot continue in the [illegible] zone, after dawn which is about 3 AM. The casualties evacuated smoothly by M.A.C. to No 10 C.C. Station, & by ambulance train. During the fighting of this period I regret to report the deaths in action of 2 Med. Officers	

Instructions regarding War Diaries and Intelligence Summaries are contained in F. S. Regs., Part II. and the Staff Manual respectively. Title pages will be prepared in manuscript.

WAR DIARY
or
INTELLIGENCE SUMMARY.
(Erase heading not required.)

Army Form C. 2118.

Place	Date	Hour	Summary of Events and Information	Remarks and references to Appendices
S.W. of VLAMERTINGHE				
	July 31.		Wounded Lieut. G. McCullum attached to 6th Bn Cornwall L.I. } in action	
			Lieut. J. Hanke " 8. King R. Rifle Corps }	
			The casualties are not known to me	
			Number of wounded passed through the Div. medical units:–	
			Officers – 25 admitted 18 evacuated.	
			Other Ranks 890 " 788 " (8 died of wounds)	
			During the period of these attacks the enemy made much use of trench mortars, & hand bombs, with the result that upper limb multiple wounds were inflicted.	
			The DADMS remained with H.Qrs. or Advanced Report Centre.	[initials]
	1st August.		Counter attack of Huns ordered to recover the trenches lost in preceding bombardment.	
			Losses of our Army. Some of these wounded, were those uncollected from fight on previous day.	
			The same arrangements made for collection & evacuation.	
			Weather cold with heavy storms. Trenches wet & very muddy so that the clothes of wounded are in a terrible state.	
	2nd Aug.		The total wounded daily treated is greatly in excess of the average. Due partly to the greater number of troops & the severity of the shell & bomb fire.	

1577 Wt. W10791/1773 500,000 1/15 D. D. & L. A.D.S.S./Forms/C. 2118.

Instructions regarding War Diaries and Intelligence Summaries are contained in F. S. Regs., Part II. and the Staff Manual respectively. Title pages will be prepared in manuscript.

WAR DIARY
or
INTELLIGENCE SUMMARY.
(Erase heading not required.)

Army Form C. 2118.

Place	Date	Hour	Summary of Events and Information	Remarks and references to Appendices
S-W of VLAMERTINGE.	3 August		The losses in this division continue to be heavy, owing to the attempts made to improve the trenches low at HOOGE. The Germans concentrate every weapon upon our trenches. The greatest mischief being done by their trench mortars. A perfect hail of shell & incessant bombardment on the trenches in ZOUAVE & Sanctuary Woods. This being at the apex of our Salient, receives bombardment from 3 sides. The position of our trenches renders removal of the wounded most difficult & dangerous but in spite of the terrific fire, all ranks have worked with unflinching devotion. The Red Cross Service also deserve the highest credit for its splendid work in taking the Amb. Cars right up to the edge of the woods. The Germans persistently shell YPRES & the MENIN Road, & every vehicle runs the gauntlet of a succession of batteries in passing along the Road. Even the main dressing Station at POPERINGHE is liable to damage, the Germans retaliating by throwing shells of all sizes into that town. Sometimes 3 times a day. Every night or early morning huge projectiles drop on the town. VLAMERTINGHE through which the wounded must pass is similarly bombarded generally with high explosive shells. Known as "Whizz bangs" – which come without warning. The YPRES Road is absolutely ranged & swept by shrapnel. Our guns have steadily bombarded the trenches & German position at HOOGE. The wounded have been evacuated with great promptness.	

1577 Wt. W10791/1773 500,000 1/15 D. D. & L. A.D.S.S./Forms/C. 2118.

WAR DIARY
or
INTELLIGENCE SUMMARY.
(Erase heading not required.)

Army Form C. 2118.

Instructions regarding War Diaries and Intelligence Summaries are contained in F. S. Regs., Part II. and the Staff Manual respectively. Title pages will be prepared in manuscript.

Place	Date	Hour	Summary of Events and Information	Remarks and references to Appendices
S.6 - VLAMERTINGHE	1915 5/ August		Of the wounded that have passed through the Field Ambulances, we have so far between the 30th July & 4 August, registered a total of:—	
			Admitted { Officers — 50; Other Ranks — 1594 } Evacuated Officers — 48; " Other Ranks 1632 }	
			This will give an idea of the amount of work performed by the Regtl Medical Officers, working under heavy fire, & the Regt Stretcher Bearers, under most trying circumstances.	
			I must also place on record my thanks to the Field Ambulances of the 46th North Midland Division, for their great assistance, in feeding & evacuating 11 Officers & 128 Other Ranks.	
			The work of evacuation was carried out under arrangements made by the DADMS of the Division Major J. Hartigan RAMC, who was untiring in his efforts, & deserves the highest credit for his arrangements.	
			The Officers of all 3 Field Ambulances rendered splendid service in dressing the wounded at the various Dressing Stations.	
			The nature of the wounds, often multiple, made the task no easy one. Especially owing to the rapid flow of cases, owing to the fact that collection & clearing the trenches has to be completed before daybreak. No time is permitted in this war, to allow the RAMC to carry out their tasks. Motor ambulance cars are liable to be fired upon	

1577 Wt. W10791/1773 500,000 1/15 D. D. & L. A.D.S.S./Forms/C. 2118.

Instructions regarding War Diaries and Intelligence Summaries are contained in F. S. Regs., Part II. and the Staff Manual respectively. Title pages will be prepared in manuscript.

WAR DIARY
or
INTELLIGENCE SUMMARY.
(Erase heading not required.)

Army Form C. 2118.

Place	Date	Hour	Summary of Events and Information	Remarks and references to Appendices
Sh a VLAMERTINGHE	6th August		Yesterday the 5th inst the Rench line of G. Sector was handed over to the 6th Division, & under orders from DDMS 6th Corps — we handed over the Asylum to them for use as an Advanced Dressing Station. The Building was handed over to No. 16 Field Ambulance at 9 pm.	
			During the afternoon & evening violent bombardment by the Germans. They shelled the road to YPRES with shrapnel. Several casualties among the Regtl Transport going up with rations. Men & horses killed. Several shells dropped into the town of POPERINGHE.	
			1 man of 49th [illegible] killed & 14 wounded.	
			Heavy attack made at 3.30 this morning.	
		10 am.	I went to Hd.Qrs 6th Corps to meet a Commission on FLIES.	
			Inspected some of the camps in our area. Houseflies actively laying eggs & maggots recovered from dung heaps — especially those manure heaps in front of farm houses.	
			The floors of pig styes offer particularly favourable breeding ground. Thousands detected in the straw.	
			The Commission pointed out the method of identifying the various species of maggot flies, & the	

Instructions regarding War Diaries and Intelligence Summaries are contained in F. S. Regs., Part II. and the Staff Manual respectively. Title pages will be prepared in manuscript.

WAR DIARY
or
INTELLIGENCE SUMMARY.
(Erase heading not required.)

Army Form C. 2118.

Place	Date	Hour	Summary of Events and Information	Remarks and references to Appendices
1915 S.W. of VLAMERTINGHE.				
	7th August.		Div'l Head Qrs. returned from the ramparts at YPRES. Heavy shelling still going on over the town.	
	8th August.		The G.O.C. inspected new drafts of 7th K.R. Rifles & 8th R. Brigade. Some of them reported to be very young & poorly developed. School at VLAMERTINGHE evacuated.	
	9th August.		This morning an attack was made by 6th Div. against the Crater & Chateau at HOOGE. Heavy casualties among that Division. 42nd Inf Brigade at Y Wood suffered from shell fire.	
	10th August.		The taking of the [illegible] Crater [illegible] arrangements made in our sector as to collecting & evacuation of wounded. A.D.M.S. [illegible] visited POTIJZE (Chateau) to see the position & working of the F. Ambulance of 6th Division.	
	12th.		This evening there [illegible] several large shells (17") into VLAMERTINGHE. At [illegible] this morning the Germans bombarded YPRES with heavy shell and one of them falling into the Cathedral Vaults where the D.C.L.I. were billetted inflicted a heavy loss. A Rescue party was also [illegible] by further bombardment & among the killed were 3 men of the 44th Field Ambulance who formed part of the rescue party. The town being heavily shelled the road is impassable for traffic. ~~[illegible]~~ [illegible] specimens.	

Instructions regarding War Diaries and Intelligence Summaries are contained in F. S. Regs., Part II. and the Staff Manual respectively. Title Pages will be prepared in manuscript.

WAR DIARY
or
INTELLIGENCE SUMMARY
(Erase heading not required.)

Army Form C. 2118

Place	Date	Hour	Summary of Events and Information	Remarks and references to Appendices
1915			& Cars are diverted to the north.	
	12th Aug		Traffic has been suspended on the YPRES Road.	
			Heavy thunderstorms with tropical rain.	[illegible]
	14th August		Sir H. Plumer & Surg. Gen. Porter visited the Div. Rest Station in the afternoon.	[illegible]
	16th August		The usual transfer of duties taking place today	
			43 F. Amb. — to assume charge of D. Rest Station vice — 42nd	
			42 F. Amb. — to Clearing & Dressing Station " — 44th	
			44 F. Amb. — to Rest area.	
			The Officer i/c Div Baths also relieved Lt. [illegible] taking over the Baths.	
			Instructions are issued as to the disposal of cases of self inflicted wounds. A special building to be opened in BOESCHEPE. to be opened shortly. These cases are NOT to be treated in the Div Rest Station.	
			[illegible] & wagon lines of 47. 48 & 7th Brigades	[illegible]

1875 Wt. W593/826 1,000,000 4/15 J.B.C. & A. A.D.S.S./Forms/C. 2118.

Instructions regarding War Diaries and Intelligence Summaries are contained in F. S. Regs., Part II. and the Staff Manual respectively. Title Pages will be prepared in manuscript.

WAR DIARY
or
INTELLIGENCE SUMMARY
(Erase heading not required.)

Army Form C. 2118

Place	Date	Hour	Summary of Events and Information	Remarks and references to Appendices
N.W. of VLAMERTINGHE [illegible]	14/5		The 14th Div. line has been altered a new front, & the [illegible] sector G has been taken over by 6th Division. The new front extends from S. end of Y. Wood. Square I 12 c. 2.0. up to the VERLORENHOEK Road exclusive. Square I 5 a 1.9 with a special area for defence, to include the town of YPRES. The consequence of this alteration being to eliminate the collection of wounded from C. D. E. R. aid posts. The 14th Div retaining A & B. aid posts with a new post, dug outs at the Chateau at POTIJZE. Square I 4 a. 6.4. The line of evacuation for cases being along the Road de WESTROOSBEKE - to the Menin Gate YPRES with alternative route by motor ambulance through SAINT-JEAN - across canal to BRIELEN.	Map Sheet 28 N.W.
			Inspected transport lines of Durham L. Inf. + 9th K.R. Rifles.	
	14th August		Heavy shelling along the YPRES Road. Some shells thrown into the town of POPERINGHE, one falling close to the large Main Dressing Station. 42 Field Ambulance. Corps orders point to the need of selecting alternative roads, & also buildings & sites for bivouacs in the event of units being compelled to evacuate their present sites. The Town of POPERINGHE offers no facilities as all the large buildings have been shelled at one time or another & are situated in the line of fire. So that one must be	

Instructions regarding War Diaries and Intelligence Summaries are contained in F. S. Regs., Part II. and the Staff Manual respectively. Title Pages will be prepared in manuscript.

WAR DIARY
or
INTELLIGENCE SUMMARY
(Erase heading not required.)

Army Form C. 2118

Place	Date	Hour	Summary of Events and Information	Remarks and references to Appendices
S. 43 C/15 VLAMERTINGHE 19th Aug			Compelled to remove altogether away from the town, & find temporary accommodation in farm houses & barns.	
			The O.C. 42 F. Amb is making inspection of suitable buildings.	
			— Lt Col. H. Simson reports his departure on 7 days leave of absence on urgent private affairs to England	
			Capt Younger Ram. reports his arrival for duty with No. 44 Field Ambulance	
			— Capt Edwards posted for duty to No. 43 Field Amb. Lt. MacKenzie to 2nd Irish Rifles	[illegible]
			— Inspected transport lines of D.C. Light Inf. & No 6 Siege Battery.	
do	20th Aug		Inspected the Div. Rest Station — now under command of O.C. 43rd Field Ambulance	
			Progress is being made with the erection of a Dining hut. This will be capable of seating 130.	
			Found the Camp very clean & all arrangements satisfactory.	
			Called at Div. Dressing Station "POPERINGHE", found 2 cases of G.S. wound of abdomen, unfit for removal. The casualties of last few days have been lighter than usual.	
			— Inspected Camp of 42. Inf Brigade 2 Battalions & found the Battalions moving out of Camp. (Shropshire L. Inf & Rifle Brigade) Camp left clean. Occupied by D. Cornwall L. Inf. — and KOYLI at 6 pm	

1875 Wt. W593/826 1,000,000 4/15 J.B.C. & A. A.D.S.S./Forms/C. 2118.

Instructions regarding War Diaries and Intelligence Summaries are contained in F. S. Regs., Part II. and the Staff Manual respectively. Title Pages will be prepared in manuscript.

WAR DIARY
or
INTELLIGENCE SUMMARY
(Erase heading not required.)

Army Form C. 2118

Place	Date	Hour	Summary of Events and Information	Remarks and references to Appendices
14/15				
S.W. of VLAMERTINGHE	21st Aug		Very heavy rain & nights turned cold	
		2.30 pm	Attended the usual Conference of 6th Corps. Surg Genl Porter was present. Discussed the means of providing better sanitation in Camps & bivouacs. Also the question as to whether the motor cycle attached to the Field Ambulances should be placed at the disposal of the O.C. of that Unit for the purpose of inter communication. The DMS II Army is strongly in favour of the existing method, & wishes the cycles to be used for rapid transmission of messages between the Dressing Stations, & all points where speed is essential to the smooth working of evacuation of wounded. This question will be referred by him to G.H.Q. for a ruling.	
			The case of Enteric fever reported by Belgian Officials – a woman residing at House O/28 on VLAMERTINGHE Road in BRANDHOEK. Woman removed to Hospl. House placed out of bounds.	
			Capt Edward [illegible] RAMC has arrived & joined the 43rd Field Ambulance.	[illegible]
	22 Aug		Accompanied the AA & QMG 14th Div on a tour of inspection to various camping grounds.	
			Inspected the Wood in G.4. & found a space had been cleared on western fringe of undergrowth for erection of 20 huts. Water in moat of farm is very foul.	
			Visited camp of 8th R. Brigade recently taken over on evening of 20th [illegible] for 2 Battalions. Occupied by Shropshire Lt Infy	

1875 Wt. W593/826 1,000,000 4/15 J.B.C. & A. A.D.S.S./Forms/C. 2118.

Army Form C. 2118

Instructions regarding War Diaries and Intelligence Summaries are contained in F. S. Regs., Part II. and the Staff Manual respectively. Title Pages will be prepared in manuscript.

WAR DIARY
or
INTELLIGENCE SUMMARY
(Erase heading not required.)

Place	Date	Hour	Summary of Events and Information	Remarks and references to Appendices
Sth of VLAMERTINGHE.			Heavy shelling last evening – 8pm – 8.30 pm the German sending Jack Johnsons to left of VLAMERTINGHE Road searching for our heavy guns. Also shrapnel over the road in BRANDHOEK. Many large shells sent in to the town of POPERINGHE.	
	22 Augt.		The ADMS – 12th Div & 4 other officers of the same, paid a visit of inspection to our S. Section to see models. And were all highly interested, & expressed themselves as much pleased with all they saw.	
			A quiet day. The number of wounded recently much reduced.	
	23 Augt.		Inspected camps of 5th Oxford & Bucks & 6th Shropshire Lt. Inf. – Found movement between the 2 Battalions. All sanitary arrangements most satisfactory.	
	24th Augt.		Orders received from 6th Corps for Lt Col Fox. RAMC to proceed to England on being relieved by Major R. D. St. Vaughan.	
			Return of sick wastage shows a marked improvement in the 14th Division. Total sick. 90. Wounded. 143. Giving a percentage to strength of .48. The figures compare favourably with the divisions comprising the 2nd Army.	
			Inspected camp of 9th KR Rifles. Only transport left there at the time. Pointed out some minor defects. Drains to be cleared out & puddles filled in with dry earth.	

Instructions regarding War Diaries and Intelligence Summaries are contained in F. S. Regs., Part II. and the Staff Manual respectively. Title Pages will be prepared in manuscript.

WAR DIARY
or
INTELLIGENCE SUMMARY
(Erase heading not required.)

Army Form C. 2118

Place	Date	Hour	Summary of Events and Information	Remarks and references to Appendices
S.E. of VLAMERTINGHE	25 August		Received telegraphic instructions from 6th Corps that on being relieved by Col Guise-Moores CB I was to proceed to England, & report to War Office. A later telegram to Q. 14 Division from 6th Corps A 883. 7.15pm 24/8/15 confirmed this. During the afternoon Col. Guise-Moore arrived to assume duties of A.D.M.S.	
	26 August		Handing over to my successor. Col Guise-Moores CB visited some of the Infantry Camps. [illegible] visited the Div Baths, & Div Rest Station.	
			Lt Col [illegible] handed over command of 43rd Field Ambulance to Major W.F.H. Vaughan RAMC. [illegible] report of the latter received.	
			Lt Col Simson 44th F Amb returned from leave to England. Weather very hot & fine.	

1875 Wt. W593/826 1,000,000 4/15 J.B.C. & A. A.D.S.S./Forms/C. 2118.

Instructions regarding War Diaries and Intelligence Summaries are contained in F. S. Regs., Part II. and the Staff Manual respectively. Title Pages will be prepared in manuscript.

WAR DIARY
or
INTELLIGENCE SUMMARY
(Erase heading not required.)

Army Form C. 2118

Place	Date	Hour	Summary of Events and Information	Remarks and references to Appendices
St. J VLAMERTINGHE	27th August		I hand over the duties of ADMS on my departure to England in accordance with telegram A.883 of 6th Corps. Leave this morning 11.30 am for BOULOGNE. 27/8/15. [illegible]	

1875 Wt. W593/826 1,000,000 4/15 J.B.C. & A. A.D.S.S./Forms/C. 2118.

14th Division

121
7/121

Sept '15.

5

H.Q. 14th Division A.D.M.S.
Vol 2

Sept 15

Summarised but not copied.
Dec. 1917.

Instructions regarding War Diaries and Intelligence Summaries are contained in F. S. Regs., Part II, and the Staff Manual respectively. Title Pages will be prepared in manuscript.

WAR DIARY
or
INTELLIGENCE SUMMARY
(Erase heading not required.)

Army Form C. 2118

Maps: sheets 27 & 28 Belgium B series 1/20,000

1

Place	Date	Hour	Summary of Events and Information	Remarks and references to Appendices
H7 C 7.7. Sheet 28 NW Belgium B series	1.9.15		Colonel S GUISE-MOORES AMS took over charge of 14th Div: as ADMS from Colonel T.G. LAVIE AMS The Division has two Brigades in the advanced area east of YPRES & one in the forward area W of that town. The FA's are placed as follows, 42nd has an advanced dressing station in the prison at YPRES situated H12 b 6.5. & a main dressing station at the COLLEGE RUE BOESCHEPE, POPERINGE 43 Field ambulance under Major VAUGHAN RAMC acting as the Divisional rest station at 27. L20 d 3-5 Farm for the reception of non evacuation cases requiring rest & no 44 FAmb: under L'COL: SIMSON RAMC at L.3. There are three aid posts A at I9c.9 5. B at I10 a.7.3 in a dug out. A is in an old mill on the YPRES-MENIN road & the POTIYZE aid post at 4a.6 3. in a chateau. The B post is approached by a communication trench called WEST LANE approached from the MENIN road There are 2 RAMC personnel per Field ambulance attached to each aid post, relieved every 24 hours. In addition 4 men proceed each night to each aid post & remain till the wounded have been evacuated. A aid post is cleared by wheeled stretcher to the PRISON during the day & by motor ambulance from thence to POPERINGE by night 10-45 pm. "B" post is cleared by wheeled stretcher & handled chairs to "A" post at dusk & from Chateau POTIYZE by motor ambulance at 10.45 pm to POPERINGE - main dressing station If a large number of wounded have to be dealt with they are first taken to the Prison at YPRES so as to allow the cars to return quickly to the posts. One motor ambulance is always kept in the PRISON at YPRES	

[signature]

1875 Wt. W593/826 1,000,000 4/15 J.B.C. & A. A.D.S.S./Forms/C. 2118.

Army Form C. 2118.

Instructions regarding War Diaries and Intelligence Summaries are contained in F. S. Regs., Part II. and the Staff Manual respectively. Title Pages will be prepared in manuscript.

WAR DIARY
or
INTELLIGENCE SUMMARY
(Erase heading not required.)

Place	Date	Hour	Summary of Events and Information	Remarks and references to Appendices
H 7 C 7 7 Sheet 28 1/20000	8/9/15		Weekly wastage Officers 5 sick, 6 wounded O.R. 79 sick, 72 wounded. Total 84 sick + 78 wounded for week ending sept 4th. SGW	
"	13/9/15		The 43rd I.B. will relieve the 42nd I.B. in the right sector on the night 15th/16th Sept. The 3rd Division is on our right & the 6th & 49th on our left. Divisional Baths are situated on the S. side of the RUE DE BOESCHEPE POPERINGE. There each unit takes its turn of a hot bath, each man has his clothes ironed & has a complete set of clean under clothing issued in the place of those he takes off. Those he discards being washed after disinfection in a Thresh's disinfector & made ready for re-issue to incoming units. Week ending Sept 11 officers sick 5 wounded 5 OR sick 68 wounded 82 Sick to hospital 37. SGW	
"	17/9/15		Sheet 27 map 1/20000. Field ambulances changed over 42nd taking place of 44th. 44th FA going into the Div: Rest camp & 43rd which was in the Div. Rest Camp taking the place of the 42nd. Lt BARR of the 42nd FA relieving Lt BROWN of the 44th FA at the Divisional Baths.	
	20/9/15		SGW Proposed scheme for collection & evacuation of wounded from H sector map Sheet 28 NW. Belgium 1/20,000 Regimental aid posts ① Dug outs in the railway embankment at I 11 b 0.5 ② Dugouts allotted for the purpose in R4 & S18 ③ Dug-outs under the MENIN ROAD at I 17 b. 1.9 Besides the regimental medical establishments two RAMC nursing orderlies will be posted at each of the above. Aid Posts (additional) will be established at the following places the personnel being found from the Field Amb I 10 A. 83 & The PRISON YPRES Week ending Sep 18 Sick officers 7 wounded 5. OR sick 56 wounded 71 Sick to hospital 32	

1875 Wt. W593/826 1,000,000 4/15 J.B.C. & A. A.D.S.S./Forms/C. 2118.

Instructions regarding War Diaries and Intelligence Summaries are contained in F. S. Regs., Part II. and the Staff Manual respectively. Title Pages will be prepared in manuscript.

WAR DIARY
or
INTELLIGENCE SUMMARY
(Erase heading not required.)

Army Form C. 2118

Place	Date	Hour	Summary of Events and Information	Remarks and references to Appendices
See preceding pages 1 + 2	20/9/15		Advanced Dressing Station THE MILL on the MENIN ROAD I.9.b.0.5. Main dressing Stations (1) THE ASYLUM at H.12.d + (2) THE COLLEGE RUE BOESCHEPE POPERINGHE. Motor ambulances will rendezvous at the road junction at I.9.D.7.4 at dusk. If circumstances permit walking cases should be evacuated during the day. They should be directed to proceed to the ASYLUM. Any requiring treatment en route can obtain same either at the Advanced dressing station or at the PRISON YPRES. As far as possible wounded unable to walk should be carried to the Regimental aid Posts by the Stretcher Bearers (regimental). Cases that cannot be so moved should be collected at suitable places & the positions of the latter & their approximate number be reported to the MO at the nearest aid post. Stretcher bearer parties will proceed at dusk to the aid posts & remove patients to motor ambulances. After the Aid posts have been cleared wounded collected in the front of the line will be similarly removed. In order that all wounded are satisfactorily removed before dawn it is most essential that the position of the wounded be reported to MOs at aid posts. Copies of operation orders will be [illegible]	
			[initials]	
	27/9/15		Operation orders Divisional no 29 dated 23 Sept. 1915 & RAMC operation (~~no 4~~) orders dated 23rd Sept 1915 connected with the former are attached as appendices 2 & 4 respectively. Wounded coming from the [illegible] S. of YPRES were if serious taken direct to the 10th or 17th CCS at L 23 a sheet 27 1/40000 other cases were sent from the Divisional collecting Station to the main dressing station at THE COLLEGE RUE BOESCHEPE POPERINGHE	

Instructions regarding War Diaries and Intelligence Summaries are contained in F. S. Regs., Part II. and the Staff Manual respectively. Title Pages will be prepared in manuscript.

WAR DIARY
or
INTELLIGENCE SUMMARY
(Erase heading not required.)

Army Form C. 2118.

Page 4.

Place	Date	Hour	Summary of Events and Information	Remarks and references to Appendices
27/9/15 see 1.2 & 3 pages		11 Am	Daily state of wounded from noon 25/9/15 to noon 26 admitted to Field Ambulances 16 officers & 1137 O.R. of these 16 officers & 958 were transferred to Nos 10 & 17 C.C. Station & 178 to Div: Rest Station: & 1 officer & 1 man died The Bearer Divisions were accommodated in the dugouts N of the MENIN GATE from the 7 pm 24th inst till 27th. The dugouts (Regimental aid post) at the BIRR X ROADS were (2 dugouts out of 4) destroyed by shell fire on 25th By midday 25th OC 42 F.A. Capt ROBERTS (OC DIV COLLECTING STATION) reports approximate numbers evacuated are 675 admitted of these 225 wounded have been dressed & evacuated to CCS. These cases are walking cases. The severely wounded are not evacuated till night fall. To evacuate the Div: Coll: Station, 197 of the 675 were passed on to the 43 F.A. without being dressed. The 43 FA formed the MAIN dressing station in POPERINGHE. The aid post at YPRES PRISON reports that up to 4-45 pm on 25th he had dressed & evacuated 130 cases of lightly wounded to main dressing station additional cars being sent every ¼ of an hour to ensure rapid evacuation. Week ending Sept 25 Officers sick 4. wounded 20 OR sick 77 wounded 297 Sick % of strength ·41	J.C.M.
27/9/15		1 pm	The Bearers of the FA's worked in advance of the aid posts during the night of 25th & 26th. Evacuated wounded by FA's ~~night~~ 26-27 noon to noon 2 officers + 86 OR of these 2 officers & 75 OR were transferred to No 10 CCS. & 7 to the Div: Rest Station.	

1875 Wt. W593/826 1,000,000 4/15 J.B.C. & A. A.D.S.S./Forms/C. 2118.

Instructions regarding War Diaries and Intelligence Summaries are contained in F. S. Regs., Part II. and the Staff Manual respectively. Title Pages will be prepared in manuscript.

WAR DIARY
or
INTELLIGENCE SUMMARY
(Erase heading not required.)

Army Form C. 2118

Place	Date	Hour	Summary of Events and Information	Remarks and references to Appendices
See previous pages.	29/9/15		See appendix 3 for note from MOs i/c: Ox & Bucks & KSLI regiments on the condition of aid posts &c. Report on work done by 42 FA on 25-27th	
	30/9/15		Sept attached appendix 3. Week ending Oct 2nd. Officers 1 (sick), wounded 23. OR 99 sick, wounded 1098. Total sick 100 wounded 1121. Sick to hospital 55.	
			J. Grew Moore Col ADMS 14 Div HQ in the Field 2/X/15.	

1875 Wt. W593/826 1,000,000 4/15 J.B.C. & A. A.D.S.S./Forms/C. 2118.

Appendix (1) Copy No 6

R.A.M.C. Operation Order No 4, by Colonel S. Guise Moores C.B., A.D.M.S., Commanding R.A.M.Corps, 14th Division.

23rd. September 1915.

Reference HOOGE Sheet 1/10,000 and Squared Map, Sheet 28.

INTENTION.

1. The G.O.C. intends to assault the enemy's position from I 12 d 2.4. to I 12 a 0.4. at dawn on September 25th.

MEDICAL ARRANGEMENTS

2. On the night 24/25th September the following arrangements will be adopted for the collection and evacuation of wounded.

REGIMENTAL AID POSTS

No 1. Dug-Outs at I 11b 0.4. (Railway embankment)
No 2. Dug-Outs at I 11d 8.6. (R. 4)
No 3. Dug-Outs at I 17b 1.9. (MENIN ROAD)

Aid Posts (the personnel of which will be found by Field Ambulances) will also be established at :- I10 a 8.3. and the PRISON, YPRES.

ADVANCED DRESSING STATION.

The MILL on the MENIN ROAD at I9 d 0.5.

DIVISIONAL COLLECTING STATION.

ASYLUM at H.12 d.

MAIN DRESSING STATION.

The COLLEGE, RUE BOESCHEPE, POPERINGHE.

ESTABLISHMENTS

3. With reference to the above O.C. 42nd Field Ambulance will arrange for the following details to be posted on the night 23/24th September.

(a) Two Nursing Orderlies at each of the regimental Aid Posts.

(b) 1 Medical Officer, 1 N.C.O and 5 men at Aid Post at I 10 a 8.3.(This Medical Officer will in addition to treating wounded brought to his post act as laison officer and keep in touch with Brigade Headquarters.

(c) 1 Medical Officer, 1 N.C.O. and 6 men(including bicycle Orderly) at the ADVANCED DRESSING STATION. In addition 6 men will be posted at the latter place on the night 25/26th Sept, to act as loading party.

(d) 2 men to act as a directing party at the dug-Out on the railway embankment at I 16 a 4.7. This party will mount at dawn 25th Sept and withdraw at 7 p.m.

The personnel at the PRISON, YPRES and at the MAIN DRESSING STATION, POPERINGHE, will continue to be found by the 43rd. Field Ambulance

Asylum
25 Bearers 43 7/A 5-45
25 Bearers 44 7/A 9/pm

O.C. 42nd. Field Ambulance will open for the reception of wounded at the DIVISIONAL COLLECTING STATION on night 24/25th Sept.

Bearer Division 43rd. Field Ambulance with 2 officers will proceed to the ASYLUM on Sept 25th arriving at the latter place at 5.45 p.m.

Bearer Division 44th Field A mbulance with 2 Officers will proceed to the A SYLUM on the same date arriving at 9p.m. Each of the a bove will carry 1. days ration and the Iron Ration. On arrival at the ASYLUM the bearer divisions will come under the orders of OC 42nd Field Ambulance

COMMUNICATION TRENCHES. 4. Communication Trenches will be used as follows:-

Eastward Tra ffic.

To No 1 Aid Post:- EAST LA NE.
To No 2 and 3 Aid Posts:- UNION STREET, BIRR CROSS ROADS.

Western Traffic.

~~To~~ From No 1 Aid Post:- WEST LANE.
~~To~~ From No 2and 3 Aid Post:- MUD LANE- CASTLE STREET.

EVACUATION 5. Walkling cases will proceed to the DIVISIONAL COLLECTING STATION. The various police posts on the roads have bea instructed to direct all such cases there.

Bearer Divisions 42nd and 43rd Field Ambulances will march in small parties from the ASYLUM at 6pm. 25th inst, to the ADVANCED DRESSING STATION whence they will proceed- one division to No 1 Aid Post and one Division to No 3 Aid Post. Wounded will be taken to the Motor Ambulance Rendezvous and loaded.. After the Aid Posts ha ve been cleared, wounded in other pa rts of the line will be collected.

Wheeled Stretchers will be used in removing cases from the Aid Posts. 2 Wheeled Stretchers will be kept at the PRISON , YPRES. The remainder at the ADVANCED DRESSING STATION.

When all wounded have been evacuated the bearer divisions 42nd and 43rd Field Ambulances will march back to the dug-outs in the Ramparts NORTH of the MENIN GATE which have been allotted to them. BearerDivision 44th. Field Ambulance will rejoin their Headquarters.

Line of evacuation by night.

From No 1 Aid Post:- RAILWAY line or path running closeto and parrallel with WEST LANEz
From 2 and 3 Aid Posts:- MENIN ROAD.

As far as possible all severe cases(especially abdominal) will be evacuated direct from ADVANCED DRESSING STATION to MAIN DRESSING STATION. Cases treated and registered at the DIVISIONAL COLLECTING STATION will be evacuated to Casualty Clearing Station by No 4 M.A.C. . under arrangements made by D.D.M.S. 6th Corps.

MOTOR AMBULANCES . All Motor Ambulances of the Division(less 2 Fords for the Divisional REST STATION) will be at the disposal of the O.C. 42nd Field Ambulance. They will be employed as follows:-

During the day Two cars at the PRISON, YPRES, for evacuation of wounded at that place. the remainder will be used for evacuatuating wounded from the ASYLUM. They will not approach that place during the day until required, but will rendezvous on the road at H. 10 c. 9.3. at 7a.m. 25th September.

Besides the above, 5 cars of the Motor Ambulance Convoy will be availa ble at the MAIN DRESSING STATION under arrangements made by D.D.M.S. 6th Corps.

AT Night. Except in great emergency, only Divisional Cars will be used to evacuatecases from the front to DIVISIONAL COLLECTING STATION. Three cars will proceed from ASYLUM at 6-15pm to the rendexvous (road junction I 9d 7.4.). 3 at 6-30pm and 3 at 6-45pm. After tha t hour cars will only be allowed to proceed as others return. Not more than 9 cars will be allowed EAST of ASYLUM at any one time.

No 4 M.A.C. will be available to remove cases from the DIVISIONAL COLLECTING STATION.

The O.C. M.A.W.Unit will arrange for a party with the necessary equipment, to proceed to the ASYLUM at 7pm. 25th Sept, so as to be available to render assistance in case a car is damaged

The A.P.M. 14th Division is arranging to post one policeman at the following places to control the traffic:- 1. Ambulance Wagon Rendezvous, 2. ASYLUM.

MAPS etc. 7 No Maps of our trenches, diaries, orders or other documents will be carried by any Officer or man employed in the evacuation of wounded.

REPORTS. 8 Reports to A.D.M.S. Advanced Divns Hdqrs at R Ramparts, Ypres, between the SALLY PORT and MENIN GATE after 6pm 24th Sept.

9. Acknowledge.

J Hartman

Major,
D.A.D.M.S. 14th Division.

Copies:-
No 1 O.C. 42nd Field Ambulance.
No 2 O.C. 43rd -:-
No 3 O.C. 44th -:-
No 4. O.C. M.A.W.Unit.
No 5 , D.D.M.S . 6th Corps.
No 6. Office File.

Appendix 2

Report on Work done by 42nd Field Ambulance on 25th 26th + 27th September 1915 and bearer divisions 43rd – 44th Field Ambulances

---

In accordance with Operation Orders issued the following arrangements were made.

An Advanced Dressing Station was established at the MILL on the MENIN ROAD Captain MAVOR. RAMC in command with 1 Sergt and 6 orderlies + one Cycle orderly with equipment for dressing cases and feeding them. Also surplus medical + surgical stores so as to be able to supply Regimental Aid Posts if called upon. Ten Petrol tins full of drinking water were available if called for by any post.

B. Post half way up West Lane was taken over by Captain Stewart RAMC who acted as LIASON Officer as well as treating any wounded who arrived there. Personnel one Officer 1 Corporal + 6 men. Water was available here in a large tank about 100 gallons which had been placed previously.

Two R.A.M.C. orderlies were sent to remain at No.1 + No 3 aid Posts to be under the command of Regimental Medical Officers + to assist in dressings of cases.

On the night of 24th-25th the Divisional Collecting Station was established by No 42nd Field Ambulance in the Cellars of the ASYLUM just west of YPRES. Two Tent sub-Divisions were employed assisted by 14 men of No 44 Field Ambulance to act as guides + in loading + unloading cases.

The Officers for Duty were

Captain	Roberts	42nd Field Ambulance
Lieut	Barr	
"	Booth	
Lieut QrMr	Brook	
~~Capt Lieut~~	MILLAR	43rd Field Ambulance.
Lieut	Birks	
Lieut	Haig	

Arrangements at Div: Collecting Station

Cases in day time entered by main entrance + proceeded down corridor. At night came by road, east side of building.

of Anti-Tetanic Serum + being entered in the A + D. book.
After the dressings had been finished the case was transferred to the Ward, where a large number of mattresses were placed which had been found in the building; and here they were given either Bully Beef, bread, biscuit, Oxo, Extract of Meat, Tea or Cocoa.

Up to 4.30 pm most of the cases had walked to the ASYLUM + were of the slightly wounded nature. Several cases who arrived at the Divisional Collecting Station had severe wounds of the upper limbs + through shock + collapse had to be evacuated as Lying Down cases.
Many Stretcher Cases were evacuated from the Advanced Dressing Station by means of Motor Ambulances during the day, as it was found possible to use these on the MENIN ROAD owing to the absence of severe shelling, but later in the afternoon owing to the presence of hostile aircraft this was discontinued + many cases were evacuated to the PRISON + ASYLUM by means of wheeled stretchers.

The available space in the cellars was divided up into 9 receiving rooms, one Dressing Room, one Large Ward.

One separate & distinct cellar was made into a Quartermaster's store.

Cooking. Tea, Cocoa, Beef Tea was made in the Cellars by use of Petrol Stoves & Primus Stoves.

Cooking for Personel was done in the court yards in three separate places so as not to have one large smoky fire.

The first Walking Case arrived at the ASYLUM at 6.45 am. 25th & cases continued to come in until 4.30 p.m when there was a lull & other cases came in very slowly until the night collection started. By 4.30 pm 800 cases had arrived at the ASYLUM

The Wounded were passed by guides to the Receiving rooms & the numbers that passed in were checked by an N.C.O.

The Dressings of as many as possible were carried out by the five Officers I had at the ASYLUM, each case dressed being Tallied, having a dose

Evacuation H10 c.9.3

Motor Ambulance Wagon Rendezvous was established at [illegible] sheet 28. Belgium 1-40,000. map, and all the cars of the Division less two Fords were there by 4 a.m on the 25th

Two Motor Cyclist orderlies were kept at the ASYLUM.

Staff. Sergt Cooper M.T.A.S.C. was posted here to regulate the traffic + orders were sent to him re the number of cars to be sent to the ASYLUM + at what intervals.

Later in the morning owing to absence of shelling on the YPRES – VLAMERTINGHE road the Rendezvous was changed to just WEST of the level Crossing YPRES – VLAMERTINGHE road.

Besides these Cars, five Motor Ambulance Wagons ~~[illegible]~~ of No 4 M.A.C. were available + were at Main Dressing Station POPERINGHE.

I sent for the M.A.C. cars at 8.12 a.m as the congestion at the ASYLUM was increasing + the Divisional Cars could not compete with the numbers. The D.A.D.M.S. arrived shortly after this message had been sent and arranged that more than the five Cars at POPERINGHE should be

so far.
The cases that were dressed at the ASYLUM were ordered to be evacuated to the C.C.S + the cases not dressed to the MAIN DRESSING STATION. Unfortunately a lot of these dressed cases were unloaded at POPERINGHE leading to congestion + double entry in A+D books, on this being noticed O.C. 43rd Field Ambulance notifying me + both he + I took steps to have this discontinued.

The evacuation at night was slightly different. The Divisional Cars evacuated from the MENIN ROAD to the ASYLUM — here any cases requiring urgent treatment were dressed + the other cases were transferred at once to waiting M.A.C. cars + sent straight to Main Dressing Station. A N.C.O was detailed to check the numbers evacuated making a distinction between those tallied + those not tallied.

Collection of WOUNDED

42nd Field Ambulance Bearer Division under the command of Captain Miller + Captain King proceeded + billeted in Dug outs in Ramparts YPRES on the night

[illegible] 25th. Unfortunately at about 10 a.m.
25th a large shell burst in the Ramparts placing out of action 9 Bearers. One killed and eight who were buried + bruised + much shaken.

On receipt of a message from Captain Stewart RAMC that there were a heavy casualties in Railway Wood Captain Miller + Captain King each went forward with a bearer sub Division. Almost at the same time as this message was received the D.A.D.M.S. visited the Ramparts + gave orders for the Bearers to go forward Captain Miller to go to BIRR X Road Aid Post + Captain KING to Railway Embankment Aid Post. These parties evacuated wounded until 7 p.m. when ~~then~~ the collection was continued by the Bearer Divisions of No 43rd + No 44th Field Ambulance under the command respectively of

43rd F.A.	Lieut TAYLOR.	RAMC
	Lieut HOPKINS	RAMC.
44th F.A.	Captain ATKINS	RAMC
	Captain FLOOD	RAMC

[illegible] collection proceeded the whole of the night 25th/26th by the bearer divisions of 43rd & 44th Field Ambulances and twelve bearers of 45th Field Ambulance. From 7 a.m. 26th the Collection was continued by 43rd Field Ambulance Bearers & 44th Field Ambulance Bearers up to the evening. The night collection of the 26th/27th being carried out by Bearers of 42nd & 44th Field Ambulances & by Bearers of 43rd Field Ambulance under Lieut Hopkins and the collection was continued by Captain MILLER 42nd Field Ambulance up to about 1 p.m. 27th when there were still 6 stretcher cases to be brought in. It was found impossible to bring these in in daylight owing to the trenches being blown in & the open spaces having to be crossed where sniping occurred.

At 10 a.m. 27th I received orders from A.D.M.S. 14th Division to withdraw my Ambulance & hand over the collection to O.C. 40th Field Ambulance.

2

I beg to call to your notice the exceedingly good work done by all the collecting Officers + bearers. Their duties were very arduous + tiring owing to the recent rain making the Trenches + surroundings very greasy + muddy + also the bombardment blowing in trenches, over which cases had to be carried. The journey for one case to be taken from the front trench to the Advanced Dressing Station + for the return of the squad taking 3 hours.

I beg to attach recommendations for your favourable consideration.

I have the honour to be
Sir
Your Obedient Servant
Fred Roberts
Capt RAMC
O.C. 42nd Field Ambulance

30-9-15.

A.D.M.S.
14th Division

Report on visit to Posts [illegible]

On arriving at [illegible] Post on Thursday night – the 23rd inst. we found that none of the 4 dug-outs were completed. There was a deficiency of [illegible] on the site and [illegible] in one there was no [illegible].

Although it had been [illegible] dug-out there [illegible] of 2" at [illegible] one end.

The roofing of all four dugouts was absolutely insufficient. Daylight could be seen between the [illegible] in one.

On Saturday morning the [illegible] was heavily shelled & 2 dug-outs were blown in, the M.O. of the [illegible] narrowly escaping complete burial.

The Water-cart [illegible] early in the morning was knocked out of action. As a result the [illegible]

& rain afterwards.

When the rain came on on Saturday, all the roofs began to leak & in a short time a deluge of mud & water came through. Consequently medical dressing was out of the question & the sufferings of the wounded were added to by these discomforts.

Later on the mud & water on the floors reached a depth of from 6" to 12".

The accomodation for wounded was reduced to one dug-out for each regiment & as a result the congestion was acute at times.

The trench leading up to the Aid Post was too narrow for stretchers & before we left was rendered impracticable by mud, rain & numerous shell holes.

As to the position of the Aid Post, from our experience we are of opinion that the wounded were seen entering the Aid Post by the enemy & that the heavy shelling in this area was in consequence of this.

The Bearers from the Field Ambulance instead of coming at 7 o'c as we expected did not arrive till after 8 o'c, thus leading to [illegible] collection.

H. L. Gillespie
Lt. R.A.M.C.
M.O. 5th Oxf & Bucks.

J. L. [illegible] – Lt. R.A.M.C.
M.O. – 5 K.S.L.I.

27 Feb: '15

2nd ATTACK ON BELLEWAARDE (BATTLE OF LOOS) 25/26th Sept. 1915.

14th DIVISION - 6th CORPS.

A.D.M.S. = Col.S.Guise Moores.

D.A.D.M.S. = Major J.A.Hartigan. H.Q. at H 7.c.7.7.(28).

Sept.

23rd. Op. Orders. R.A.M.C. Order No 4 issued giving medical arrangements for coming attack. For copy see Appendix 1 attached to diary.

25/26th. Casualties.) Evacuation.) Wd. coming from waggon rendez- vous E. of YPRES were if serious taken direct to Nos 10 & 17 C.C.S's. at L 23.a.(27) Other cases were sent from Div. Col. Station to M.D.S. at the College, Rue Boeschepe, POPERINGHE.
Br. Divs. were accommodated in dugouts N. of Menin Gate from 7 p.m. 24th - 27th.
By midday 25th, 42 F.A. evacd. 675 cases from Div. Col. Station, 227 of which went direct to C.C.S and 197 to M.D.S.
Up to 4.45 p.m. 25th, 130 lightly wd. cases were evacd. from A.P. at Prison, YPRES to M.D.S. additional cars being sent every ¼ hour to ensure rapid evacuation.
Brs. of F.A's worked in advance of A.P's during night 25/26th.

From noon 25th - Noon 26th 17 & 1137 wd. were admitted to F.A's.

27th. Casualties. Noon 26th - Noon 27th 2 & 86 wd. admitted to F.A's.

Report of work of F.A's.) For report of work of F.A's during operations see Appendix 2 attached to diary.

No 42 FIELD AMBULANCE - 14th DIVISION.

O.C. = Capt.F.E.Roberts.

H.Q. at L 3.a.5.8.(27)

Sept.

22nd. Med. Arr. As it was suggested in case of an attack to take over Asylum, YPRES as Div.Col.Station, a detachment was sent there to make necessary preparations. 200 stretchers & 4 wheeled stretchers were also taken there.
A detachment also proceeded to road leading from Railway Wood A.P. I 11.b.2.5.(28) to Menin Rd., to make good passage ways for wheeled stretchers.
A detachment also proceeded to prepare dugouts in Ramparts YPRES, just N. of Menin Gate, which are to be taken over as billets for bearers.

24th. " Medical & surgical equipment sent to Asylum.
A.D.S. formed at Mill on Menin Rd. I 9.d.0.5.(28) and A.P. formed at I 10.a.8.3.(28).
Bearer Div. proceeded to Ramparts, YPRES at 4.30 p.m.
Asylum, YPRES taken over as Div.Col.Station at 7.30. p.m. by 2 T.S.D's of No 42 F.A. and 14 men of No 44 F.A.

No 42 FIELD AMB. - 14th DIVISION.(contd.)

Sept.

25th. Casualties.) Evacuation.) Collection of wd. carried out by brs. of No 42 F.A. under Capts.S.Miller & D.R.King.
First wd. arrived at Div.Col.Station at 6.45 a.m. and from then onwards large numbers came in until by 4.30 p.m. 820 had been admitted.
Div.F.A.M.Ambs. and 5 cars of No 4 M.A.C. evacuated cases as follows:- Those who had been dressed to C.C.S. and those requiring dressing to M.D.S. By 4.30 p.m Div. Col.Station was clear and from then onwards until night cases came in slowly.
In addition about 90 cases were evacuated from A.D.S. some on wheeled stretchers to the Prison,YPRES and then by M.Amb. to M.D.S., and some by M.Amb. straight from A.D.S. to M.D.S.

Cas.R.A.M.C. 0 & 1 killed. 0 & 1 wd.

26th. Casualties.) Evacuation.) Collection of wd. during the night 25/26th was carried out by bearers of No 43 F.A. under Lts.W.A.Taylor & P.S. Hopkins and bearers of No 44 F.A. under Capts. F.G.Flood & R.P.G.Atkins with 12 bearers of No 42 F.A.
From 7 a.m. onwards the collection was continued by brs. of No 42 F.A. & No 44 F.A. Cases collected were mostly lying down and were taken to A.D.S. and from there evacuated by Div.F.A.M.Ambs. to Div.Col.Station and there transferred to M.A.C. cars which evacuated to M.D.S. & C.C.S. Cases requiring urgent treatment were dressed at Div.Col.Station.

Cas. R.A.M.C. 0 & 2 wd.

27th. Casualties.) Evacuation.) Collection of wd. during night 26/27th was carried out by brs. of No 42 F.A. with a few brs. of Nos 43 & 44 F.A's. Cases brought in were evacd. to M.D.S. by M.A.C. cars.

Moves. At 4.50 p.m. collection of wd. was handed over to No 43 F.A. and unit moved to L 3.a.5.8.(27).

No 43 FIELD AMB. - 14th DIVISION.

O.C. = Major W.F.Vaughan.

H.Q. at POPERINGHE.

Sept.

25th. Ops.R.A.M.C. Unit in charge of M.D.S. at College,POPERINGHE and A.P. at Prison,YPRES.

Casualties. 12 & 164 admitted.

26th. Moves det. Bearer Div. under Lt. W.A.Taylor left for Asylum,YPRES at 3 p.m.

Casualties. 11 & 764 admitted.

27th. Moves det. Bearer Div. rejoined at 1 p.m.
1 B.S.D. under Lt. P.S.Hopkins left for Asylum,YPRES at 3.30 p.m.

Casualties. 1 & 47 admitted.

28th. Moves det. 1 B.S.D. sent to Asylum,YPRES at 6 p.m.

Cas.R.A.M.C. 0 & 1 d. of w. - wd. whilst acting as S.B. at YPRES.

Casualties. 1 & 66 admitted.

No 44 FIELD AMBULANCE - 14th DIVISION.

O.C. = Lt.Col.H.Simson.

H.Q. at HILHOEK.

Sept.

25th.	Ops.R.A.M.C.	Unit in charge of D.R.S. at HILHOEK.
	Moves det.	Capts.F.G.Flood & R.P.G.Atkins with 72 brs. & 3 H.Ambs. proceeded to Asylum,YPRES (42 F.A.) at 6 p.m. to assist in collection of wd. Returned during 26th.
26th.	Cas.R.A.M.C.	0 & 3 wd. evacd. 0 & 2 suffering from shock.

Oct '15

121
7518

HQ. 14th Div: A.D.M.S.

Vol 3

Oct 15

5

Army Form C. 2118

Instructions regarding War Diaries and Intelligence Summaries are contained in F. S. Regs., Part II. and the Staff Manual respectively. Title Pages will be prepared in manuscript.

WAR DIARY
or
INTELLIGENCE SUMMARY
(Erase heading not required.)

Place	Date	Hour	Summary of Events and Information	Remarks and references to Appendices
		Belgium & France Scenes Sheets 27 NE & 28 NE 1/20000		
BRANDHOEK	1/X/15		Aid post I11 C8.2 is to be evacuated the next morning to I12 C2.5 about 8.15 hrs. the DGS having this as too close to the firing line to be of use & recommended that the dug out in the Railway EMBANKMENT I11 A 10.5 be used & one made in the EMBANKMENT. Sam	
	4.X.15		The 43 Infantry Brigade is placed at the disposal of the 15th Corps with effect from Oct 4th. Arranged with DDMS 5th Corps that all evacuation should be carried out from their area by Ambulances of the 5th Corps. We have therefore not sent any ambulances with the Brigade though it had been arranged to send 2 sections of the 43rd FAmb. The 43rd I B relieved the 50th I.B. 19 Div: from O 36 b 5.3. the wood running south through O 7 B.6.8. Sam	
	5/X/15		Return of wastage (sick & wounded) from Divisions for week ending Oct 2nd shows that the 14th Div. is 5th in the list in the 6th Corps of the units as regards sick per centage to strength. Officers sick 1, wounded 23, Other ranks sick 99 wounded 1098 Totals sick 100 wounded 1121 Sick % to strength .55 Sam	
	6/X/15		The aid posts of the Division are as follows No 1 aid post railway embankment 7th RB (LT DUNLOP) A aid Post at the MLL MENIN RD 7th KRR (Lt HEWAT) In trenches at I12 C2.5 8th RB (2Lt DUNKERLEY. At CHATEAU POTIJZE I 4A 9.5. 2Lt O'LOUGHLIN (8 KRR). At I 6.6.0 LT DUDGEON 10th DLI at the PRISON YPRES 1 Officer 43 FA 2 NCOs & 6 men relieved every 8 days	

1875 Wt. W593/826 1,000,000 4/15 J.B.C. & A. A.D.S.S./Forms/C. 2118.

Instructions regarding War Diaries and Intelligence Summaries are contained in F. S. Regs., Part II. and the Staff Manual respectively. Title Pages will be prepared in manuscript.

WAR DIARY
or
INTELLIGENCE SUMMARY
(Erase heading not required.)

Army Form C. 2118

6

Place	Date	Hour	Summary of Events and Information	Remarks and references to Appendices
			Map References, Sheet 28 Belgium 1/40,000	
ERANDHOEK	6/X/15		At the ASYLUM. YPRES a bearer subdivision of No 43 FA is kept in readiness for duty in evacuation. The subdivision sleep there. [initials]	
			The 6th Division will relieve the 14 Division from A3 to A5 on the night of Oct. 6th & 7th. The POTIJZE aid post will therefore be evacuated on that evening & handed over to the new appointed of that Division at A.D.M.S. [initials]	
"	10/X/15		It had been arranged by G.S. 14th Division to commence the construction of the following dug outs in H Sector for the use of regimental medical officers as aid posts.	
			(1) 3 dug outs under the railway embankment about I 11 a.5.1. These are for use as an overflow to the aid posts now existing under the railway embankment I 11 a 10.5	
			(2) 5 dug outs about I 11 d 3.4 South of WITTEPOORT FARM & just east of MUDDY LANE. These will be for use as an aid post to the right Batt: in H Sector. The dug outs about BIRR X roads are not satisfactory. They are easily "crumped" & let in a good deal of water. [initials]	
	11/X/15		Weekly return. Officers 5 sick, wounded 4. O.R. sick 77 wounded 46. Totals wounded 50 sick 82. Sick % to strength .43 [initials]	

1875 Wt. W593/826 1,000,000 4/15 J.B.C. & A. A.D.S.S./Forms/C. 2118.

Instructions regarding War Diaries and Intelligence Summaries are contained in F. S. Regs., Part II. and the Staff Manual respectively. Title Pages will be prepared in manuscript.

WAR DIARY
or
INTELLIGENCE SUMMARY
(Erase heading not required.)

Army Form C. 2118 7

Place	Date	Hour	Summary of Events and Information	Remarks and references to Appendices
BRANDHOEK	16/10/15		Return of wastage sick & wounded for week ending 16th Oct 1915 shews Officers sick 6 wounded 3. OR sick 82 wounded 62 Totals sick 88 wounded 65 Sick % to strength ·45.	
	17/10/15		The 6th Division will relieve the 14th Division in the present Divisional front as follows night Oct 21-22 Centre & left sectors in front & support line X1 to X3 & KAAIE Salient	
			night Oct 22-23 Right sector. F13 X 1a, L FARM, BRIELEN HOUSES & L4 [illegible]:	
			The ADMS 6th Div: called & arranged for the OC of the FA's collecting in the 14th Div: area when taken over, to accompany the OC FA collecting 14th Div: on his nightly round & for officers who will take over the existing regimental aid posts to also accompany him. SAW	
	18/10/15		It was pointed out to G.S. that the new dugouts already mentioned had not been constructed. So arrangements were made that 9 OC Brigade 6th Div: taking over the sector in which they were to have been made to be informed of our intention.	

Army Form C. 2118

WAR DIARY
or
INTELLIGENCE SUMMARY
(Erase heading not required.)

Instructions regarding War Diaries and Intelligence Summaries are contained in F. S. Regs., Part II. and the Staff Manual respectively. Title Pages will be prepared in manuscript.

Place	Date	Hour	Summary of Events and Information	Remarks and references to Appendices
BRANDHOEK	23/4/15		All regimental medical officers in the Div: Front area withdrew from their aid posts on night 23rd-24. The 43 FA collecting also withdrew from the PRISON & ASYLUM. The F Ambulances are disposed as follows 42nd in Div: Rest area N of the POPERINGHE-WATOU ROAD. 44th FA at HILHOEK POPERINGHE ABELE road 43rd in the COLLEGE BOEBOESCHEPE POPERINGHE	
	24/4/15		The Brigades are located as follows: 41st 7th & 8th KRR in huts at H1 d 8 8 known as A huts & huts at G 6 d as B huts respectively 7th & 8th R.B. in 49th Divisional area	
			42nd Brigade 6th DCLI at F27 A 5 8 Lt MORTON MO now called A Standing Camp	
			X DLI at F27 C 6 8 Lt DUDGEON MO " " B " "	
			6th SOMERSET at L3 c 10 4 Lt HOPKINS MO now called C " "	
			6th YLI " L3 d 4 5 Lt MORRISON MO now called D " "	
			43rd Brigade are in camps round HOUTKIRK & HAZEELE NW of WATAU.	
			1 Section of FA 42nd on the HOUTKIRT-HAZEELE Rd which collects sick daily & evacuates to 42nd FA.	
			Sick of the 2 Battalions in 49th Div: area are evacuated daily by motor ambulance sent by 42nd FA.	

1875 Wt. W593/826 1,000,000 4/15 J.B.C. & A. A.D.S.S./Forms/C. 2118.

Instructions regarding War Diaries and Intelligence Summaries are contained in F. S. Regs., Part II. and the Staff Manual respectively. Title Pages will be prepared in manuscript.

WAR DIARY
or
INTELLIGENCE SUMMARY
(Erase heading not required.)

Army Form C. 2118 9

Place	Date	Hour	Summary of Events and Information	Remarks and references to Appendices
BRANDHOEK	24/4/15		Wastage return shows officers sick 6. wounded 3. OR sick 93 wounded 49. Totals sick 99 wounded 52 sick % to strength .50 for week ending 23/4/15.	
	25/4/15		42nd F Amb: are still in tents without boards. They take in all scabies cases of the division an average of 20 being in residence. Permanent wooden latrines, drying shed & ablution places are erected. There is also a wattle hut erected for the transport near the transport lines which have standings of brick with head covers. The 44th (Divisional rest station) have 2 huts erected for patients holding 20 each the remainder are in tents in the F Amb: portion of the camp. The DRS portion is still in bell tents without boards. The dining shed, latrines, wash house, drying room & ablution rooms are all wooden erections. The transport lines are shale flooring with galvanised iron roofing. 8 more huts are to be erected for this unit. 43rd FA in buildings in POPERINGHE transport lines in a field just north W of the town. transport personnel in tents. Horse lines similar to the 44th FA. [signature]	
	26/4/15		Soldiers club Home being opened in POPERINGHE room allotted for concert room, reading & writing, also refreshment room with tables & bars. Sanitary arrangements made by OC 25 San Sect to include pail system of latrines in the stables & urinals with soakage pits in the yard. also incinerator to be constructed [signature]	

1875 Wt. W593/826 1,000,000 4/15 J.B.C. & A. A.D.S.S./Forms/C. 2118.

Army Form C. 2118

10

Instructions regarding War Diaries and Intelligence Summaries are contained in F. S. Regs., Part II. and the Staff Manual respectively. Title Pages will be prepared in manuscript.

WAR DIARY
or
INTELLIGENCE SUMMARY
(Erase heading not required.)

Place	Date	Hour	Summary of Events and Information	Remarks and references to Appendices
BRANDHOEK	31/4/15		Sick cases in the Division requiring treatment are to be sent to No 43 F Amb in Poperinghe. Cases which cannot be dealt with there must be sent to No 10 Casualty Clearing Station in charge of a NCO from the Field Amb. A nominal roll in duplicate to be sent with them.	
			Those cases requiring stretcher or minor attention will be attended to & returned to F Amb the same day. Those requiring prolonged attention will be admitted to CCS & treated or evacuation from the Div. area.	
			J [illegible] Col ADMS 14th Div	
			Note	
			A map is attached shewing the aid posts &c from which the wounded were evacuated after collection, also the Advanced Dressing Station, Divisional Collecting Station, Main Dressing Station & Casualty Clearing Stations taking part in the evacuation. Period 25–27th Sept/15	
			[illegible]	

1875 Wt. W593/826 1,000,000 4/15 J.B.C. & A. A.D.S.S./Forms/C. 2118.

Map shewing the method of collection & evacuation of wounded during the action 25–27th Sept 1915

SHEET 27.

SHEET 28.

POPERINGHE

YPRES

Scale 1:40,000

Magnetic

Note

The arrow points, leading from the Red Cross circle indicate the exact spots where the aid posts &c. were placed

II

HQ. 14th Division

A & Q.

Vol: 4

121/7678

Nov 1915

Nov 15.

Instructions regarding War Diaries and Intelligence Summaries are contained in F. S. Regs., Part II. and the Staff Manual respectively. Title Pages will be prepared in manuscript.

WAR DIARY
or
INTELLIGENCE SUMMARY
(Erase heading not required.)

Army Form C. 2118

Part II

Place	Date	Hour	Summary of Events and Information	Remarks and references to Appendices
			Sheet 28 NW Belgium "B" series 1/20000	
BRANDHOEK. HQ. 14th Div	17/XI/15		The Division has been resting for the past month.	
			The 14th Division will relieve the 6th Division from Junction of A1 & A2 (I5 d.3.2) to junction D18 & D19 (C15 c.7.6) as follows.	
			(a) On night 18th/19th Nov: The 42 I.B. & one Batt. attached from 43rd I.B. will relieve the 18th I.B. in the right sector from junction A1 & A2 to junction of GARDEN Street & B11 (exclusive)	
			On the same night the 41st I.B. will relieve the 16th I.B. in the left sector from junction B15 & B16 (C21.b.3.4) to junction of D18 & D19 (C15.c.7.6) the present left of the 6th Div.	
			(b) On the night 19/20 Nov: The 43rd I.B. & one Batt. attached from 41st I.B. will relieve the 71st I.B. in the centre sector from Junction of Garden Street & B11 inclusive to junction B15 & B16 (C21.b.3.4).	
			The 11th Kings LIVERPOOL REGT (Pioneers) will reoccupy their old quarters between bridges 10 & 7 on the night 19/20 Nov: i.e. I7c 4.8 to I7a.6.3	
			The 57th I.B. 17th Div: is on the right of the 6th Div. The 146th I.B. 49th Div: is on the left of the 6th Div. [initials]	

1875 Wt. W593/826 1,000,000 4/15 J.B.C. & A. A.D.S.S./Forms/C. 2118.

Instructions regarding War Diaries and Intelligence Summaries are contained in F. S. Regs., Part II. and the Staff Manual respectively. Title Pages will be prepared in manuscript.

Army Form C. 2118

WAR DIARY
or
INTELLIGENCE SUMMARY
(Erase heading not required.)

Place	Date	Hour	Summary of Events and Information	Remarks and references to Appendices
			Sheet 27 + 28 NW } "B" series POPERINGHE – YPRES.	
BRANDHOEK.	18/4/15		The following will be the arrangement for the collection & evacuation of sick & wounded of the Division.	
			(1) Main dressing station COLLEGE, RUE BOESCHEPE POPERINGHE.	
			(2) Advanced dressing station {PRISON, YPRES I 7 B. 1. 1.} at which one motor ambulance will be kept.	
			(3) Collecting Post at REIGERSBURG CHATEAU H.6.6. at which one motor ambulance will be kept.	
			4 Collection from aid Posts	
			Motor ambulances will call at (a) LA BRIQUE at C 26. d. 8 0.	
			(b) ST JEAN at C 27. d. 0. 7.	
			(c) POTIJZE at I 4 C. 2. 9.	
			at 8.45 pm nightly & each morning at 5–30 Am	
			The motor ambulance at REIGERSBURG CHATEAU will call at I. 6 0 9 at 3 pm daily & evacuate direct to MAIN dressing station	
			S[illegible]	

1875 Wt. W593/826 1,000,000 4/15 J.B.C. & A. A.D.S.S./Forms/C. 2118.

Instructions regarding War Diaries and Intelligence Summaries are contained in F. S. Regs., Part II. and the Staff Manual respectively. Title Pages will be prepared in manuscript.

WAR DIARY
or
INTELLIGENCE SUMMARY
(Erase heading not required.)

Army Form C. 2118

Part 12

Place	Date	Hour	Summary of Events and Information	Remarks and references to Appendices
			Ref: Map Belgium 1/40000 Sheet 28.	
BRANDHOEK. H7c 8.5 HQ.	18/XI/15		The following instructions were issued for evacuation of urgent cases (wounded & sick)	
			A" Infantry units occupying trenches	
			(1) By night send a message to advanced dressing station THE PRISON c/o TOWN MAJOR YPRES or c/o LIVERPOOLS asking for motor amb. to be sent to be sent to aid Posts at POTIJZE ST JEAN or POTIJZE as required.	
			2 By day send a message as above in (1) asking as for a motor ambulance to be sent in the case of POTIJZE are to MENINGATE I8.1.10. in case of ST JEAN or LA BRIGUE areas to WELL CROSS ROADS I 2.d.1.7 Cases will be carried on wheeled stretchers from aid Posts to these points by the RAMC detachments	
			B" Units occupying banks of YPERLEE & the areas between that & YPRES LA BRIQUE road. Send cases to road junction I 16.0.9 & message to collecting post REIGERSBURG CHATEAU asking for motor ambulance to proceed to that point	
			C" Artillery area west of the YPERLEE canal send cases to the collecting Post at REIGERSBURG CHATEAU	
			D" Artillery area EAST of YPRES. message to advanced dressing station THE PRISON c/o TOWN MAJOR YPRES or LIVERPOOLS asking for stretcher bearers	

1875 Wt. W593/826 1,000,000 4/15 J.B.C. & A. A.D.S.S./Forms/C. 2118.

Instructions regarding War Diaries and Intelligence Summaries are contained in F. S. Regs., Part II. and the Staff Manual respectively. Title Pages will be prepared in manuscript.

WAR DIARY
or
INTELLIGENCE SUMMARY
(Erase heading not required.)

Army Form C. 2118.

Part 13

Place	Date	Hour	Summary of Events and Information	Remarks and references to Appendices
			Ref Map Sheet 28 1/20000 NE Belgium Ands	
BRANDHOEK HQ 14th DIV	18/XI/15		to meet at a named point -	
			E. Wards in YPRES and cases to advanced dressing station THE PRISON	
			In the case of the Battalion on the extreme left flank of the Division send cases to ESSEX FARM & dispatch message C25 a.3.9 via bridge 4 & dispatch message to Collecting Post REIGERSBURG CHATEAU asking for motor ambulance to be sent to that point.	
	19/XI/15		Extract from RAMC Operation orders dated 17th XI/15 - Ref Map Belgium 1/40000 Sheet 28	
			(2) No 44 Field ambulance will form the MAIN DRESSING STATION COLLEGE RUE BOESCHEPE POPERINGHE from 18th inst inclusive	
			(3) The OC 44 F Amb will arrange to form an advanced dressing Station at the PRISON YPRES with the following personnel & necessary Equipment 1 Officer, 1 NCO & 10 men.	
			He will relieve the party of No 18 F Amb now there on the morning of 19th inst by arrangement with OC No 18 F Amb.	
			(4) OC No 44 FA will arrange direct with OC No 17 FA to take over the COLLECTING POST at REIGERSBURG CHATEAU on the morning of the 19th inst & will detail the following personnel & necessary Equipment 1 NCO & 2 men	

1875 Wt. W593/826 1,000,000 4/15 J.B.C. & A. A.D.S.S./Forms/C. 2118.

Instructions regarding War Diaries and Intelligence Summaries are contained in F. S. Regs., Part II. and the Staff Manual respectively. Title Pages will be prepared in manuscript.

WAR DIARY
or
INTELLIGENCE SUMMARY
(Erase heading not required.)

Army Form C. 2118.

Pow 14

Place	Date	Hour	Summary of Events and Information	Remarks and references to Appendices
			Ref: Map Sheet 28 1/40000 Belgium	
BRANDHOEK	19/11/15		OC No 44 Field Amb. will take over from OC No 18 F Amb at the PRISON YPRES all wheeled stretchers belonging to the 14th Div: (Cent) after their distribution is arranged the remainder will be held as a reserve at the main dressing station	
			(6) No 44 Field ambulance will detail three parties of stretcher bearers each consisting of 1 NCO + 3 men with two wheeled stretchers to proceed to the aid posts at POTIJZE ST JEAN + LA BRIQUE respectively on the night of 18th inst and will arrange for their rationing + for a supply of drinking water to be maintained to them. They should report to the senior regimental medical officer at each place.	
			7 For the night 19-20 Nov: inclusive until further orders the OC 44th Field Amb: will arrange to collect from the Divisional front as follows	
			POTIJZE two motor ambulances — leaving main dressing station 8pm — leaving main dressing station one motor amb: — 4-45 AM	
			ST JEAN do — 8pm — do — 4-45 AM	
			LA BRIQUE " — 8pm — do — 4-45 AM	
			One or more motor ambulances will call at the PRISON on the return journey from POTIJZE.	
			The motor ambulance at REIGERSBURG CHATEAU will collect from the canal bank at road junction I 6.0 9 at 3pm & 9pm daily & evacuate direct to the main dressing station commencing on the 19th inst	

1875 Wt. W593/826 1,000,000 4/15 J.B.C. & A. A.D.S.S./Forms/C. 2118.

Army Form C. 2118

Page 15

Instructions regarding War Diaries and Intelligence Summaries are contained in F. S. Regs., Part II. and the Staff Manual respectively. Title Pages will be prepared in manuscript.

WAR DIARY
or
INTELLIGENCE SUMMARY
(Erase heading not required.)

Place	Date	Hour	Summary of Events and Information	Remarks and references to Appendices
			Ref map Sheet 28 Belgium N.W. 3rd Series.	
ERANDHOEK.	19/XI/15		OC 44th F Amb will detail 3 motor ambulances to report to OC 44th Field Amb at 7-45 pm nightly commencing 19th inst. – Sam	
	20/XI/15		The stretcher party detailed for LA BRIQUE will proceed via ESSEX FARM & BRIDGE 4. (C 25. 7 10) & report to Lt O'LOUGHLEN the M.O. i/c: 8th KRRC at his aid post (C 20 d. 8-4.) The motor ambulance at REIGERSBURG CHATEAU will also call at ESSEX FARM (C25 a 3. 9) at 9 pm daily. Sam	
	21/XI/15		Aid posts are as follows 2 at POTIJZE one in a dug out & another in a cellar close to CHATEAU 1 in the village of ST JEAN C27 d .01 1 in the village of LA BRIQUE C26 d 5.0 1 in C25 a 2.9 the [illegible] batt on the left flank. Sam	

1875 Wt. W593/826 1,000,000 4/15 J.B.C. & A. A.D.S.S./Forms/C. 2118.

Instructions regarding War Diaries and Intelligence Summaries are contained in F. S. Regs., Part II. and the Staff Manual respectively. Title Pages will be prepared in manuscript.

WAR DIARY
or
INTELLIGENCE SUMMARY
(Erase heading not required.)

Army Form C. 2118

Page 16

Place	Date	Hour	Summary of Events and Information	Remarks and references to Appendices
			Map 27 & 28 Belgium N.W. "B" Series	
BRANDHOEK. HQ C 8 [illegible]	22/4/15		43rd Field ambulance is in the rest area at L 3 a. 5. 8 (map 27) 42nd Field amb. is at L 20. d (map 27) forming the Divisional Rest station 44th Field amb. is at the COLLEGE RUE BOESCHEPE POPERINGHE doing the collection work for the front & forming the MAIN dressing station & advanced dressing station at the PRISON YPRES.	
	23/4/15		Wounded admitted into main dressing station rifle 11, other wounds 21 = 32. Ordered the 43 FA to take over the WHITE CHATEAU west end of VLAMERTINGHE village on N side of YPRES - POPERINGHE RD 1 officer & 10 men sent to take over from 16th FA 6th Division preparatory to 2 sections of the 43rd going in residence. Visited the aid posts at ST JEAN in cellars & also the advanced dressing station at the PRISON at 9-4 pm.	
	24/4/15		On the 26th inst. the 43rd Field ambulance less one section will move & open an advanced dressing station at the WHITE CHATEAU VLAMERTINGHE (H 2 d. 9.1)	

1875 Wt. W593/826 1,000,000 4/15 J.B.C. & A. A.D.S.S./Forms/C. 2118.

Instructions regarding War Diaries and Intelligence Summaries are contained in F. S. Regs., Part II. and the Staff Manual respectively. Title Pages will be prepared in manuscript.

WAR DIARY
or
INTELLIGENCE SUMMARY
(Erase heading not required.)

Army Form C. 2118.

Page 17

Place	Date	Hour	Summary of Events and Information	Remarks and references to Appendices
			Ref Map Belgium 1/20000 Sheet 28	
BRANDHOEK	24/X/15		2 On the night 26-27 inst the 43rd F Amb will take over from the 44 F Amb the collection & evacuation of sick & wounded from Battalions whose aid posts are at LA BRIQUE & ST JEAN. Motor ambulances leaving the Advanced dressing station (Room 1 above) at 8-15 pm & 5 am.	
			3 From the 27th inst inclusive the 43rd F Amb will also take over from the 44th Field Amb the collection of sick from the Cantonments in Squares A30c & d; H1d, G12c & for Medical Detention Hut at G6d 4.2 employing 2 horse drawn ambulances which will call at these places between 10-30 & 11-30 am daily. The OC 43rd FA will arrange with OC 44 F Amb to relieve the RAMC detachment at LA BRIQUE & ST JEAN on the evening of the 26th inst. All cases for evacuation from the Dressing Station (VLAMERTINGHE) will be cleared by motor amb. direct to C.C. Station.	
	28/X/15		The 43rd F Amb less 1 section now installed in WHITE HOUSE VLAMERTINGHE. The DRS at HILLHOEK are not to move. The CRE	

1875 Wt. W593/826 1,000,000 4/15 J.B.C. & A. A.D.S.S./Forms/C. 2118.

Instructions regarding War Diaries and Intelligence Summaries are contained in F. S. Regs., Part II. and the Staff Manual respectively. Title Pages will be prepared in manuscript.

WAR DIARY
or
INTELLIGENCE SUMMARY
(Erase heading not required.)

Army Form C. 2118.

Nov 18.

Place	Date	Hour	Summary of Events and Information	Remarks and references to Appendices
			Ref Map Belgium 1/20000 Sheets 27 + 28 Divisional Rest Station	
BRANDHOEK	28/XI/15		6th Corps is providing material for 10 huts. The [illegible] approved to the 7 Fd Amb (DRS) is to be constructed so that the station will be made suitable for reception of men convalescing. The existing huts are 2 for patients holding 20 a hut dispensary, a hut QrMrs Store & a shed for dining patients & personnel Room. The Kitchen, Latrines, Washhouse, Bathing shed, drying & ironing rooms are all of permanent structure with concrete floors. Brushwood is being placed as a foundation for the intercommunication paths & trench boards for the same.	
DRS				
	30/XI/15		The hut material is arriving & the trench boards are coming from the unoccupied permanent Camps of the Division.	
			[illegible signature] [illegible]	

1875 Wt. W593/826 1,000,000 4/15 J.B.C. & A. A.D.S.S./Forms/C. 2118.

A.D.M.S. 14th Div:
Vol: 5

121/7931

Dec. 1915

Instructions regarding War Diaries and Intelligence Summaries are contained in F. S. Regs., Part II. and the Staff Manual respectively. Title Pages will be prepared in manuscript.

WAR DIARY
or
INTELLIGENCE SUMMARY
(Erase heading not required.)

Army Form C. 2118

Place	Date	Hour	Summary of Events and Information	Remarks and references to Appendices
			Ref map BELGIUM 1/20,000 sheet 27, 28	
BRANDHOEK	1/XII/15		Army Commander inspected the Divisional Rest Station (42nd Field Amb) at HILLHOEK & the Divisional Baths at 10-45 Am. [initials]	
	2/XII/15		Visited DRS with Dr Genl LUDLOW: It was decided that 10 huts additional for patients should be supplied by CRE 6th Corps: eight huts are at present erected holding 40 patients in all. [initials] Visited 43rd F Amb now in the WHITE HOUSE VLAMERTINGHE	
	3/XII/15		Visited 43rd Field Amb. Same as 2/XII/15. They are quite settled & this is a going concern. [initials]	
	4/XII/15		Visited DDMS 6th Corps at CHATEAU COUTHOVE on the POPERINGHE - PROVEN Rd. for fortnightly conference: Shewed a new pattern trench cooker made from a creosol drum containing sawdust. It lasts 8-10 hours & with oil water. Not much radiant heat from it. But the centre flame gives off a good heat. [initials]	

1875 Wt. W593/826 1,000,000 4/15 J.B.C. & A. A.D.S.S./Forms/C. 2118.

Instructions regarding War Diaries and Intelligence Summaries are contained in F. S. Regs., Part II. and the Staff Manual respectively. Title Pages will be prepared in manuscript.

Army Form C. 2118

WAR DIARY
or
INTELLIGENCE SUMMARY
(Erase heading not required.)

Place	Date	Hour	Summary of Events and Information	Remarks and references to Appendices
			Reference map BELGIUM. 1/20,000 Sheet 27 & 28.	
BRANDHOEK	5/XII/15		Called a conference of OSC Field ambulances at 11-15. Captain LANGRISHE DADMS proceeded on leave Major ROBERTS OC 42nd FA acting for him. 10 minutes at 8 pm came to say that shell at YPRES had wounded OC 11 LIVERPOOLS Col BAILEY, the MO Capt. WHITE & the quartermaster who were in the canal bank that day out of the line – [illegible]	
	6/XII/15		Visited No 10 CCS & saw Colonel Bailey (wounded) & Capt White RAMC (wounded yesterday in YPRES. [illegible]	
	8/XII/15		Visited section of Field Amb: (43rd) on the POPERINGHE - WATOU RD also the Motor Amb: workshop unit at ST JEAN TER BRIESEN. [illegible]	
	9/XII/15		2 officers & 30 men wounded at LA BRIQUE last night & 20 killed by shelling. Visited DDMS 6th Corps & DRS (42nd F Amb) [illegible]	

1875 Wt. W593/826 1,000,000 4/15 J.B.C. & A. A.D.S.S./Forms/C. 2118.

Instructions regarding War Diaries and Intelligence Summaries are contained in F. S. Regs., Part II. and the Staff Manual respectively. Title Pages will be prepared in manuscript.

WAR DIARY
or
INTELLIGENCE SUMMARY
(Erase heading not required.)

Army Form C. 2118

Place	Date	Hour	Summary of Events and Information	Remarks and references to Appendices
			Ref: map: BELGIUM 1/20000 sheets 27 & 28	
BRANDHOEK	10/XII/15		Visited A & B camp in the Lst area. Mud up to ankles & halfway up legs. Many huts have no floors & tents have tent boards sunk in the ground. Now occupied by 8th KRR & 6 KSLI respectively. [signature]	
	11/XII/15		Visited 6th Corps HQ. Saw DMS 2nd Army re the question of MOs who have not 3 months to run before their contracts expire – must sign for another year or be transferred to another Division in case the Div: leaves the country. Also received instructions re renewal of part worn unexpendable articles in the panniers. [signature]	
	12/XII/15		Saw OsC 3 Ambs went over the question of the Division moving elsewhere. Spoke about all men being inoculated against enteric. Operation orders for bringing in & clearing of Field Ambulances when the Division leaves the trenches on nights 15-16 & 16-17th inst. Spoke about equipment renewal of Expendable & inexpendable articles. Issued instructions to MOs of units re the question of panniers & their replenishment. [signature]	

1875 Wt. W593/826 1,000,000 4/15 J.B.C. & A. A.D.S.S./Forms/C. 2118.

Army Form C. 2118

WAR DIARY
or
INTELLIGENCE SUMMARY
(Erase heading not required.)

Instructions regarding War Diaries and Intelligence Summaries are contained in F. S. Regs., Part II. and the Staff Manual respectively. Title Pages will be prepared in manuscript.

Place	Date	Hour	Summary of Events and Information	Remarks and references to Appendices
			Ref: Map BELGIUM 1/40,000 Sheet 27/28	
BRANDHOEK	12/12/15		1 The 6th Division will commence to relieve the 14th Division on the night Decr 15/16. Extract from RAMC Operation order 14th Division	
			2 (a) On the night Decr 15/16	
			18th I B will relieve 42nd I B.	
			71st I B " relieve 43rd I B	
			(b) On the night Decr 16/17	
			16th I.B will relieve 41st I B.	
			(c) RA units will be relieved on the nights Decr 16/17 & 17/18 & proceed to their present Battery lines (Wagon)	
			3 On relief Brigades will be accommodated as follows	
			41st I.B. A & B huts, "B" camp in square A 30 & 1 Batt in POPERINGHE	
			42nd I B former billets in HOUTKERQUE & HERZEELE	
			43rd I B Divisional Camps A B C D.	
			Brigadiers will occupy their former Head Quarters	

1875 Wt. W593/826 1,000,000 4/15 J.B.C. & A. A.D.S.S./Forms/C. 2118.

Instructions regarding War Diaries and Intelligence Summaries are contained in F. S. Regs., Part II. and the Staff Manual respectively. Title Pages will be prepared in manuscript.

WAR DIARY
or
INTELLIGENCE SUMMARY
(Erase heading not required.)

Army Form C. 2118

Place	Date	Hour	Summary of Events and Information	Remarks and references to Appendices
			Ref: Map: 1/40000 BELGIUM Sheets 27 & 28	
BRANDHOEK	12/XII/15		4 The 11th Kings Liverpool Regt will be withdrawn on the evening of Decr 15 to their former billets in WATOU	
			5 On Decr 17th	
			(a) 42 Field Amb will close.	
			(b) 43 Field Amb: less 1 section will hand over the dressing station to a Field Amb: of 6th Division withdraw to their camp at L3.a.5.8 (Sheet 27) & close.	
			(c) 44th Field Amb. will withdraw the detachments at the PRISON YPRES & the REIGERSBERG CHATEAU on relief by detachments from 6th Division	
			(d) 43rd & 44th Field Ambulances will withdraw the detachments at Regimental aid posts.	
			6 The 44th Field Amb. will remain open & admit all sick of the Division.	

Army Form C. 2118

Instructions regarding War Diaries and Intelligence Summaries are contained in F. S. Regs., Part II. and the Staff Manual respectively. Title Pages will be prepared in manuscript.

WAR DIARY
or
INTELLIGENCE SUMMARY
(Erase heading not required.)

Place	Date	Hour	Summary of Events and Information	Remarks and references to Appendices
			Ref map BELGIUM 1/40,000 Sheets 27 + 28.	
BRANDHOEK	12/12/15		The sick of the Division will be collected as under & conveyed to 44th Field Amb.	
			From / By / Calling about / At / Commencing	
			A & B Huts, B Camp, H 30, Medical [illegible] Hut } Motor Ambulances of 43rd F Amb — 10.30 am — Huts — Dec 17th	
			HERZEELE, HOUTKERQUE } Motor Amb of 42nd F Amb } 10.00	
			WATOU } 11 am — GRAND PLACE — Dec 16	
			CAMPS A & B } Horse Amb 44th F Amb — 10.30 am — F 21 c 2.1 Sheet 27 — Dec 16	
			CAMPS C & D — Horse Amb of 43 F Amb — 10.30 am — IN DE ZAND PUTTEN L 3 a 7.4 Sheet 27 } Dec 16	
			[Signature] Col. AMS	

1875 Wt. W593/826 1,000,000 4/15 J.B.C. & A. A.D.S.S./Forms/C. 2118.

Instructions regarding War Diaries and Intelligence Summaries are contained in F. S. Regs., Part II. and the Staff Manual respectively. Title Pages will be prepared in manuscript.

WAR DIARY
or
INTELLIGENCE SUMMARY
(Erase heading not required.)

Army Form C. 2118

Place	Date	Hour	Summary of Events and Information	Remarks and references to Appendices
BRANDHOEK	13/12/15.		Col JOISE - MOORES proceeded on leave to England - I reported in morning to G.O.C 14th Divn, arranged with him for 44th F. A. to take over baths on 18th inst. visited A & B huts & B camp & A.30 A.D.M.S. VIth Divn called in forenoon & arranged personally with regard to taking over - sent out ammendments to operⁿ orders re collection of sick.	H.S
do	14/12/15.		Rainy S. wind - A.D.M.S. VIth Divn called again and left a copy of his programme - visited D.D.M.S VIth Corps. arranged for disposal of wheeled stretchers and trench stretchers. Called for return of transport & animals in F.A.'s - discrepancies require adjustment.	H.S
do	15/12/15		Inspected outfits at 9.30 - at 11 saw various M.O.s of units & instructed them in ~~their~~ duties of M.O. i/c regt especially with regard to duties on board ship & in tropical countries. Saw O.C. train and arranged about adjustment of animals in F.A.'s, and he also promised to send a W.O. ASC to each	H.S
do	16/12/15		~~met O.C.~~ Rainy S. wind - met O.C.'s. F.A.'s at 11 a.m. discussed arrangements for handing over to F.A.'s of VIth Divn, progress with regard to transport & equipment of Amb^ces satisfactory - with exception of tents - operation tents all unserviceable - and most of bell tents.	

1875 Wt. W593/826 1,000,000 4/15 J.B.C. & A. A.D.S.S./Forms/C. 2118.

Army Form C. 2118

Instructions regarding War Diaries and Intelligence Summaries are contained in F. S. Regs., Part II. and the Staff Manual respectively. Title Pages will be prepared in manuscript.

WAR DIARY
or
INTELLIGENCE SUMMARY
(Erase heading not required.)

Place	Date	Hour	Summary of Events and Information	Remarks and references to Appendices
BRANDHOEK	16/12/15 cont		arranged for 9 operating + 18 bell to be requisitioned by DADOS from base. Wired to D.G. for 3 officers RAMC + 20 men to complete establ. Went to baths in afternoon - two new pumps required. I have asked CRE to supply these. Lieut A. HEGARTY (TC) RAMC killed in action to day serving with 49th Bde R.F.A.	
do	17/12/15		S.W. wind some rain Saw remaining Regl M.O's at HQ this morning - following points dealt with. duties of M/Os i/c units. duties on board ship. Sanitation. inoculation. tropical diseases med. equipment unfits. at 2.30 saw large number of unfits at College. Pop. about 50% were returned to duty with regiments. opened letter from G.O.C. 41st Bde to Col Guise Moores enclosing private letter from O.C 8th KRR. describing gallantry of Capt MILLER RAMC. attached - Brigr asked what should be done in the matter - I replied recommendation should be submitted officially through him to G.O.C Divn.	

1875 Wt. W593/826 1,000,000 4/15 J.B.C. & A. A.D.S.S./Forms/C. 2118.

Instructions regarding War Diaries and Intelligence Summaries are contained in F. S. Regs., Part II. and the Staff Manual respectively. Title Pages will be prepared in manuscript.

Army Form C. 2118

WAR DIARY
or
INTELLIGENCE SUMMARY
(Erase heading not required.)

Place	Date	Hour	Summary of Events and Information	Remarks and references to Appendices
BRANDHOEK	17/12/15 (cont)		reports rendered that PRISON. YPRES – REIGERSBERG Chateau & Dress. Statn at VLAMERTINGHE have been handed over to 17th & 18th F. A.s of VIth Divn. All bearers withdrawn from aid posts – wheeled stretchers handed over & receipts given – VIth Divn collects to night.	
do	18/12/15		~~went to~~ S. W. wind went to ~~gas~~ H Q 41st Bde saw Brigr re Capt MILLER – inspected mess unfits at ~~H Q~~ received secret memorandum re arrangements for 14th Divn when in reserve	
do.	19/12/15.		N. E wind – fine & clear. awakened about 5 am by heavy firing at 6 am. strong fumes of gas passed over H Q camp – very irritating with sweetish taste – this lasted about an hour. at 7. am received message from G.S. 'German attack with gas on 6th Corps front from about WARWICK Farm' very heavy artillery fire all morning. at 12.40 received following message. from G.S. German gas attack lasted about one hour. AAA. no serious infantry attack followed though a few German infantry advanced opposite the MORTELDJE salient and were driven back AAA. Smoke helmets were very satisfactory. AAA units of 14th Divn	

1875 Wt. W593/826 1,000,000 4/15 J.B.C. & A. A.D.S.S./Forms/C. 2118.

Army Form C. 2118

WAR DIARY
or
INTELLIGENCE SUMMARY
(Erase heading not required.)

Instructions regarding War Diaries and Intelligence Summaries are contained in F. S. Regs., Part II. and the Staff Manual respectively. Title Pages will be prepared in manuscript.

Place	Date	Hour	Summary of Events and Information	Remarks and references to Appendices
			Map 27 & 28 Sheets Belgium 1/20000 Map HAZEBROUCK 5 A BELGIUM 1/100000	
BRANDHOEK	19/12/15 Cont.		need not be ready to move at short notice. AAA men should not be allowed in VLAMERTINGHE or POPERINGHE except on duty. AAA. addressed all units 14th Div. Went to HOUTKERQUE at 2.30 pm. and inspected unfits of 42nd Bde. Between 40 & 50 brought up from each regt about 50% found unfit.	KS.
	21/12/15		Visited 43rd F.A. now closed & also 6th Corps HQ. Returned from leave yesterday 20th [illegible]	
	22/12/15		Visited water tanks in the brick fields, also church army hut & [illegible] VLAMERTINGHE POP: road found there were no urinals supplied.	
	23/12/15		Issued instructions as follows. To F Amb: OC San: Sec: & OC M A W C [?] (1) The 14th Div: Supply Column, including San: Sect: Lorry, Ammunition Park, Motor Ambulances / Ambulance Workshop of the 14th Div: will embark at HAVRE (2) 14th Div: Supply Col including Sanitary Sect Lorry will join the Div: Supply Column at ESQUELBECQ on 25th by 2 pm	

1875 Wt. W593/826 1,000,000 4/15 J.B.C. & A. A.D.S.S./Forms/C. 2118.

Instructions regarding War Diaries and Intelligence Summaries are contained in F. S. Regs., Part II. and the Staff Manual respectively. Title Pages will be prepared in manuscript.

WAR DIARY
or
INTELLIGENCE SUMMARY
(Erase heading not required.)

Army Form C. 2118

Place	Date	Hour	Summary of Events and Information	Remarks and references to Appendices
			Maps { Sheets 27 & 28 Belgium 1/20000 HAZEBROUCK 5A 1/100000	
BRANDHOEK	24/12/15		3 The motor amb. workshop unit ~~accompanied~~ with 21 motor ambulances attached from 42, 43rd & 44 Field ambs will accompany the Div. Supply Column. The motor ambulance wagons of 42, 43 & 44 Field Ambs will report to O.C. M.A.W.U at 44 F.A. at 2 pm 25th Dec. carrying rations for their drivers for 26th. The Div. Supply Column will draw at CAESTRE 3 days supplies for itself the San: Sec: lorry the M.A.W.U & the motor ambulance wagons in addition to the current day's ration & will arrange for carriage & distribution. The D.S.C. will also arrange for the petrol for the same units & vehicles.	
			4 Four motor ambulances from 4 M.A.C. will report to O.C. 44th F.A. at 4 pm 25th inst. These will be employed & & from the 26th inst to perform the collection of sick from 41st & 42nd I Bs & from WATOU.	
			5. OC 44th Field amb: will detail two wagon orderlies to report to O.C. 42nd F Amb: at 8 AM 24th inst: They will accompany the motor ambulances of 42nd FA for instruction as to points at which sick of 42nd Brigade & other units at WATOU are collected. These orderlies will rejoin 44th F Amb on 25th after completion of that day's collecting & proceed on subsequent days with the motor ambulances attached from No 4 M.A.C. which are detailed to collect from 42 Brigade area.	

1875 Wt. W593/826 1,000,000 4/15 J.B.C. & A. A.D.S.S./Forms/C. 2118.

Army Form C. 2118

WAR DIARY
or
INTELLIGENCE SUMMARY

(Erase heading not required.)

Instructions regarding War Diaries and Intelligence Summaries are contained in F. S. Regs., Part II. and the Staff Manual respectively. Title Pages will be prepared in manuscript.

Place	Date	Hour	Summary of Events and Information	Remarks and references to Appendices
			Maps: Sheets 27 & 28 Belgium 1/20000 HAZEBROUCK 5A. 1/100000	
BRANDHOEK	25/xii/15		Notification has been received of the following movements GROUP I Entrain 27th Decbr 1915 41st Infantry Brigade less all transport except cookers & water carts XXXXXXX 44 Field ambulance less all transport except 1 cook wagon. GROUP II entrain on 28th Decbr 43rd Infantry Brigade less all transport except cookers & water carts XXXXXXX 43rd Field ambulance less all transport except 1 cook wagon GROUP III entrain 29th Decbr. 42nd Infantry Brigade less all transport except cookers & water carts XXXXXXX 42nd Field Amb: less all transport except 1 cook wagon GROUP I will be billeted between NORDAUSQUES & BONNINGUES LES ARDRES GROUP II will be billeted in the triangle WATTEN - EPERLECQUES - SALPERWICK GROUP III will be billeted between RECQUES & WESTROVE All these places are marked on HAZEBROUCK Sheet 5, squares A, B, 3 & C3.	

1875 Wt. W593/826 1,000,000 4/15 J.B.C. & A. A.D.S.S./Forms/C. 2118.

Instructions regarding War Diaries and Intelligence Summaries are contained in F. S. Regs., Part II. and the Staff Manual respectively. Title Pages will be prepared in manuscript.

WAR DIARY
or
INTELLIGENCE SUMMARY
(Erase heading not required.)

Army Form C. 2118

Place	Date	Hour	Summary of Events and Information	Remarks and references to Appendices
			Maps { Sheet 27/28 Belgium 1/20000; HAZEBROUCK 5A 1/100000	
BRANDHOEK	25/XII/15		The 24th Div: is relieving the 49th Div: in the line. The relief will commence on the night 28/29 Dec & will be completed on the morning 1st January. The 14th Div: will be moved back into the 2nd Army area & the 24th Div: comes into the 6th Corps area and take over the billets vacated by the 24th Div:	
	25/XII/15	4-20pm	All orders regarding the move are held in abeyance until further orders.	
	26/XII/15		The movement is Cancelled	
	27/XII/15		The 14th Division will relieve the 49th Division in the line from C15c 7.6 to B12b 8.2 as follows.	
			(a) On the night 28/29th Dec 3 Battalion 41st I B will relieve 148th I B in the centre sector.	
			(b) On the night 29/30th Dec 2 Battns 43rd I B will relieve 146th I B in the right sector.	
			(c) On the night 30/31st Dec 2 Battns 42 I B will relieve 147th I B in the left sector.	
			(d) The 14th Div: Art: will relieve 49th Div: Art: on the night Dec 30/31 & Dec 31/Jany 1st.	
			The 6th Division will be on our right & the French Division on our left.	

1875 Wt. W593/826 1,000,000 4/15 J.B.C. & A. A.D.S.S./Forms/C. 2118.

Instructions regarding War Diaries and Intelligence Summaries are contained in F. S. Regs., Part II. and the Staff Manual respectively. Title Pages will be prepared in manuscript.

Army Form C. 2118

WAR DIARY
or
INTELLIGENCE SUMMARY
(Erase heading not required.)

Place	Date	Hour	Map BELGIUM 1.40000 Sheet 28 Summary of Events and Information	Remarks and references to Appendices
BRANDHOEK	27/xii/15		The field ambulances of the 14th Div: will relieve those of the 49th Div: as follows:—	
			29th Decr. One section 42nd Field Amb: to relieve 3rd (WEST RIDING) Field Amb at A28 a. [illegible] Reliefs to be arranged directly between O.C. & units [illegible] hour & day of relief	
			30th Decr. 43rd Field Ambulance (less one tent subdivision) to relieve 2nd (W.R) Field Amb: A 23 a & c	
			OC 43rd Field amb: will detail a detachment of 1 NCO & 4 men to report on Decr 30th to OC 1st (W.R) Field amb: at A21 a.5.5 to take over charge of the camp and vacation of that unit on Decr 31st	
			The OC 44 Field Amb will arrange direct with O.C. 2nd & 3rd (W.R) Field ambulances to relieve the 4 detachments at Regimental Aid Posts in the front line on the night of Decr 28th each detachment to consist of 4 stretcher bearers	
			OC 44th Field ambulance will arrange direct with O.C. 3rd [illegible] (W. Riding) Field Ambulance to relieve to take over on the night 28th Decr the collecting Post in dug outs C19.c.40. (Takes 20 lying down cases) Personnel required will consist of 1 Officer 1 Sergeant & 4 other ranks	

1875 Wt. W593/826 1,000,000 4/15 J.B.C. & A. A.D.S.S./Forms/C. 2118.

Instructions regarding War Diaries and Intelligence Summaries are contained in F. S. Regs., Part II. and the Staff Manual respectively. Title Pages will be prepared in manuscript.

WAR DIARY
or
INTELLIGENCE SUMMARY

(Erase heading not required.)

Army Form C. 2118

Place	Date	Hour	Summary of Events and Information	Remarks and references to Appendices
			Reference map BELGIUM 1/40,000 Sheet 28.	
BRANDHOEK H7 C77	27/12/15		OC 43rd Field Amb. will arrange with OC 2nd (WR) Field Amb. to relieve the motor ambulances at the collecting Post at BRIELEN on 29 Dec. the personnel required will consist of 1 NCO & 2 other ranks.	
			OC 43rd Field Amb: will arrange with 3rd (WR) Field Amb to take over the farm at B19 d 8.8 on the 28th inst and establish there a Medical Detention room with a personnel of 1 NCO & 2 men. He will also detail an officer daily to visit the room at 10 Am to see such sick as may be paraded there. Sick for Hospital will be conveyed from thence to the main Dressing Station	
			The 44 Field ambulance will form the main Dressing Station at the COLLEGE RUE BOESCHEPE POPERINGHE & will be responsible for the collection & disposal of sick & wounded	
			The collection of sick & wounded from the front line will be taken over by the 14th Div: from 10 Am on Dec 30th all patients being conveyed to the main Dressing Station. Motor ambulances will work as follows	
			For ESSEX FARM (C19c.4.0) 4 ambulances depart from main Dressing Station at	8 pm
			" " 2 " " " " " " at	4-30 Am
			For Cross roads B23 a 9.9. 2 " " " " "	8 pm
			" " 1 " " " " "	4.30 Am

Army Form C. 2118

WAR DIARY
or
INTELLIGENCE SUMMARY
(Erase heading not required.)

Instructions regarding War Diaries and Intelligence Summaries are contained in F. S. Regs., Part II. and the Staff Manual respectively. Title Pages will be prepared in manuscript.

Place	Date	Hour	Summary of Events and Information — Reference map BELGIUM 1/40000 Sheet 28	Remarks and references to Appendices
BRANDHOEK	27/xii/15		Commencing Decr 29th OC 43rd FA will detail motor ambulances to call daily as follows	
			one motor amb: calling at ELVERDINGHE 11 am.	
			" " " calling at REST CAMP No 1 at A16 a 7.6 11 am.	
			Commencing Dec 30th OC 42nd F Amb. will detail 2 motor ambs to report to OC 44 FA at 7-45 pm each night	
			The motor amb at BRIELEN will call daily as under commencing Decr 30th	
			ESSEX FARM 3 pm.	
			ROAD JUNCTION B22 C.7 8 3.30 pm.	
			The daily collection of sick as at present carried out will cease after the dates mentioned below.	
			From A 30 & B & C camps Decr 28th	
			" HAZELLE 29th "	
			" HOUTKERQUE 30th "	
			From Decr 29th inclusive horsed ambulances will be substituted for motor ambulances for the collection made from A & B huts & 43rd F Amb will collect with horsed ambulances from A & D camps only	

1875 Wt. W593/826 1,000,000 4/15 J.B.C. & A. A.D.S.S./Forms/C. 2118.

Instructions regarding War Diaries and Intelligence Summaries are contained in F. S. Regs., Part II. and the Staff Manual respectively. Title Pages will be prepared in manuscript.

WAR DIARY
or
INTELLIGENCE SUMMARY
(Erase heading not required.)

Army Form C. 2118

Place	Date	Hour	Summary of Events and Information	Remarks and references to Appendices
			Map BELGIUM 1/40,000 Sheet 28	
BRANDHOEK.	31/XII/15		Evacuation from the front line is done on trolleys on field railway from trenches to collecting post at C19 C4.0 (ESSEX FARM) where motor ambulances meet. The line continues to ~~?~~ RLY COTTAGES B 30.B.3.3. called LABELLE ALLIANCE LINE. ~~Intermediate~~ This clears the aid post at C 20.b.0.9. & starts at B 30 A 8.9.	
			Aid posts are at C13 a 1.7. C13 b 3 3 (GLIMPSE COTTAGE) C 13 d 9.2 (GLIMPSE COTTAGE LINE) (LANCASHIRE FARM) (LANCASHIRE FARM LINE) + the one already mentioned at C 20 b 09. The trolley line (trolleys take 5 wounded lying down) for the GLIMPSE COTTAGE & LANCASHIRE FAM Posts meet at C19 a 4.0	
			A motor ambulance is now kept permanently at ELVERDINGHE CASTLE No 43 FA (Ad. Dressing Station) is on the telephone & can be called up if more than one car is required. If any one is required the BRIELEN VILLAGE car can be requisitioned by telephone from 42nd Brigade HQrs. Each aid post is to have 200 ammonia ampoules & 500 are to be kept in reserve for emergencies at C19 C4.0. (Collecting Post)	
			Geo Moores Colonel ??? ADMS 14th Div.	

1875 Wt. W593/826 1,000,000 4/15 J.B.C. & A. A.D.S.S./Forms/C. 2118.

S.
Jan 1916.

F/31/1

Adv. 14th Div.
Vol: 6

14 DIV.

Instructions regarding War Diaries and Intelligence Summaries are contained in F. S. Regs., Part II. and the Staff Manual respectively. Title Pages will be prepared in manuscript.

WAR DIARY
or
INTELLIGENCE SUMMARY
(Erase heading not required.)

Army Form C. 2118

Place	Date	Hour	Summary of Events and Information — Reference Map BELGIUM 1/40,000 Sheet 28.	Remarks and references to Appendices
BRANDHOEK	2/1/16		Commencing on the night January 2/3rd 43rd Field Amb. will take over the collection of sick & wounded from the "left sector" & admit all patients collected by them both from the front line & from the areas at present cleared by them as detailed below. Two motor ambulances of 43rd Field Amb. will call daily at X roads B23 a 9.9 at 9 pm & one at same point at 5.30 Am. On January 2nd the 43rd FA will post 4 stretcher bearers at SARAGOSSA FARM (B24a.1.4) with orders to proceed each night as soon as it is dark to Regimental aid post at C13a 1.7 to evacuate patients from there to Cross roads B23a 9.9. Commencing on Jany 3rd 42nd FA will take over the following collections & will the patients to 44 FA. From Camp A 1 horse drawn ambulances From Div: Rest Camp No 1 motor ambulance (A16 A & C) The collection from Camp D will cease from Jany 3rd inclusive OC. 44 Field Amb. will direct the 3 motor ambulances from 42nd Field Amb. to rejoin their unit at once [illegible signature]	

1875 Wt. W593/826 1,000,000 4/15 J.B.C. & A. A.D.S.S./Forms/C. 2118.

Instructions regarding War Diaries and Intelligence Summaries are contained in F. S. Regs., Part II. and the Staff Manual respectively. Title Pages will be prepared in manuscript.

WAR DIARY
or
INTELLIGENCE SUMMARY
(Erase heading not required.)

Army Form C. 2118

Place	Date	Hour	Summary of Events and Information	Remarks and references to Appendices
			Ref: map BELGIUM 1/40000 Sheet 28	
BRANDHOEK	3/1/16.		One motor ambulance with one NCO & 2 men posted at ELVERDINGHE CHATEAU (B14 b 1.1. This ambulance to perform the duty which was told off to the amb. detailed daily by OC 43rd FA to call at 11 am at same place – see 27/xii/15	Scm
	4/1/16		Divisional cyclists & cavalry are moved from WATOU area to ST SIXTE A.1.a.1.5. OC 42nd F Amb detailed to send an officer at 10 am daily to see sick there	
			OC 43rd Field Amb ordered to collect sick with horse ambulance from the undermentioned camps calling at 10 am to convey them to 44th Field amb (Rue BOESCHEPE POPERINGHE) Camp no 1 A16a. Camp no 2 A16c. Camp no 4 A8a (calling at cross roads A9a 0 4 ([illegible] Corner) Ambulance should also halt on return journey at point A14 d.5.1 to collect sick from HQ entrenching Battn (A14.c 9 6). It has been arranged for sick from the following units to go to 44th Field Amb as under 33rd Brigade RGA (A22 d 8 4) & 4th entrenching Batt (A23 b 5.6 to main dressing station. The 4th Siege Battery (B21.d 9 9) to KART FARM These 3 units are corps troops	

1875 Wt. W593/826 1,000,000 4/15 J.B.C. & A. A.D.S.S./Forms/C. 2118.

Army Form C. 2118

Instructions regarding War Diaries and Intelligence Summaries are contained in F. S. Regs., Part II. and the Staff Manual respectively. Title Pages will be prepared in manuscript.

WAR DIARY
or
INTELLIGENCE SUMMARY
(Erase heading not required.)

Place	Date	Hour	Summary of Events and Information	Remarks and references to Appendices
			Reference Maps BELGIUM "B" Series Sheet 28 1/40000 & BOESINGHE 1/10000	
BRANDHOEK.	6/1/16		On the night January 8/9 the 14th Div. extends its front & takes over the line from 6th Division up to junction of trenches B15 & B16 (C 21.b.2.3) the 43rd I.B. extending its right to the point named.	
			The OC 44th FA will arrange to take over the dug out near Bridge 4 occupied by 6th Div. Collecting Post on their withdrawal at 9 am on 9th inst.	
			The OC 44th FA will direct the Stretcher bearer detachment at Aid Post of Batt: in right section of 43rd Brigade to relieve RAMC personnel of 17th Field Amb. at LA BELLE ALLIANCE which is to be withdrawn at second [illegible] & morning of 9th	[illegible]
	7/1/16		Had to withdraw the motor ambulance plying between BRIELEN VILLAGE & ESSEX FARM arriving latter at 3 pm on account of its being followed on the road by terrible High explosive shell fire.	
			Visited No 10 C.C.S. this afternoon to see O.C. re the loss of General Sandeman's Servant's kit which was lost between 41 Brigade HQ where he was wounded & the C.C.S.	
			Saw O.C. 9th? re the extension of 14th Div: line to the right. Also spoke about having an officer to inspect motor cycles daily & also motor cars	[illegible]

1875 Wt. W593/826 1,000,000 4/15 J.B.C. & A. A.D.S.S./Forms/C. 2118.

Instructions regarding War Diaries and Intelligence Summaries are contained in F. S. Regs., Part II. and the Staff Manual respectively. Title Pages will be prepared in manuscript.

WAR DIARY
or
INTELLIGENCE SUMMARY
(Erase heading not required.)

Army Form C. 2118

Place	Date	Hour	Summary of Events and Information	Remarks and references to Appendices
			Map BELGIUM 1/40000 Sheet 28 + 27	
BRANDHOEK 9/1/16			Our laundry work for underclothing after men bathing is done by contract at WESTOUTRE. The contractor arranges to have the articles as they come back from the washerwoman. She also issues the clothing, sees that it is correctly returned, mended & pays the employees. We send for it daily from Baths by G.S. wagon. The work is done in the 1/Canadian Div: area & Q branch decided us to remove the shirt room elsewhere. I saw the AA&QMG Can. Div: & settle matters. Things remain as they were. The Baths now used were taken over from the 49th Div. Consist of shower baths with changing rooms, soiled linen room &c. It is a hutted structure. The water used coming from a well. The soap is extracted by lime & the water charcoal filtered is used once more again.	[illegible]
10/1/16			Visited the camp of No 1 Company Div: Train Z 21 C (Sheet 27). The sanitary arrangements require looking into.	[illegible]
11/1/16			Visited GHQ.	
12/1/16			Note from Capt Couchman asking for wheeled stretchers for use in the right sector (LA BELLE ALLIANCE). CAPT COUCHMAN to No 6th SOMERSET L.I. Wheeled stretchers can be used in the PILKHEM ROAD from DAWSON CITY (trench map BOESINGHE) to CANALBANK. They can be left during the day at side of road (PILKHEM ROAD) just W of DAWSON CITY. Two could be sent & also two kept in the ruins of LA BELLE ALLIANCE during the day. Applied to ordnance for extra wheeled stretchers	

Instructions regarding War Diaries and Intelligence Summaries are contained in F. S. Regs., Part II. and the Staff Manual respectively. Title Pages will be prepared in manuscript.

WAR DIARY

or

INTELLIGENCE SUMMARY

(Erase heading not required.)

Army Form C. 2118

Place	Date	Hour	Summary of Events and Information	Remarks and references to Appendices
			Map BELGIUM Sheets 27-28. 1/40000 also trench map BOESINGHE	
BRANDHOEK	12/1/16		GOC 42nd Brigade asked for a medical officer to call at MALAKOFF FARM B 22 d 1.10 (Sheet 28 NW) daily to see sick from his units in farms W of the canal. Arranged that MO collecting from left sector (43rd FA) nightly at 8-9 pm should stop there & see any sick.	
			Also wounded seen at C 13 a 1.7 and post E canal bank should be sent by wheeled stretcher to BARD COTTAGE B 24 b 9.3 instead of by trolley as previously arranged owing to trolley line being out of order.	
			Arranged that these wounded should be taken up by MO collecting from collecting post near Bridge 4 nightly. OC No 43 FA sending an additional motor amb: nightly for this purpose & the wounded from this area. The motor amb: to be under the MO collecting for 44 F Amb: (centre right sector).	
	13/1/16		Propose to use 42nd Field Amb. C section at A 23 a for men who are unable to return to the trenches but who are not sick. They will be detained & bring their rations with them first day. F Amb to provide for 3 subsequent days. The men to return to units when they come out of the trenches 3 days later.	

1875 Wt. W593/826 1,000,000 4/15 J.B.C. & A. A.D.S.S./Forms/C. 2118.

Instructions regarding War Diaries and Intelligence Summaries are contained in F. S. Regs., Part II. and the Staff Manual respectively. Title Pages will be prepared in manuscript.

WAR DIARY
or
INTELLIGENCE SUMMARY
(Erase heading not required.)

Army Form C. 2118

Place	Date	Hour	Summary of Events and Information	Remarks and references to Appendices
			Map Reference BELGIUM 1/40,000 Sheet 28. Trench map BOESINGHE 2nd Army Sheet 1	
BRANDHOEK	16/1/16		Asked CRE to build a trolley line to connect WINDSOR CASTLE LINE via BARD COTTAGES with new line from GLIMPSE COTTAGE + LANCS FARM LINE which is passing over bridge 6 to AUSTERLITZ FARM. This would allow wounded to be evacuated either from BRIELEN X Roads or DAWSONS CORNER.	
	17/1/16		Asked G to arrange for Battalion aid posts of the right + centre sections to be located in the CANAL BANK, as the accommodation in the trenches is very limited + does not lend itself to efficient treatment. French dug-out accommodating 8-10 stretchers in such cases are required. A small dug out might be retained in the trenches where medical officers could inspect sick in the evenings.	[illegible initials]
			Telephone Stations Exist at ELVERDINGHE CHATEAU MORDACQ FARM B17.c.9.3 Visual station BRIELEN	
			Visual a central station in the red brick house just SE of the Church in BRIELEN B29A81.	
			Wireless Stations (1) 41 I B H.Q. Canal Bank C19 C4.2 (2) + ELVERDINGHE CHATEAU	

1875 Wt. W593/826 1,000,000 4/15 J.B.C. & A. A.D.S.S./Forms/C. 2118.

Instructions regarding War Diaries and Intelligence Summaries are contained in F. S. Regs., Part II. and the Staff Manual respectively. Title Pages will be prepared in manuscript.

WAR DIARY
or
INTELLIGENCE SUMMARY
(Erase heading not required.)

Army Form C. 2118

Place	Date	Hour	Summary of Events and Information	Remarks and references to Appendices
			Ref Map BELGIUM 1/40000 Sheet 28 & Sheet 27 & French map BOESINGHE 1/10000	
BRANDHOEK			Defence scheme emergency arrangements attached.	
	20/1/16		The camp at A 28 a (Sheet 28) has been taken over by a section of 43rd from 42 FA Field Amb: The 42nd Field Ambulance has taken over the camp at L 3 a (Sheet 27) from the 43rd Field Amb: They have exchanged camps. [signature]	
	21/		In order to complete supervision of sanitation in the Division the areas occupied by units will be supervised by Field Ambulance commanders as follows	
			OC 42nd Field Amb: area bounded on the North by the International boundary on the East by POPERINGHE CANAL on the West by the POPERINGHE - CROMBEKE ROAD (passing through F 10 d Sheet 27) & on the South by the Interdivisional Boundary (Sixth Div: is on right 87th French Division on our left)	
			OC 43rd Field Amb: area bounded as follows: - N International boundary East KEMMEL BECK stream. S. Interdivisional boundary (14th & 6th Divisions) W. POPERINGHE CANAL	
			OC 44th Field Amb: area in occupation of 14th Div: with the following boundaries N Interdivisional Boundary 14th & 6th Division. W. POPERINGHE CANAL & Road POPERINGHE - ABEELE South Intercorps boundary VI & V Corps EAST KEMMELBECK stream [signature]	

1875 Wt. W593/826 1,000,000 4/15 J.B.C. & A. A.D.S.S./Forms/C. 2118.

Instructions regarding War Diaries and Intelligence Summaries are contained in F. S. Regs., Part II. and the Staff Manual respectively. Title Pages will be prepared in manuscript.

WAR DIARY
or
INTELLIGENCE SUMMARY
(Erase heading not required.)

Army Form C. 2118

Place	Date	Hour	Summary of Events and Information	Remarks and references to Appendices
			Map 28 (Sheet) 1/40,000 Belgium	
BRANDHOEK 23/1/16			Saw OC 40 Field Amb with regard to making a 2nd entrance by which motor ambulances could approach & leave the dressing station from the front line & also those from the MDS taking cases to CCS. This would prevent blocking of the main road by motor amb traffic as the "drive" would be in the ambulance precincts. [signature]	
25/1/16			ADMS approached with regard to above plan submitted to CRE Divn to get the matter in hand. [signature]	
26/1/16			Each Field Amb has now been supplied with three wheeled stretchers	
			Visited GHQ & saw DDMS (personnel) about Lt Col Simson OC 44 F Amb who has gone sick since he has been to England on leave. also arranged with Lt Col Cummins RAMC for him to visit the Field ambulances on 30th inst.	
27/1/16			Visited No 1 Camp & saw Lt DUNKERLEY MO i/c 8 RB which is occupying the camp. Inspected it & pointed out sanitary improvements. Decided to bring out a set of rules for sanitation of standing camps standardising the procedure for all. [signature]	

1875 Wt. W593/826 1,000,000 4/15 J.B.C. & A. A.D.S.S./Forms/C. 2118.

Instructions regarding War Diaries and Intelligence Summaries are contained in F. S. Regs., Part II. and the Staff Manual respectively. Title Pages will be prepared in manuscript.

WAR DIARY
or
INTELLIGENCE SUMMARY
(Erase heading not required.)

Army Form C. 2118

Place	Date	Hour	Summary of Events and Information	Remarks and references to Appendices
			Map BELGIUM Sheet 28 1/40000	
BRANDHOEK	29/1/16		Instructions for sanitation of camps standardising the procedure typed & circulated. Sam	
	30/1/16		Visited with Col CUMMINS 44th Field Amb (main dressing station) 43rd Field Amb A.D.S. Section 43rd Field Amb: now taking in Scabies cases & men detained till their units come from the trenches & discharged from the D.R.S. The Baths (which are to be taken to pieces & sent to 49th Division which are here) & the D.R.S.	
			The new Baths are to be opened in POPERINGHE in the empty rooms belonging to the (5) of the COLLEGE now occupied by the 44th Field Amb:	
			Tubs are being obtained & also boilers through D.A.D.O.S. Water is to be pumped from the stream close by by pump supplied by R.E. into a water tank in the courtyard. Coal is being supplied by A.S.C. The drying rooms will be fitted with wire & stoves by R.E. The washing of the men's underclothing will continue to be done at WESTOUTRE by contract. The baths should be opened by Monday 31st inst.	
			The R.E. have also supplied apparatus to fit up 7 shower baths. Sam	

1875 Wt. W593/826 1,000,000 4/15 J.B.C. & A. A.D.S.S./Forms/C. 2118.

Instructions regarding War Diaries and Intelligence Summaries are contained in F. S. Regs., Part II. and the Staff Manual respectively. Title Pages will be prepared in manuscript.

WAR DIARY
or
INTELLIGENCE SUMMARY
(Erase heading not required.)

Army Form C. 2118

Place	Date	Hour	Map BELGIUM Sheet 28 1/40000 Summary of Events and Information	Remarks and references to Appendices
BRANDHOEK			Instructions for sanitation of camps standardising the procedure typed & issued to all concerned. [illegible]	
	29/1/16		Visited with Col CUMMINS 44th Field Amb (main dressing station)	
	30/1/16		43rd Field Amb A.D.S. Section 43rd Field Amb: now taking in Scabies cases & are detained till their cure – come from the Trenches & discharged from the D.R.S. The Baths (which are to be taken to pieces & sent to 49th Division which are there) & the D.R.S. The new Baths are to be opened in POPERINGHE in the empty rooms belonging to behind (S) of the COLLEGE now occupied by the 44 Field Amb. Tubs are being obtained & also 80 yds stores of DADOS. Water is to be pumped from the stream close by by pump supplied by RE into a water tank in the courtyard. Coal is being supplied by ASC. The drying rooms will be fitted with wire & stoves by RE. The washing of the men under clothing will be continue to be done at WESTOUTRE by contract. The baths should be opened by Monday 31st inst. The RE have also supplied apparatus to fit up 7 Shower baths [illegible]	[illegible] Col [illegible] ADMS 14 Div.

1875 Wt. W593/826 1,000,000 4/15 J.B.C. & A. A.D.S.S./Forms/C. 2118.

DEFENCE SCHEME.

Emergency arrangements.(Medical)

Reference: Maps Belgium Sheet 28, 1 in 40,000 & BOESINGHE, 1/10,000.

1. On the receipt of the message "defend" the existing arrangements will be augmented, and additional measures put into force, as mentioned below :-

2. Collecting Posts.
   i. near Bridge 4 (West Bank)
   ii. near Bridge 6 (West Bank)(site to be selected).

No. 1 will be found by the Field Ambulance in occupation at the time, and the personnel increased to One Officer, One N.C.O., and 6 men.

No. 2 will be found by the Field Ambulance at the time clearing the left sector, and will be constituted, as regards personnel etc., as is No. 1.

Only dressings that are absolutely necessary should be done at these Collecting Posts. Arrangements must be made for providing hot drinks for wounded, and a supply of drinking water should be maintained.

3. Loading Points.
   (a) By day,(for walking cases only - see paras4 & 7b)
   (i) B.29.d.1.8.)Personnel at existing collect-
   (ii) B.22.a.3.8.(approx))ing Posts at ELVERDINGHE & BRIELEN should be stationed at these points.
   (b) By Night - as in routine, plus the above, which will remain.

4. Divisional Collecting Station: KARTE F^m (B.19.d.7.7)
O.C. Field Ambulance at D.R.S. will despatch a detachment consisting of One Officer, One N.C.O. and 10 men to this place, who will take over the equipment there, and establish a dressing station for walking cases. Extra dressings and Oxygen cylinders will be required. The existing detachment will be relieved, and rejoin their Field Ambulance. An A & D Book will be kept, and trivial cases sent to D.R.S; others should be evacuated direct to C.C.S. If necessary this collecting station will be used at night as a Dressing Station for sitting cases. * careful that cases are not admitted twice over

5. Dressing Stations.
   (a) Advanced: (i) A.23.c.2.8.
   (ii) A.28.a.3.6.

No.(ii) will deal by night with sitting cases only, No.(i) being free to admit stretcher cases.
   (b) Main: The College, POPERINGHE.

6. Collection of Wounded.

(a) The O.C., 44th Field Ambulance will superintend the collection of wounded from the Trenches and Aid Posts. He will be located at HOSPITAL FARM. (B.19.b.1.1.) and will establish communication with collecting Posts, and A.D.M.S. by means of Motor Cyclists.

(b) One bearer sub-division from each Field Ambulance will immediately proceed to KARTE F^m (B.19.d.7.7) and report to the collecting Officer for use and distribution as required.

(c) One hour after the departure from the Field Ambulances of the bearer sub-divisions, a second bearer sub-division from each will proceed to KARTE F^m and remain there in reserve. The remaining bearer sub-divisions will be kept in readiness by Officers Commanding Field Ambulances to meet any further requirements.

(over)

7. Clearing of Collecting Posts.

(a) Stretcher cases - such cases as can be moved by daylight will be taken to the collecting post near Bridge 4, whence they will be evacuated by motor ambulances working along the road running parallel to the Canal on its West Bank, and taken direct to the main Dressing Station. By night, the Collecting Posts will be cleared as in routine, an augmented service of motor ambulances being instituted as below (para 8b)

(b) Walking cases: (i) by day - these will be directed, in parties of not more than six, to the Divisional Collecting Station - KARTE FARM. The "Stragglers posts" have instructions to direct them along the roads. Those unable to proceed further than the ELVERDINGHE - YPRES road, will be loaded on to Motor Ambulances at the "Loading Points" and taken, in the case of No. 1 Point, to the Main Dressing Station: in that of No. 2, to the Advanced Dressing Stations.
(2) by night - cases will be directed to the Loading Points, (para 3(a)) where all will be loaded on to Motor Ambulances - those from No. 1 Point will be taken to Divisional Collecting Station, and those from No. 2 point to No. 2 Advanced Dressing Station.

8. Motor Ambulances.

(a) All available motor ambulances in the Division will be sent at once to HOSPITAL FARM and report to the Officer i/c Collecting. They will park along the road at intervals of not less than 50 yards from road-junction A.18.d.2.7. to HOSPITAL FARM. Motor Ambulances proceeding eastwards from there will move via road junctions B.20.b.3.7. and B.14.b.9.1. No Motor Ambulances are to park on this road.

Should additional Motor Ambulances be required by day, the Officer i/c Collecting will notify A.D.M.S. stating number required.

(b) By day, a service of at least 4 Motor Ambulances per hour will probably be required at each Loading Point for walking cases unable to proceed further. To maintain this service, the following will probably be the number required:-
from No. 1 Loading Point 6 Motor Ambulances.
No. 2 " " 4 Motor Ambulances.

(c) By night, 10 extra Motor Ambulances will be required from M.A.C: those should report to Officer i/c Collecting at HOSPITAL FARM and park as in subpara (a)

NOTE. Motor Ambulances convoying walking cases from No. 1 Loading Point to KARTE FARM at night, will proceed via YPRES & VLAMERTINGHE or via ELVERDINGHE, and road junction at HOSPITAL FARM, completing the circuit via route as in subpara(a).

(d) The following will probably be the minimum services required by night to maintain a continuous stream of evacuation from Loading Points:-

		Cars per hour.	Cars required.
Right Sector	(a)Stretcher cases	4	6
	(b)Walking cases	6	6
Left Sector:	(a)Stretcher cases,	4	4
	(b)Walking cases,	6	6

The Collecting Officer with Motor Ambulances clearing the Left Sector will post himself at Cross roads B.23.a.9.8. and will utilize the Signal Office at that place for communicating with Officer i/c Collection at HOSPITAL FARM, and with Regimental Headquarters in the Left Sector.

(Continued.)

9. <u>Evacuation to D.R.S. and C.C.S.</u>
Probable requirements from M.A.C.

	Motor Amblces.
(1) By day :-	
at Divl Collecting Station	6.
Dressing Stations:	
Main,	4.
No. 1 Advancod,	4.
No. 2.Advancod,	4.
Total,	18.

(2) By night :-	
at Divl Collecting Station,	4.
Dressing Stations,	
Main,	3.
No. 1 Advancod,	3.
No. 2.Advanced,	4.
Total.	14.

Further requirements to be notified to the A.D.M.S. by the Officers Commanding the Dressing Stations and Divisional Collecting Station.

10. <u>Communications.</u>
Motor Cyclists will be posted as follows :-

A.D.M.S.	2 (42nd Field Amblce = 1 (43rd " " = 1.
Officer i/c Collecting,	1 - 44th Field Ambulance.
Collecting Post, Bridge 4,	1 - 42nd Field Ambulance.

11. The D.R.S. will be prepared to receive 200 slightly wounded.

S. Guise Moores.
COLONEL, A.M.S.
A. D. M. S.
14TH (LIGHT) DIVISION.

18th January, 1916.

5 Feb 1916

A.D.M.S. 14th Div

Instructions regarding War Diaries and Intelligence Summaries are contained in F. S. Regs., Part II. and the Staff Manual respectively. Title Pages will be prepared in manuscript.

WAR DIARY
or
INTELLIGENCE SUMMARY
(Erase heading not required.)

Army Form C. 2118

Place	Date	Hour	Sheet 28 / N W Belgium 1/20000 — Summary of Events and Information	Remarks and references to Appendices
BRANDHOEK	1/2/16		Visited DRS at HILLHOEK run by 42 Field Amb: Saw OC 44th F Amb: told him to send his cases direct to CCS & not through ~~Div:~~ Rest Station. SAW	
	2/2/16		Visited No 4 Camp saw CAPT COUCHMAN RAMC at Somerset LI re certain sanitary improvements connected with the camp. Saw OC 9th KRR re his large number of sick. SAW	
	3/2/16		As the DRS at HILLHOEK has been partially closed on account of the state of camp (mud) & the approaches to it being impassable for traffic the Div Army arranged with 12 CCS to take in D.R.S. cases. All cases to be sent there till the DRS fit to receive cases. Visited CCS at HAZEBROUCK today to arrange about discharge of men to 14th Div: Cases to be collected in one or two batches. Sent two clerks to 12 CCS for this purpose. OC 12 CCS to notify Div 14th Div: when cases are admitted to duty or evacuated to L of C. SAW	
	4/2/16		Scabies cases to be sent to 50th ~~N Mid~~ CCS at HAZEBROUCK. Saw OC & arranged for cases discharged to be sent to RTO at the Station to come on to HQ a refilling point in case of a move of the Division. SAW	
	5/2/16		Visited 43rd & 44th Field Ambs: chose a spot for the erection of a new French hut which the Corps had at the Scabies Branch of the 43rd Field Amb on the POPERINGHE - ELVERDINGHE Rd. SAW	

1875 Wt. W593/826 1,000,000 4/15 J.B.C. & A. A.D.S.S./Forms/C. 2118.

Instructions regarding War Diaries and Intelligence Summaries are contained in F. S. Regs., Part II. and the Staff Manual respectively. Title Pages will be prepared in manuscript.

WAR DIARY
or
INTELLIGENCE SUMMARY
(Erase heading not required.)

Army Form C. 2118

Place	Date	Hour	Summary of Events and Information — Ref map NW BELGIUM 1/20,000	Remarks and references to Appendices
BRANDHOEK	4/2/16		Had to give up billets in the POPERINGHE - ELVERDINGHE Road as they belonged to the 49th Div: who were out of the line resting & who required them on moving to another area	
			An Opening Bathing in COLLEGE POPERINGHE behind 44th Field Amb: for Division, Tubs, Soyers stoves, drying rooms, coal, & personnel arranged	SAW
	7/2/16		Visited HAZEBROUCK saw Col GRECH re complaint about DURHAM C.O. their mens kits at No 12 CCS not being returned complete	SAW
	8/2/16		Bomb fell in A.D. Camp yesterday which farm House wounded one girl aged about 15. Went to Belgian Civil Hospl after dispatching her there in motor amb: to enquire re treatment of injuries &c.	SAW
	9/2/16		Visited D.D.M.S. at CHATEAU COUTHOVE (14th Corps) The Division is now under 14th Corps (MAJ GEN LORD CAVAN	
	10/2/16		Visited 44th Field Amb: at COLLEGE & also MAWU at St JEAN TER BIEZEN.	SAW
			Orders issued to move	SAW
	11/2/16		One Sectn 44th Field Amb: marched with 41st Brigade into WINNIEZEELE today the others have moved as follows	SAW

Army Form C. 2118

Instructions regarding War Diaries and Intelligence Summaries are contained in F. S. Regs., Part II. and the Staff Manual respectively. Title Pages will be prepared in manuscript.

WAR DIARY
or
INTELLIGENCE SUMMARY
(Erase heading not required.)

Place	Date	Hour	Summary of Events and Information	Remarks and references to Appendices
			Ref Map: NW BELGIUM 1/20000 Sheets 27 & 28	
BRANDHOEK	12/2/16		43rd on 12th to WATOU 44th Field Amb. on 14th to WORMHOUDT [initials]	
ESQUELBECQ	13/2/16		Head Quarters Division moved to ESQUELBECQ [illegible] prior to a move South. [initials]	
	14/2/16		Visited 44 Field Amb now in the Schools in WINNIEZEELE also the 42 Field Amb. at WORMHOUDT (Schools). Brigade Baths opened at latter place for 42nd Brigade. Tubs & coal provided the former already exist in the building lent by Brigade Supply Officer. Sick moved by Div[isional] Army to 10 & 17 CCS by motor ambulance, collected in WATOU, HOUTKERQUE & WINNIEZEELE [initials]	
	15/2/16		Billeting officers 7 Amb. [illegible] went to [illegible] area in advance of 17th Div. C [illegible] 42 F Amb. with 42nd Brigade on parade 43rd F Amb. [illegible] from WATOU to HOUTKERKE to allow a [illegible] Div. Field Amb. to go in there [initials]	
	17/2/16		Visited 42, 43, 44 Field ambulance today	
	18/2/16		The FAWC with 21 motor ambulances & 3 motor cycles will move under ch. of OC FAWC on 21st to FLESSELLES (Ref Map LENS 1/100000) [initials]	

1875 Wt. W593/826 1,000,000 4/15 J.B.C. & A. A.D.S.S./Forms/C. 2118.

Instructions regarding War Diaries and Intelligence Summaries are contained in F. S. Regs., Part II. and the Staff Manual respectively. Title Pages will be prepared in manuscript.

WAR DIARY
or
INTELLIGENCE SUMMARY

(Erase heading not required.)

Army Form C. 2118

Place	Date	Hour	Summary of Events and Information	Remarks and references to Appendices
			Ref map Belgium NW Sheets 27 + 28 1/40000	
ESQUELBECQ	18/2/16.		44th Field Amb entraining at CASSEL on Feb 21st 42nd Field Amb: entraining at ESQUELBECQ on Feb 21st 43rd Field Amb entraining at CASSEL on Feb 21st [illegible initials]	
Ref map LENS 1/100000	20/2/16		Left ESQUELBECQ for FLESSELLES to join 3rd Army area arrived 7 pm. [illegible initials]	
FLESSELLES	22/2/16		All the Field ambulances arrived in the 3rd Army area: 44th are now at FLESSELLES, 43rd at VIGNACOURT & 42nd at BERTHACOURT. C.C.S at ST OUEN (30th) VILLERS (Highland CCS) [illegible initials]	
	23/2/16		Saw all O.i/C F Ambs arranged for ambulances to call at villages to collect sick daily for C.C.S. Called at ST OUEN saw Major Kelly RAMC the OC 30th C.C.S also visited a Jute Factory & arranged for Divisional Baths there [illegible initials] Received orders for the Division to move North near ARRAS & take over French lines in that area [illegible initials]	
Ref Sheet LENS 1/100000	24/2/16		The Division marched to area CANDAS, – BEAUVAL, – AUTHIEULE – DOULLENS HEM, – OCCOCHES – AUTHIEUX – FIENVILLIERS & there [illegible] [illegible initials]	

1875 Wt. W593/826 1,000,000 4/15 J.B.C. & A. A.D.S.S./Forms/C. 2118.

Instructions regarding War Diaries and Intelligence Summaries are contained in F. S. Regs., Part II. and the Staff Manual respectively. Title Pages will be prepared in manuscript.

WAR DIARY
or
INTELLIGENCE SUMMARY
(Erase heading not required.)

Army Form C. 2118

Place	Date	Hour	Summary of Events and Information	Remarks and references to Appendices
			Ref map LENS 1/100000	
FLESSELLES	24/5/16		44th Field amb: marches with 41st Brigade group and will be billeted at DOULLENS	
			43 Field amb: marches with 40th Brigade group and will be billeted at BEAUVAL	
			42 Field amb: marches with 42 Brigade group " " " at GERAINCOURT.	
			Divisional HQ at DOULLENS. CCS at BEAUVAL & DOULLENS [illegible] the sick [illegible] evacuated to	
			[signature]	
DOULLENS	25/5/16		The Division marches today further north.	
			41st Infantry Brigade with 44th Field amb: to SOMBRIN	
			43rd Infantry Brigade with 43rd Field amb: to COULLEMONT.	
			42 Infantry Brigade with 42 Field amb to SUS St LEGER	
			HQrs at SUS St LEGER	
SUS St LEGER	26/5/16		HQrs will close at SUS St LEGER at 10 AM & open at BARLY at 11 Am Feb 29th [signature]	
			[signature]	
BARLY	29/5/16		On the 28th the 42nd Field amb [illegible] march to WANQUETIN & take over the French Field amb: Huts in that village	
			The 44 Field amb remains at SOMBRIN till further orders (moved on 29/5/16 to FOSSEUX)	
			43rd Field amb moves to DARLEY	
			[signature] Colonel [illegible] ADMS 14 DN	

1875 Wt. W593/826 1,000,000 4/15 J.B.C. & A. A.D.S.S./Forms/C. 2118.

War Diaries

of

A.D.M.S 14th Division

for

March }
April } 1916

COMMITTEE FOR THE
MEDICAL HISTORY OF THE WAR
Date 9-JUN.1916

ADMS
14 DW
Vol 8

Instructions regarding War Diaries and Intelligence Summaries are contained in F. S. Regs., Part II. and the Staff Manual respectively. Title Pages will be prepared in manuscript.

WAR DIARY
or
INTELLIGENCE SUMMARY
(Erase heading not required.)

Army Form C. 2118

Place	Date	Hour	Summary of Events and Information — Ref map France 1/100000 LENS 11.	Remarks and references to Appendices
BARLY	3/3/16		Remained at Barley (BARLEY) from 1st to 3rd inclusive left for Div: HQrs at BERNEVILLE on morning 4th. Snowing all day for the past 3 days. Saw ADMS 5th Division COL HARDY & arranged to carry out the work of the advanced dressing station for the 5th & 14th Division at the ECOLE NORMALE ARRAS. This is situated in the RUE D'AMIENS at the NW end of the town. The HQ section of the 42nd Field amb: under MAJOR SMEETH RAMC to be installed. No 14th F Amb: 5th Division to supply 1 officer 1 NCO & 35 men as stretcher bearers drivers of cars (3 motor amb:) to live on the premises. The 5th Division wounded to be interned in the ADS [illegible] of the 14th Field amb: Evacuation from the ADS to be undertaken by the 15th CCS at LUCHEUX to the CCS at DOULLENS & LUCHEUX	
BERNEVILLE	4/3/16		The French ambulance have not been able to evacuate the Ecole Normale & are remaining until today though the 42nd was to have taken over on the 1st month at 9 a.m. So far the French have been attending to our wounded brought into the ECOLE & we have evacuated them also any French soldiers wounded	
	5/3/16		Have control of the ADS the French medical personnel having left. At present the field ambulances are disposed as follows 42nd HQ: section ECOLE NORMAL ARRAS B & C " BARLEY CHATEAU 43rd BARLEY CHATEAU & huts adjoining 44th FOSSEAU VILLAGE (Billets)	

WAR DIARY
or
INTELLIGENCE SUMMARY
(Erase heading not required.)

Army Form C. 2118

Instructions regarding War Diaries and Intelligence Summaries are contained in F. S. Regs., Part II. and the Staff Manual respectively. Title Pages will be prepared in manuscript.

Place	Date	Hour	Summary of Events and Information	Remarks and references to Appendices
			Ref: Map 1/100000 Lens 11	
BERNEVILLE	5/3/16		With regard to the B & C sections 42nd Field Amb: they moved to WANQUETIN hutted hospital on the 28/2/16 & took over from the French medical unit there but owing to the town being considered in the 5th Div: area the 2 sections moved out on the 2/3/16 to allow the 14th Field Amb to come in. The sections moved to BARLEY (see 4/3/16) & opened a reception room for the sick of the Div area. The ADS evacuates by 15th MAC to LUCHEUX (officers) & DOULLENS (men). The cars come right up to the ADS. SGM	
	6/3/16		Arranged with ADS army for local baths in villages of BERNEVILLE & SIMENCOURT to open shower baths. 1/2 ton coal to be supplied to each as a beginning. Also 4 Soyers stoves for heating purposes. SGM	
	7/3/16		43rd Field Amb: are to be ready to move for BARLY & LIGNEREUIL & billet there. Two sections of 42nd now at WANQUETIN to go to FOSSEUX in place of 43rd to allow 14th Field Amb. to take over WANQUETIN huts as CRS in the 5th Div area. The MAWU to go to FOSSEUX chateau with the 44th Field Amb: SGM	

1875 Wt. W593/826 1,000,000 4/15 J.B.C. & A. A.D.S.S./Forms/C. 2118.

Instructions regarding War Diaries and Intelligence Summaries are contained in F. S. Regs., Part II. and the Staff Manual respectively. Title Pages will be prepared in manuscript.

WAR DIARY
or
INTELLIGENCE SUMMARY
(Erase heading not required.)

Army Form C. 2118

Place	Date	Hour	Summary of Events and Information	Remarks and references to Appendices
BERNVILLE			Ref Map 1/100000 LENS 11	
	8/3/16		Am appointing men to FOSSEUX, DAINVILLE BERNVILLE SIMENCOURT to look after sick details, Baths, laundry & sanitation. Sgd	
	9/3/16		Taken over the Ecole normale as ADS for the French since 4th inst: all evacuations from 5th & 14th Division being carried out by the 42nd Field amb under Major SMEETH ROMO who is also supplying all necessary drugs & dressings to the units of both divisions in the front line. Baths have been found in ARRAS at the Ecole COMMUNALE which can be used for 41 Brigade. Chaplain BARR who has been appointed OC Baths & Laundry has to make arrangements by which the women of ARRAS are to wash the soiled underlinen at contract rates in conjunction with Mayor & Town Major (Capt: SCOTT) Sgd	
	10/3/16		All charges connected with Baths & Laundry to be submitted through me [illegible] OC [illegible] imprest account.	
	11/3/16		Visited aid posts in the AGNY & ACHICOURT sectors saw 9th RB, SOMERSETS, CORNWALLS & YORKSHIRE. The Somersets and [illegible] post was a dugout, the remainder in derelict houses Sgd	

1875 Wt. W593/826 1,000,000 4/15 J.B.C. & A. A.D.S.S./Forms/C. 2118.

Instructions regarding War Diaries and Intelligence Summaries are contained in F. S. Regs., Part II. and the Staff Manual respectively. Title Pages will be prepared in manuscript.

WAR DIARY
or
INTELLIGENCE SUMMARY
(Erase heading not required.)

Army Form C. 2118

Place	Date	Hour	Summary of Events and Information	Remarks and references to Appendices
BERNVILLE 12/3/16.			Drugs are short. Visited the advanced depot at DOULLENS & brought back a large quantity with me in the car. Visited the ADS at the ECOLE-NORMALE in ARRAS & went on to the ECOLE des JEUNES FILLES & saw baths there. Decided to take over for 42nd I.B. & placed 1 NCO & 4 men RAMC for that purpose. The Baths have 8 cubicles with 2 showers in each. & drying rooms attached. [illegible]	
13/3/16			Arrangements have been completed for washing clothes by contract in both ARRAS & WANQUETIN. Stock can be got from FOSSEUX (44th Field Amb) & also disinfection of blankets and clothes to be done there in the FODEN LORRY which is there. [illegible]	
14/3/16			Visited LIGNEREUIL with DDMS 6th Corps & saw chateau there. The DMS 3rd army wishes it to take over direct as a CCS for infectious cases. Told OC 43rd Field Amb to put a section in & clean up. The DMS army to find 50 beds, pans, sheets, stretchers &c &c. & to have a mobile laboratory sent there for diagnostic purposes. [illegible]	
15/3/16			Decided that WANQUETIN is to be our area & BARLY is 50th. Ordered 42nd at BARLY chateau to take over huts at WANQUETIN (two sections) [illegible]	

1875 Wt. W593/826 1,000,000 4/15 J.B.C. & A. A.D.S.S./Forms/C. 2118.

Instructions regarding War Diaries and Intelligence Summaries are contained in F. S. Regs., Part II. and the Staff Manual respectively. Title Pages will be prepared in manuscript.

WAR DIARY
or
INTELLIGENCE SUMMARY
(Erase heading not required.)

Army Form C. 2118

Place	Date	Hour	Summary of Events and Information	Remarks and references to Appendices
WARLUS	16/3/16		Head Qrs DW: moved to WARLUS. Decided that ECOLE NORMALE used as 14th Div: area in ARRAS to find other quarters. Also a smaller series of cellars in ACHICOURT for collecting post for AGNY & ACHICOURT sectors of the line	
	17/3/16		Moved today from BERNVILLE. Infectious Hospital maintained at LIGNEREUIL. Visited FOSSEUX & LIGNEREUIL	
	18/3/16		A case of Cerebro spinal meningitis occurred in an officer of the RE Lt ROWLEY. OC No 8 Mobile Lab: confirmed diagnosis by lumbar puncture. Visited Adv Depot [illegible] at DOULLENS to hurry up indents for drugs. Still very short of supplies	
	19/3/16		A case of C.S.M. at WANQUETIN (civilian child) OC 8 Mobile Laboratory investigating case	
	20/3/16		DDMS conference at NOYELLE VION. Visited LIGNEREUIL & FOSSEUX & WANQUETIN. Scabies cases to be transferred to latter Field Amb & the FODEN LORRY also	
	21/3/16		Capt BARR RAMC OC [illegible] Laboratory confirmed Cerebro Spinal meningitis [illegible] Infectious Hospital (43 Field Amb) at LIGNEREUIL	

1875 Wt. W593/826 1,000,000 4/15 J.B.C. & A. A.D.S.S./Forms/C. 2118.

Instructions regarding War Diaries and Intelligence Summaries are contained in F. S. Regs., Part II. and the Staff Manual respectively. Title Pages will be prepared in manuscript.

WAR DIARY
or
INTELLIGENCE SUMMARY
(Erase heading not required.)

Army Form C. 2118

Place	Date	Hour	Summary of Events and Information	Remarks and references to Appendices
WARLUS	21/3/16		Visited with DDMS 6th Corps aid posts at BLAGNY, RONVILLE & ST SAVEUR also new public baths at ARRAS. The baths in ARRAS are now plentiful for all requirements. Visited the Sugar Refinery in DAINVILLE with a view of putting a section 43rd in here to hold as a Divisional collecting station. Good cellars & dry and accommodation available	
	22/3/16		Visited new Adv. Depot Med Stores at FREVENT & ordered all Field Ambs to [illegible] for their drugs still short. [illegible]	
	23/3/16		42nd Field Amb (1 sect) moving to Sugar Refinery DAINVILLE to form DCS & take over new collecting post at ACHICOURT. Capt. BARR died this morning. Capt BROWNRONE to take on duties of Bath[illegible] & Laundry & obtained motor cycle for purpose. [illegible]	
	24/3/16		Major VAUGHAN of 43rd Field [illegible]	
	25/3/16		HAUTVILLE to take over douche baths [illegible] for troops there	
	26/3/16		Collecting Post at ACHICOURT equipped & ready for taking over collecting of wounded (43rd from 42nd Brigades)	
	28/3/16		43rd Field Amb. took over from 42nd Field Amb. the evacuation of wounded [illegible] orderlies (3) at each aid post were to be relieved tonight. Sugar Refinery DAINVILLE now ready for DIV: Collecting post. Billiard room [illegible] as a dressing room & 3 horsed ambulances & 2 motor ambulances left there	
	29/3/16		To move from ECOLE NORMALE & take over cellars in RUE AMIENS at the Convent as ADS	
	30/3/16		Major Vaughan visited aid posts & wounded collecting post at ACHICOURT	

[illegible] Col. [illegible] ADMS 14 Div

1875 Wt. W593/826 1,000,000 4/15 J.B.C. & A. A.D.S.S./Forms/C. 2118.

(6414) Wt. W3906/P1607 2,500,000 7/18 McA & W Ltd (E 3591) Forms W3091/4.

Army Form W.3091.

Cover for Documents.

Nature of Enclosures.

W.D. M. S. 14th B.W

Notes, or Letters written.

June 1916

ADMS. 14 Div

Army Form C. 2118

Vol 9

PAGE I

Instructions regarding War Diaries and Intelligence Summaries are contained in F. S. Regs., Part II. and the Staff Manual respectively. Title Pages will be prepared in manuscript.

WAR DIARY or ~~INTELLIGENCE SUMMARY~~

(Erase heading not required.)

Place	Date	Hour	Summary of Events and Information	Remarks and references to Appendices
	1916 April			
WARLUS.	1st	8 p.m.	Visited WANQUETIN, discussed with O.C. 42nd F.A. proposed scheme for improving Scabies camp. R.E. are going to construct a bath house with drying & ironing room. Water to be led from neighbouring well in pipes.	W.S. Vaughan Lt Col RAMC for ADMS 14th Div.
" "	2nd	8 pm	This afternoon visited AID POSTS in left sector	W.S.V.
" "	3rd	4 pm	Met DDMS. 6th Corps & ADMS 56th Div. at FOSSEUX to discuss whether a 2nd F.A. should be put in chateau or grounds. Decided to be impracticable	W.S.V.
" "	4th	8 pm	Col Guise Moores C.B. returned from leave yesterday at 5 pm. He visited 44th F.A. at FOSSEUX & 42nd F.A. at WANQUETIN. arranged for separate baths for Scabies cases.	W.S.V.
" "	5th	8 pm	Visited A.D.S. at ARRAS. & in afternoon DDMS Third Army.	W.S.V.
" "	6th	8 pm	Attended DDMS. conference – prevention of flies – dung incinerators	W.S.V.

1875 Wt. W593/826 1,000,000 4/15 J.B.C. & A. A.D.S.S./Forms/C. 2118.

Instructions regarding War Diaries and Intelligence Summaries are contained in F. S. Regs., Part II. and the Staff Manual respectively. Title Pages will be prepared in manuscript.

WAR DIARY
or
~~INTELLIGENCE SUMMARY~~

(Erase heading not required.)

Army Form C. 2118

PAGE II

Place	Date	Hour	Summary of Events and Information	Remarks and references to Appendices
WARLUS	1916 April 7th	8pm	Recommended retention of leather jerkins until end of month - cold & dry.	W.A.V.
" "	8th	8pm	Col Guise Moores CB. was admitted to DRS FOSSEUX today. I take over duties of ADMS. 12th Div. temporarily	W.A.Vaughan Lt Col RAMC
" "	9th	8pm	Visited WANQUETIN & SIMONCOURT to inspect sanitary improvements also OC. TRAIN at BERNEVILLE re. issue of coal	W.A.V.
" "	10th	8pm	Saw 4 men of 44th FA. who are applying for commissions. Visited FOSSEUX in morning; in afternoon went to SUGAR REFINERY & COLL. POST at ACHICOURT. Unused 'dugouts' are being repaired by 43rd FA.	W.A.V.
" "	11th	8pm	Went to FOSSEUX & WANQUETIN.	W.A.V.
" "	12th	8pm	Visited FOSSEUX, & WANQUETIN with Surg Gen. O'DONNELL, DDMS 6th Corps & SIR ANTHONY BOWLBY.	W.A.V.

1875 Wt. W593/826 1,000,000 4/15 J.B.C. & A. A.D.S.S./Forms/C. 2118.

Instructions regarding War Diaries and Intelligence Summaries are contained in F. S. Regs., Part II. and the Staff Manual respectively. Title Pages will be prepared in manuscript.

WAR DIARY
or
INTELLIGENCE SUMMARY
(Erase heading not required.)

Army Form C. 2118

PAGE III.

Place	Date	Hour	Summary of Events and Information	Remarks and references to Appendices
WARLUS	1916 April		Conference at DDMS 6th Corps. Contents of box for 'gas cases'	
	13th	8pm	Visited FOSSEUX & WANQUETIN with DMS Third Army & DDMS. 6th Corps	WW
"	14th	8pm	Visited FOSSEUX & Isolation Hospt at LIGNEREUIL (90 patients)	WW
"	15th	8pm	Visited WANQUETIN.	WW
"	16th	8pm	Visited FOSSEUX & LIGNEREUIL. Col. GUISE MOORES CB was discharged Hospital today & proceeded on leave to WIMEREUX.	WW
"	17th	8pm	Visited WANQUETIN to see 'Temporary Units' – great improvement in camp. LIEUT J.J. O'KELLY RAMC 42nd F.A. was last night put under close arrest for drunkeness by O.C. 8th R.B. Saw Lt Col Sweath & directed that a 'Summary of evidence' be taken & a G.C.M. applied for.	WW
			Took Russian General round D.R.S. at FOSSEUX in afternoon	
"	19th	8pm	Saw 'dental cases' for MO's. Read over summary of evidence for Lieut J.J. O'KELLY. It was unsatisfactory & I recommended that more evidence for prosecution should be taken	WW

1875 Wt. W593/826 1,000,000 4/15 J.B.C. & A. A.D.S.S./Forms/C. 2118.

Instructions regarding War Diaries and Intelligence Summaries are contained in F. S. Regs., Part II. and the Staff Manual respectively. Title Pages will be prepared in manuscript.

WAR DIARY
or
INTELLIGENCE SUMMARY
(Erase heading not required.)

PAGE IV.

Army Form C. 2118

Place	Date	Hour	Summary of Events and Information	Remarks and references to Appendices
WARLUS	1916 April 20th	8 pm	'Summary of evidence' forwarded to DAA + QMG 14th Div. Attended 'Gas' conference at Army Hd Qtrs St POL.	WH
"	21st	8 pm	'Summary of evidence' returned, more evidence required. Returned to O.C. 42nd F.A. Visited 43rd Bde H Qtrs re sanitation of AGNY. Inspected Sugar refinery.	WH
"	22nd	8 pm	Attended conference at D.D.M.S. 6th Corps. Visited LIGNEREUIL.	WH
"	23rd	8 pm	Summary of evidence returned forwarded to DAA + QMG. Visited 42nd at WANQUETIN. A case died in WARLUS on 21st inst. P.M. examination was made & cultures taken. Report just received from O.C. 20th Mobile Lab.y states case was one of meningococcal septicaemia. Instructions issued that all troops are to vacate the farm for 1 month. Disinfection of quarters by San.y section.	WH
"	24th	8 pm	Inspected men's billets at BERNEVILLE + SIMONCOURT. Unsatisfactory. Nothing has been done to increase their comfort; spoke to RE in charge of these 2 villages.	WH
"	25th	8 pm	Met D.M.S. Third Army at LIGNEREUIL. It is proposed to increase the accommodation up to 150 beds. This will allow cases of German measles to be kept for 10 days instead of evacuating them. This will reduce the number of evacuations for infectious disease to a very marked extent.	WH

1875 Wt. W593/826 1,000,000 4/15 J.B.C. & A. A.D.S.S./Forms/C. 2118.

Instructions regarding War Diaries and Intelligence Summaries are contained in F. S. Regs., Part II. and the Staff Manual respectively. Title Pages will be prepared in manuscript.

WAR DIARY
or
~~INTELLIGENCE SUMMARY~~
(Erase heading not required.)

Army Form C. 2118

PAGE V

Place	Date	Hour	Summary of Events and Information	Remarks and references to Appendices
WARLUS	1916 April 26th	8pm	Visited FOSSEUX - cooking arrangements are improved. Bath house nearly completed. Visited ADMS 56th Div. to discuss various points.	WGV
"	27th	8pm	Visited ADS in ARRAS - Saw their drill in case of 'Gas attack'. Arrangements are quite adequate. All windows etc are closed with double curtains. Vermoral sprayers are sufficient. Visited 42nd FA at WANQUETIN with DDMS 6th Corps. Great improvements were noticed. Paths have been laid out & a bath house & Pack store are in process of erection -	WGV
"	28th	8pm	'Summary of Evidence' re Lieut J.J. O'KELLY returned. G.O.C. Third Army does not consider there is sufficient evidence to justify the trial of this officer - & orders him to be released forthwith. O.C. 42nd FA. notified accordingly & correspondence returned to DAA&QMG. 14th Div	WGV.
"	30th	8pm	Visited ARRAS today with DDMS 6th Corps to select suitable buildings for C.C.S. in case of an advance - 3 buildings selected.	WGV.

for W G Vaughan
Lt Col RAMC
ADMS 14th Div

1875 Wt. W593/826 1,000,000 4/15 J.B.C. & A. A.D.S.S./Forms/C. 2118.

MAY 1916

A.D.M.S 14th DIVISION

COMMITTEE FOR THE
MEDICAL HISTORY OF THE WAR
Date 26 JUN. 1916

Instructions regarding War Diaries and Intelligence Summaries are contained in F. S. Regs., Part II. and the Staff Manual respectively. Title Pages will be prepared in manuscript.

WAR DIARY
or
~~INTELLIGENCE SUMMARY~~
(Erase heading not required.)

ADMS 14 Div

PAGE I

Army Form C. 2118

Vol 10

Place	Date	Hour	Summary of Events and Information	Remarks and references to Appendices
WARLUS	1916 MAY 1st	8pm.	Attended conference of A.D's of MS at DMS Third Army ST POL	W.T. Vaughan Lt Col RAMC for ADMS 14th Div.
" "	2nd	8pm	Visited ADMS 5th Div. to arrange about handing over two Regimental AID POSTS in I Sector (BLANGY & FAUBERG ST SAVEUR) on night 4/5 May.	W.T.V.
" "	4th	8pm	Visited ADMS 55th Div at COUY then ADMS 56th Div & O.C. DRS at LIENCOURT to arrange about handing over FOSSEUX CHATEAU to 55th Div. & taking over D.R.S. at LIENCOURT from 56th Div. In afternoon went to FOSSEUX to discuss arrangements for move	W.T.V.
" "	5th	8pm	Div' Cavalry moved to SARS LEZ BOIS. Visited LIGNEREUIL to arrange that M.O. of 43rd F.A. should go daily to see their sick. C.C.S is not going to take over from 43rd FA.	W.T.V.
" "	6th	8pm	To day at noon FOSSEUX & SIMONCOURT were handed over to 55th Div. 1 section of 2/1 Wessex F.A. proceeds to DRS FOSSEUX. Visited 42nd FA. at WANQUETIN. great improvements	W.T.V.
" "	7th	8pm	Visited LIGNEREUIL & FOSSEUX	W.T.V.
" "	8th	8pm	Visited SARS-LEZ-BOIS. Saw billets of Divisional Cavalry. also IZEL-LEZ-HAMEAU saw billets of Divisional Cyclists.	W.T.V.
" "	9th	8pm	CAPTAIN LANGRISHE D.ADMS. proceeds on leave. CAPTAIN CLARK RAMC has reported to take over his duties. 2 Sections of 44th FA. have now taken over D.R.S at LIENCOURT. all patients having been transferred from FOSSEUX	W.T.V.

1875 Wt. W593/826 1,000,000 4/15 J.B.C. & A. A.D.S.S./Forms/C. 2118.

Instructions regarding War Diaries and Intelligence Summaries are contained in F. S. Regs., Part II. and the Staff Manual respectively. Title Pages will be prepared in manuscript.

WAR DIARY
or
~~INTELLIGENCE SUMMARY~~
(Erase heading not required.)

Army Form C. 2118

PAGE II

Place	Date	Hour	Summary of Events and Information	Remarks and references to Appendices
WARLUS	1916 MAY. 10th	8pm	The move of 44th F.A. to LIENCOURT is completed. Visited this morning COLLECTING POSTS at ACHICOURT. 5 Dugouts under railway embankment have been very well repaired. Visited Sugar refinery. They are working on dugouts there also.	W.A.V.
" "	11th	8pm	Visited WANQUETIN also 44th at LIENCOURT. Inspected a batch of 16 'Temporary unfits' for road control: A good many improvements are required in the camp. Visited 43rd FA. at LIGNEREUIL. The returning of cases of German measles to their respective railheads is now working smoothly. 4 MO's proceed to ST POL for course of instruction in 'gas'.	W.A.V.
" "	12th	8pm	Interpreter VANDROY attached to 61st Field Coy RE developed C.S.M. while on leave. His clothes & those of 'contacts' will be disinfected also his quarters. O.C. No 20 Mobile Laboratory will take swabs from throats of all contacts (9). Quarters will be put out of bounds for one month.	W.A.V.
" "	13th	8pm	CAPTAIN KITCHEN RAMC & 2 stretcher bearers were detailed to attend execution of a soldier at WARLUS on 15th inst. They are to report to A.P.M. WARLUS at 3:45 am	W.A.V.
" "	14th	8pm	Handed over to Lt. Colonel PRYNNE RAMC. ADMS 14th Division	

W.A. Vaughan Lt Col RAMC
a/ ADMS 14th Division

1875 Wt. W593/826 1,000,000 4/15 J.B.C. & A. A.D.S.S./Forms/C. 2118.

Instructions regarding War Diaries and Intelligence Summaries are contained in F. S. Regs., Part II. and the Staff Manual respectively. Title Pages will be prepared in manuscript.

WAR DIARY
or
~~INTELLIGENCE SUMMARY~~
(Erase heading not required.)

Army Form C. 2118

PAGE III

Place	Date	Hour	Summary of Events and Information	Remarks and references to Appendices
WARLUS	14.5.16	8pm	Took over from Lt Col. W. F VAUGHAN. R.A.M.C. [signature] Lt Col. R.A.M.C. A.D.M.S. 14 Division.	
	15.5.16		Visited 42, 43 & 44 F. Ambulances. Visited C.R.E. 14 Division, who was reported to be sick.	[initials]
	16.5.16		Visited Advanced Dressing Station. ARRAS. Visited Sugar Refinery (Collecting Post) DAINVILLE, and Aid Posts 1, 2, 3 & 4	[initials]
	17.5.16		Visited Baths for Officers & men, ARRAS, and Aid Post 5 at RONVILLE. Visited Baths, DAINVILLE. Visited 37 C C Station.	[initials]
	18.5.16		Visited baths BERNEVILLE. Met D D M S at 43 F.A. LIGNEREUIL, & proceeded with him to 44 F Amb at LIENCOURT.	[initials]
	19.5.16		Visited Sugar Refinery, DAINVILLE, and inspected sanitation & medical arrangements of R. battalion of R. sector in the line.	[initials]

1875 Wt. W593/826 1,000,000 4/15 J.B.C. & A. A.D.S.S./Forms/C. 2118.

Army Form C. 2118

WAR DIARY
or
~~INTELLIGENCE SUMMARY~~
(Erase heading not required.)

Instructions regarding War Diaries and Intelligence Summaries are contained in F. S. Regs., Part II. and the Staff Manual respectively. Title Pages will be prepared in manuscript.

PAGE IV

Place	Date	Hour	Summary of Events and Information	Remarks and references to Appendices
WARLUS	20.5.16		Visited 42 F.A. WANQUETIN, and inspected SCHOOLS, WANQUETIN.	[illegible]
		3.30 pm	Accompanied D.D.M.S at inspection of 42 F.A., WANQUETIN.	[illegible]
	21.5.16		Visited 44 F.A., LIENCOURT & 43 F.A. LIGNEREUIL.	
	22.5.16		Visited GRANDE RULLECOURT & HAUTEVILLE to inspect possible sites for D.R.S. Visited Baths, HAUTEVILLE & 55 Div' LAUNDRY	[illegible]
	23.5.16		Visited 37 C.C.S. Visited Advanced Dressing Station & dugouts, DAINVILLE.	[illegible]
	24.5.16		Visited proposed site for Div' Laundry, WANQUETIN & also baths, WANQUETIN. Inspected sanitation & medical arrangements of L. battalion of R. sector in the line	[illegible]
	25.5.16		Visited billets BERNEVILLE. Visited billets HAUTEVILLE & Div' SCHOOL of INSTRUCTION	[illegible]
	26.5.16		Visited billets WARLUS. Visit by D.G.M.S.	[illegible]
	27.5.16		Visited billets WANQUETIN. Visited C. Post, ACHICOURT & No 1 AID POST.	[illegible]

1875 Wt. W593/826 1,000,000 4/15 J.B.C. & A. A.D.S.S./Forms/C. 2118.

Army Form C. 2118

WAR DIARY
or
~~INTELLIGENCE SUMMARY~~
(Erase heading not required.)

Instructions regarding War Diaries and Intelligence Summaries are contained in F. S. Regs., Part II. and the Staff Manual respectively. Title Pages will be prepared in manuscript.

Place	Date	Hour	Summary of Events and Information	Remarks and references to Appendices
WARLUS	28.5.16		Visited 42 F. Ambulance + baths WANQUETIN. Visited 44 F.A. LIENCOURT	[illegible]
	29.5.16		D.D.M.S. visited ACHICOURT, AID POSTS, BATHS + destructor at BERNEVILLE, BATHS at WANQUETIN + School of Instruction at WANQUETIN.	[illegible]
	30.5.16		Visited proposed sites for Officers' Rest Station at FOSSEUX, BARLY + MANIN.	[illegible]
	31.5.16		Visited 44 F.A., LIENCOURT, and 43 F.A., LIGNEREUIL.	[illegible]

~~July 1916~~

June 1916.

A. D. M. S., 14th Division

COMMITTEE FOR THE
MEDICAL HISTORY OF THE WAR
Date 19 OCT. 1916

Instructions regarding War Diaries and Intelligence Summaries are contained in F. S. Regs., Part II. and the Staff Manual respectively. Title pages will be prepared in manuscript.

WAR DIARY
or
~~INTELLIGENCE SUMMARY.~~
(Erase heading not required.)

ADMS 11th D
Army Form C. 2118.

Vol 11

Place	Date	Hour	Summary of Events and Information	Remarks and references to Appendices
WARLUS	1.6.16		Visited St. POL to obtain stores for baths	S.v.Pr.... Col. ADMS.
	2.6.16.		Visited R. battalion of L. Sector. Visited baths + 42 F.A. WANQUETIN	S.v.P.
	3.6.16.		Inspected sanitation and medical arrangements L. battalion of R. sector. Met O's C. 42, 43 + 44 F.A's + visited D.D.M.S. VI Corps.	S.v.P.
	4.6.16.		Visited 1, 2, 3, + 4 Aid posts.	S.v.P.
	5.6.16.		Attended conference at office of D.M.S. 3rd ARMY. Met C.R.E at WANQUETIN about proposed Divisional Laundry there.	S.v.P.
	6.6.16.		Visited aid posts, and medical arrangements HILL 105 with D.D.M.S. Inspected sanitation M.M.G. section, + MOBILE VET. Section. CAPT. EDMISTON R.A.M.C. (D.A.D.M.S. 57 DIVISION) reported for 3 days' instruction	S.v.P. S.v.P.
	7.6.16.		Accompanied by CAPT. EDMISTON visited AID POSTS 1, 2, 3 + 4, Collecting post, ACHICOURT, and A.D.S. ARRAS, also 42 F.A. baths, site of proposed Div'l Laundry, and SCHOOLS, WANQUETIN.	S.v.P.
	8.6.16.		Accompanied by CAPT. EDMISTON visited 44, + 43 F.A., also baths + Sugar Refinery, DAINVILLE, and baths for officers and men, ARRAS.	S.v.P.

1577 Wt. W10791/1773 500,000 1/15 D. D. & L. A.D.S.S./Forms/C. 2118.

Army Form C. 2118.

WAR DIARY
or
~~INTELLIGENCE SUMMARY~~.

(Erase heading not required.)

Instructions regarding War Diaries and Intelligence Summaries are contained in F. S. Regs., Part II. and the Staff Manual respectively. Title pages will be prepared in manuscript.

Place	Date	Hour	Summary of Events and Information	Remarks and references to Appendices
WARLUS	9.6.16		Visited baths BERNEVILLE.	H.P.
	10.6.16.		Visited Aid post, RONVILLE, & Collecting post ACHICOURT. Visited No 12 STATIONARY HOSPITAL to arrange treatment of cases of disease of nose, throat & ear.	H.P.
	11.6.16		D.M.S. III ARMY visited A.D.S., Collecting post, ACHICOURT, No 1, 2, 3 & 4 Aid posts, Sugar Refinery, DAINVILLE, baths BERNEVILLE, & 44 F.A.	H.P.
	12.6.16.		Visited billets, DAINVILLE, & 42 F.A. re "unfits".	H.P.
	13.6.16.		Memorial Service LORD KITCHENER.	H.P.
	14.6.16		Visited billets Heavy Artillery, DAINVILLE & ARRAS. Visited WAGNONLIEU & DUISANS re medical attendance R.A. units	H.P.
	15.6.16.		Visited billets 48 Bde R.F.A. Visited 43 & 44 F.A.	H.P.
	16.6.16		Inspection proposed P.B. men 42nd & 43rd Bdes & Pioneer battalion. Attended D.D.M.S. Conference.	H.P.
	17.6.16.		Inspected men proposed for P.B. 41st Bde.	
	18.6.16.		Received orders to arrange for new front — G sector to be given up, & H. I. J. & K. to represent new front	H.P.

1577 Wt. W10791/1773 500,000 1/15 D. D. & L. A.D.S.S./Forms/C. 2118.

Instructions regarding War Diaries and Intelligence Summaries are contained in F. S. Regs., Part II. and the Staff Manual respectively. Title pages will be prepared in manuscript.

WAR DIARY
or
~~INTELLIGENCE SUMMARY.~~

(Erase heading not required.)

Army Form C. 2118.

Place	Date	Hour	Summary of Events and Information	Remarks and references to Appendices
WARLUS.	19.6.16		Visited A.D.S. 5 Divn. ECOLE NORMALE, ARRAS, collecting post ST NIKOLAS, and post J1 sector. Visited 42, 43, & 44 F.A., & inspected transport.	[illegible]
	20.6.16		Inspection of 42, 43, 44 F.A's & A.D. Station by Corps Commander	[illegible]
	21.6.16		Visited aid posts K1 & K2 sectors. Conference at D.D.M.S. Visited special hospital HABARCQ with A.D.M.S. 5th Division.	[illegible]
	22.6.16.		Visited special hospital HABARCQ.	[illegible]
	23.6.16.		Section 42 F.A. moved from ST SACREMENT, and established Advanced Dressing Station at ECOLE NORMALE. ARRAS, & handed over ST SACRAMENT to 55 Divn. H.Q. of 42 F.A. moved from WANQUETIN, which was handed over to 55 Divn., and took over CHATEAU, HABARCQ, including special hospital from 14 F.A. 5th Division. Section of 43 F.A. handed over SUGAR REFINERY and dugouts to 55 Divn. and rejoined unit.	
	24.6.16.		Made reconnaissance of ST VAAST, ST CATHERINE & BOYAU DE LILLE.	[illegible]
	25.6.16.		The following moves completed – one bearer subdivision 43rd F.A. &	[illegible]

Instructions regarding War Diaries and Intelligence Summaries are contained in F. S. Regs., Part II. and the Staff Manual respectively. Title pages will be prepared in manuscript.

WAR DIARY
or
~~INTELLIGENCE SUMMARY~~.
(Erase heading not required.)

Army Form C. 2118.

Place	Date	Hour	Summary of Events and Information	Remarks and references to Appendices
WARLUS	25.6.16.		1 cyclist, under an officer distributed – Officer and 3 squads and cyclist, ACHICOURT; 1 Sergt. + remainder at Collecting post, Corner of RUE ST MICHEL + RUE DE DOUAI, ARRAS. One bearer subdivision 44 F.A. under officer with 1 cyclist to re-inforce Collecting post, ST NICOLAS – one bearer subdivision 43 F.A. held in reserve at A.D. Station, ARRAS. Wheeled stretchers distributed to collecting posts, + additional motor ambulances to A.D. Station. Visited aid posts H_2, I_1 + I_2, + 44 F.A. Visited AGNEZ-LEZ-DUISANS and DUISANS to select sites for Div. Collecting Station + second MAIN DRESSING STATION	[initials]
	26.6.16.		Inspected 5/Oxford + Bucks L.I., whose health had been reported unsatisfactory. Found their general condition satisfactory.	
	~~26.6.16.~~		Visited HAUTEVILLE + WANQUETIN to inspect men proposed for P.B. Visited 43 F.A.	[initials]
	27.6.16.		Inspected proposed P.B. men, ARRAS: also aid post H_2. Inspected P.B. men BERNEVILLE. Visited 42 F.A. + Special hospital, HABARCQ.	[initials]

1577 Wt. W10791/1773 500,000 1/15 D. D. & L. A.D.S.S./Forms/C. 2118.

Army Form C. 2118

WAR DIARY

or

~~INTELLIGENCE SUMMARY~~

(Erase heading not required.)

Instructions regarding War Diaries and Intelligence Summaries are contained in F. S. Regs., Part II. and the Staff Manual respectively. Title Pages will be prepared in manuscript.

Place	Date	Hour	Summary of Events and Information	Remarks and references to Appendices
WARLUS.	28.6.16.		Three officers, necessary personnel & equipment detailed from 43 F.A. established Divl. Collecting Station for lightly wounded cases & MAIRIE & CINEMA HALL, DUISANS, to which cases will be conveyed by horse ambulance from St. VAAST. Visited experimental latrine, manure dump, and disposal area, HAUTEVILLE.	[initials]
	29.6.16.		Visited proposed Divl. Collecting Station, DUISANS. Orders issued for 1 N.C.O, 6 men, 2 stretchers & blankets, dressings and equipment for providing hot drinks to be sent to cellar G15. a 2.4 & dug out G15 a. 0.6 to establish collecting post.	[initials]
	30.6.16.		Visited special hospital HABARCQ, & inspected arrangements for MAIN DRESSING STATION. Visited St. CATHERINE & St. VAAST to reconnoitre roads for ambulances	[initials]

July 916

A.D.M.S. 14th Division

July 1916

COMMITTEE FOR THE
MEDICAL HISTORY OF THE WAR
Date 5 - SEP. 916

Instructions regarding War Diaries and Intelligence Summaries are contained in F. S. Regs., Part II. and the Staff Manual respectively. Title Pages will be prepared in manuscript.

WAR DIARY
or
~~INTELLIGENCE SUMMARY~~
(Erase heading not required.)

ADMS 14 D. Army Form C. 2118 July

Vol 12

Place	Date	Hour	Summary of Events and Information	Remarks and references to Appendices
WARLUS	1.7.16.		Visited Collecting Post, ST NICOLAS, aid post J2 sector, collecting post RUE ST MICHEL and aid post H2 sector. Inspected sanitation mobile Veterinary Section	S. R. Pepper Col A.M.S.
	2.7.16.		Visited VI Corps, where Inspector of Drafts saw men from Division. Visited HAUTEVILLE re removal of baths. Visited 44 F.A. & baths, LOUEZ	S.R.P.
	3.7.16		Visited new aid posts I1 & H2, also H1 aid post and new dug-outs, and stretcher trenches this sector.	S.R.P.
	4.7.16.		Visited AVESNES re Divisional Laundry	S.R.P.
	5.7.16.		Visited Baths & Clothing depot, WANQUETIN. Visited VI Corps & 44 F.A.	S.R.P.
	6.7.16.		Visited Advanced Dressing Station, & tunnels proposed for the accomodation of wounded.	S.R.P.
	7.7.16.		Visited sanitation 47 Bde R.F.A., LATTRE ST QUENTIN	S.R.P.
	8.7.16		Visited special hospital, HABARCQ and 43 F.A., also AGNEZ-LEZ-DUISANS re baths. Visited disposal area and Medical Inspection Room, DUISANS.	S.R.P.
	9.7.16.		Visited Advanced Dressing Station. Inspected sanitation of 47 Bde R.F.A waggon lines	S.R.P.

1875 Wt. W593/826 1,000,000 4/15 J.B.C. & A. A.D.S.S./Forms/C. 2118.

Instructions regarding War Diaries and Intelligence Summaries are contained in F. S. Regs., Part II. and the Staff Manual respectively. Title Pages will be prepared in manuscript.

WAR DIARY
or
~~INTELLIGENCE SUMMARY~~
(Erase heading not required.)

Army Form C. 2118

Place	Date	Hour	Summary of Events and Information	Remarks and references to Appendices
WARLUS.	10.7.16.		Visited 42 F.A. at LIGNEREUIL.	T.R. Sypner Col A.D.M.S.
	11.7.16		Visited sanitation BERNEVILLE + DAINVILLE re stretchers	T.R.S.
	12.7.16		Visited 43 F.A, HABARCQ. Visited laundry, LOUEZ and disposal area, DUISANS.	T.R.S.
	13.7.16.		Inspected sanitation, WARLUS. Attended conference at D.D.M.S. office. Visited 44 F.A.	T.R.S.
	14.7.16.		Visited 43 F.A., and special hospital. Visited AGNEZ-LEZ-DUISANS. + laundry LOUEZ.	T.R.S.
	15.7.16.		Inspected sanitation 47 Bde R.F.A. waggon lines.	T.R.S.
	16.7.16.		Visited sanitation BERNEVILLE + disposal area	T.R.S.
	17.7.16		Visited disposal area, HAUTEVILLE and baths + depot WANQUETIN	T.R.S.
	18.7.16.		Visited DUISANS.	
	19.7.16.		Visited Advanced Dressing Station, Collecting Post, ACHICOURT, and aid posts H_1 + I_2. Visited baths AGNEZ-LEZ-DUISANS	T.R.S.
	20.7.16.		Visited sanitation 47 Bde R.F.A. at St. CATHERINE'S + ANZIN.	T.R.S.

1875 Wt. W593/826 1,000,000 4/15 J.B.C. & A. A.D.S.S./Forms/C. 2118.

Instructions regarding War Diaries and Intelligence Summaries are contained in F. S. Regs., Part II. and the Staff Manual respectively. Title Pages will be prepared in manuscript.

WAR DIARY
or
~~INTELLIGENCE SUMMARY~~
(Erase heading not required.)

Army Form C. 2118

Place	Date	Hour	Summary of Events and Information	Remarks and references to Appendices
WARLUS	21.7.16		Visited 42, 43 and 44 F. Ambulances. Sanitary adviser visited ARRAS, DUISANS and WARLUS.	[initialled]
	22.7.16		Visited laundry, LOUEZ. D.D.M.S. visited 43 F.A. and special hospital.	[initialled]
	23.7.16		Visited 56 Division re medical arrangements	[initialled]
	24.7.16		Visited Div! S.C. and inspected sanitation	[initialled]
	25.7.16		Visited Advanced dressing station, collecting posts RUE St MICHEL + St NICOLAS, baths ARRAS and 43 F.A. with A.D.M.S. 21 Divn.	[initialled]
	26.7.16		Attended conference at D.D.M.S. Office.	[initialled]
	27.7.16		A.D.S., St NICOLAS, C. Post. St CATHERINE, and collection J+K. sectors handed over to 21 Divisions, I sector to 11 Division. 42 F.A. relieved by 64 F.A. 42 F.A. moved to GRAND RULLECOURT. 43 F.A. relieved by 63 F.A.	[initialled]
	28.7.16		44 F.A. relieved by 65 F.A. 43 F.A. to SOMBRIN. 42 F.A. to BARLY	[initialled]
	29.7.16		42 F.A. to BARLY.	[initialled]
SUS-St LEGER	30.7.16		D.H.Q to SUS-St LEGER. 44 F.A to IVERGNY. 43 F.A to VILLERS L'HOPITAL	[initialled]
FROHEN LE.GRAND.	31.7.16		D.H.Q to FROHEN LE GRAND. 42 F.A. to St HILAIRE. 44 F.A. to BARLY.	[initialled]

[signature]
Col. A.M.S.

1875 Wt. W593/826 1,000,000 4/15 J.B.C. & A. A.D.S.S./Forms/C. 2118.

August 1916

5

A.D.M.S., 14th Division

COMMITTEE FOR THE
MEDICAL HISTORY OF THE WAR
Date -5 OCT. 1916

Instructions regarding War Diaries and Intelligence Summaries are contained in F. S. Regs., Part II. and the Staff Manual respectively. Title Pages will be prepared in manuscript.

WAR DIARY
or
~~INTELLIGENCE SUMMARY~~
(Erase heading not required.)

14 ADMS 14 D

Army Form C. 2118

Vol 13

Place	Date	Hour	Summary of Events and Information Map reference Albert Combined 1/40,000.	Remarks and references to Appendices
BERNAVILLE	1.8.16.		D. H. Q moved to BERNAVILLE, 43 F.A. to LE MEILLARD, 44 F.A to GEZAINCOURT.	[signature] Col. AMS
	2.8.16.		Visited St OUEN to arrange for Divisional laundry.	[signature]
	3.8.16.		Visited 43 F.A. at LE MEILLARD.	[signature]
	4.8.16.		Visited A.D.M.S. 7th Division to ascertain medical arrangements	[signature]
	5.8.16.		Visited 42 F.A at St HILAIRE. Visited AMIENS, BOVES + SALEUX re washing clothes.	[signature]
	6.8.16.		Visited D.D.M.S. XV Corps, and A.D.M.S. 17 Division preliminary to move of Division.	[signature]
	7.8.16.		Division left BERNAVILLE for BUIRE-SUR-ANCRE.	[signature]
	8.8.16.		D.H.Q. at D.29 c 4.7. 42 F.A. at BUIRE-SUR-ANCRE, 44 F.A at DERNANCOURT, and 43 F.A. at E16.c.2.5. SAN SECTION at D.29c.4.7.	[signature]
	9.8.16.		Visited A.D.M.S. 17 Division, and Divisional Collecting Station at BECORDEL.	[signature]
	10.8.16.		Visited Advanced Dressing Station, bearer posts, and regimental aid posts of 14 Division, and Corps Main Dressing Station	[signature]
	11.8.16.		Visited Corps Main Dressing Station.	[signature]
	12.8.16.		Visited Bearer Post, BERNAFAY WOOD to select new post for relay bearers at S22 d.7.1.	[signature]

Instructions regarding War Diaries and Intelligence Summaries are contained in F. S. Regs., Part II. and the Staff Manual respectively. Title Pages will be prepared in manuscript.

WAR DIARY
or
~~INTELLIGENCE SUMMARY~~
(Erase heading not required.)

Army Form C. 2118

Place	Date	Hour	Summary of Events and Information Map reference Albert Combined 1/40000	Remarks and references to Appendices
BELLE VUE FARM. E5 C.5.5.	13.8.16		D.H.Q moved to BELLE VUE FARM. E5. C.5.5. 42 F.A. to E5. d.0.0. as F.A. in reserve. 43 F.A. to Divisional Collecting Station F.7 d.9.9. 44 F.A. to Advanced Dressing Station at F.6a 1.1. with transport lines at F.7.d 8.8 Sanitary Section to E5. C.7.5. Visited 42 F.A, Divisional Collecting Station, + Advanced Dressing Station	H.P.
	14.8.16.		Visited Advanced Dressing Station, also 3 regimental aid posts + Collecting Post in Quarry at S22 c.1.2., and bearer post at A.2.6.1.9.	H.P.
	15.8.16.		Visited 42 F.A., Divisional Collecting Station, and Advanced Dressing Station, also H.Q. 41, 42 + 43 Brigades re medical arrangements	H.P.
	16.8.16.		Visited sanitation of administrative area for sanitation. Visited Advanced Dressing Station for conference with Regimental Medical Officers.	H.P.
	17.8.16		Operation orders 14 Divn. received. Visited D.C.S and A.D.S. Operation orders issued as per appendix No 1.	H.P.
	18.8.16.		Visited A.D. Station, Collecting Post, and Divisional Collecting Station.	H.P.
	19.8.16		Visited A.D.S, Collecting Post, Bearer Post in MONTAUBAN ALLEY, and Divl. Collecting Station. Visited Main Dressing Station + Divl. Baths	H.P.

1875 Wt. W593/826 1,000,000 4/15 J.B.C. & A. A.D.S.S./Forms/C. 2118.

Instructions regarding War Diaries and Intelligence Summaries are contained in F. S. Regs., Part II. and the Staff Manual respectively. Title Pages will be prepared in manuscript.

WAR DIARY

or

~~INTELLIGENCE SUMMARY~~

(Erase heading not required.)

Army Form C. 2118

Place	Date	Hour	Summary of Events and Information Map reference ALBERT COMBINED 1/40,000.	Remarks and references to Appendices
BELLE VUE FARM F.5. C.5.5.	20.8.16.		Visited Advanced Dressing Station. Visited 42 F.A., and transport lines with A.D.M.S 5th Division attached.	A.P.
	21.8.16.		Visited A.D.S., Collecting Post, new aid post CRUCIFIX CORNER, Divisional Collecting Station, Divisional Baths, and Corps Main Dressing Station with A.D.M.S. 5th Division.	A.P.
	22.8.16.		Visited A.D.S. and O.C. Station.	A.P.
	23.8.16.		Visited A.D. Station, Collecting Post and Aid posts. Operation orders issued in accordance with Appendix 2.	A.P.
	24.8.16.		Active operations in DELVILLE WOOD.	A.P.
	25.8.16.		Operations successfully completed.	A.P.
	26.8.16.		41st Brigade relieved by 22nd Brigade, 7 Division.	A.P.
	27.8.16.		New aid posts selected.	A.P.
	28.8.16.		Visit from A.D.M.S 24 Division re handing over.	A.P.
	29.8.16.		Orders issued to 42, 43 + 44 F.A. re relief by 74th, 73rd + 72nd F.A. respectively.	A.P.
	30.8.16.		42, 43, + 44 F.A. to bivouacs D.30 b.	A.P.
	31.8.16.		Div. H.Q. to BELLOY ST LEONARD — 25 SAN. Section to BELLOY ST LEONARD. 42 F.A. to ETREJUST — 43 F.A. to BOISRAULT — 44 F.A. to L'ARBRE A MOUCHE. 4th Army Administrative Map. Sheet 3.	A.P.

1875 Wt. W593/826 1,000,000 4/15 J.B.C. & A. A.D.S.S./Forms/C. 2118.

Appendix 1.

RAMC Operation Order No 38 by Colonel H H [illegible]
Commanding RAMC Corps
14th Division 17.8.1916.

Reference Map
ALBERT 1:40,000

1. On 18th August the 14th Division is taking part in a simultaneous attack on the enemy lines.

2. Officers Commanding 42nd and 43rd Field Ambulances will each detail one bearer subdivision under an Officer to report to O.C. Advanced Dressing Station at noon 18th inst.

3. OC 44th Field Ambulance will arrange for "Runners" to be posted at each Regimental Aid Post in front line by noon 18th inst, and will detail three Officers for duty with bearers taking up their post at Collecting Post in QUARRY S 22 c 0.5.

4. OC 43rd Field Ambulance will detail one Officer accompanied by an orderly and motor cyclist to form a Loading Point at MAMETZ at road junction F 5 c 8.3. at 3pm.

5. All horsed Ambulances and G.S. Wagons of 42nd and 44th Field Ambulances will report to OC 43rd Field Ambulance at 2pm Aug 18th and will be utilized in conjunction with all those of 43rd Fld Ambulance in conveying slightly wounded from Loading Point to Collecting Station for lightly wounded. The G.S. Wagons will be held as a reserve in case the horsed Ambulances are unable to clear all cases as they arrive, and if required will move off at intervals of 5 minutes between the horsed Ambulances.

6. All walking cases will be directed through the Collecting Post to Loading Point, MAMETZ either via CATERPILLAR VALLEY or MONTAUBAN ALLEY

7. On the arrival of first walking cases at Collecting Post a message is to be despatched to Officer i/c Loading Point notifying him of the fact.

RAMC Operation Order No 38 by Colonel H.V. Prynne RAMS
Commanding RAMC Corps
14th Division 17.8.1916.

Reference Map
ALBERT 1.40,000

1. On 18th August the 14th Division is taking part in a simultaneous attack on the enemy lines.
2. Officers Commanding 42nd and 43rd Field Ambulances will each detail one bearer subdivision under an Officer to report to O.C. Advanced Dressing Station at noon 18th inst.
3. OC 44th Field Ambulance will arrange for "Runners" to be posted at each Regimental Aid Post in front line by noon 18th inst, and will detail three Officers for duty with bearers taking up their post at Collecting Post in QUARRY S 22 c 0.5.
4. OC. 43rd Field Ambulance will detail one Officer accompanied by an orderly and motor cyclist to form a Loading Point at MAMETZ at road junction F 5 c 8.3 at 3pm.
5. All horsed Ambulances and G.S. Wagons of 42nd and 44th Field Ambulances will report to OC 43rd Field Ambulance at 2pm Aug 18th and will be utilized in conjunction with all those of 43rd Fld Ambulance in conveying slightly wounded from Loading Point to Collecting Station for lightly wounded. The G.S. Wagons will be held as a reserve in case the horsed Ambulances are unable to clear all cases as they arrive, and if required will move off at intervals of 5 minutes between the horsed Ambulances.
6. All walking cases will be directed through the Collecting Post to Loading Point, MAMETZ either via CATERPILLAR VALLEY or MONTAMBAN ALLEY.
7. On the arrival of first walking cases at Collecting Post a message is to be despatched to Officer i/c Loading Point notifying him of the fact.

8. On receipt of message referred to in Paragraph 7 Officer i/c Loading Point will immediately despatch a message to O.C. 43rd Fld Ambulance demanding horsed Ambulances for transport of walking cases to Collecting Station for lightly wounded. Horsed Ambulances will move off at intervals of 15 minutes and continue working so long as cases continue to arrive at loading Point.

9. All "Ford" Motor Ambulances will be parked at Advanced Dressing Station at 3 pm. All other Motor Ambulances, except one which will remain with 42nd Field Ambulance, will park at 43rd Field Ambulance at the same hour until called for by O.C. Advanced Dressing Station.

10. All slightly wounded and alleged "gassed" cases &c who are considered fit for duty will be handed over to A.P.M's Stragglers Collecting Station which will be at 43rd Fld Ambulance.

11. O.C. 42nd Fld Ambulance will detail one Officer to report to O.C. 43rd Fld Ambulance at 3 pm August 18th to assist at the Divisional Collecting Station for slightly wounded.

12. Attention is called to the importance of strict adherence to the routes laid down on traffic circuit maps.

13. Please acknowledge.

[signature]
Captain
D.A.D.M.S.
14th Division

Copies to:-
A.D.M.S. XV Corps
14th Div G
14th Div A
O.C. 42nd Fld Amb
" 43rd Fld Amb
" 44th Fld Amb
A.P.M. 14th Division

Appendix 2/

R.A.M.C. Operation Order No 39 by Colonel H.V. Prynne A.M.S.
Commanding R.A.M. Corps 14th Division.
23rd August 1916.

Reference Trench MAP 1/10,000 LONGUEVAL

1. On 24th August 14th Division will take part in a renewed attack on the enemy's line; the 41st Infantry Brigade being on the right and 42nd Infantry Brigade on the left.

2. O.C. 44th F. Amb. will be in charge of the collection of wounded.

3. The 43rd F. Amb. will collect from the 41st Brigade area & 44th F. Amb from 42nd Brigade area, and runners selected from bearer division of these units will be posted to battalion Aid Posts in front line by 12 noon 24th Aug.

4. The one bearer subdivision under an Officer from each of the 43rd & 44th F. Amb. will take post in CRUCIFIX alley about point S.23.A.7.7 and R.E. alley about point S.17.C.3.6. respectively, at 4 p.m. Aug 24th. The remainder of Bearer Division of these Field Ambulances will report at Advanced Dressing Station at 6 p.m. and will be moved up ONE subdivision at a time to the above points on the moving forward of the subdivision in front of them.
O.C. Advanced Dressing Station will establish Stretcher "DUMP" at S.23.A.7.7. with an initial number of 50 stretchers.

5. The whole bearer Division 42nd F. Amb will be held in readiness from 6 p.m. Aug 24th, to move off at five minutes notice.

6. O.C. 43rd F. Amb. will detail One Officer accompanied by an orderly and Motor Cyclist to form a loading point at MAMETZ at road junction F.5.C.8.3 at 6 p.m. Aug 24th.

7. All Horsed ambulances & G.S. Waggons of 42nd & 44th F. Ambs will report to O.C. 43rd F. Amb. at 5 p.m. August 24th & will be utilized in conjunction with all those of 43rd F. Amb. in conveying slightly wounded from loading point to collecting Station for lightly wounded. The G.S. Waggons will be held as a reserve in case the Horsed Ambulances are unable to clear all cases as they arrive, and if required will move off at intervals of 5 minutes between the Horsed ambulances.

8. All walking cases will be directed through the collecting post to loading point MAMETZ either by VIA CATERPILLAR VALLEY or MONTAUBAN ALLEY.

9. On the arrival of first walking cases at Collecting Post a message is to be despatched to Officer i/c Loading Point notifying him of the fact.

10. On receipt of message referred to in paragraph 9. Officer i/c Loading Point will immediately despatch a message to O.C. 43rd F. Amb demanding Horsed Ambulances for transport of walking cases to Collecting Station for lightly wounded. Horsed ambulances will move off at intervals of 15 minutes and continue working so long as cases continue to arrive at loading Point.

11. All "Ford" Motor Ambulances will be parked at Advanced Dressing Station at 6. p.m. All other Motor Ambulances, except one which will remain with 42nd Field Ambulance, will park at 43rd Field Ambulance at the same hour until called for by O.C. Advanced Dressing Station.

12. All slightly wounded and alleged "gassed" cases &c who are considered fit for duty will be handed over to A.P.M's Stragglers Collecting Station which will be at 43rd F. Ambulance. O.C. Advanced Dressing Station will arrange for the Medical examination of such men as are brought there from Stragglers Posts.

13. O.C. 42nd F. Ambulance will detail one Officer to report to O.C. 43rd F. Ambulance at 6 p.m. August 24th to assist at the Divisional Collecting Station for lightly wounded.

14 Attention is called to the importance of strict adherence to the routes laid down on traffic circuit maps.

15 Please acknowledge.

J.W. [illegible]
Captain.
D.A.D.M.S.
14th Division.

Copies to:–
D.D.M.S.
14 Div. G.
42 F. Amb
43 "
44 "
41 Infy Bde
42 "
43 "
A.P.M.

Sept. 1916

S

Confidential

14

140/1734

A D M S Vol. 14
42 F amb Vol 17
43 " " 16
44 " " 17
25 San Sec. 17

War Diary of ADMS
14th (Light) Division
for
month of
September 1916

COMMITTEE FOR THE
MEDICAL HISTORY OF THE WAR
Date 26 OCT. 1916

Instructions regarding War Diaries and Intelligence Summaries are contained in F. S. Regs., Part II. and the Staff Manual respectively. Title Pages will be prepared in manuscript.

WAR DIARY
or
~~INTELLIGENCE SUMMARY~~
(Erase heading not required.)

Army Form C. 2118

Ref: 4th Army Area administrative map. Sheet 3. + ALBERT Combined 1/40,000

Place	Date	Hour	Summary of Events and Information	Remarks and references to Appendices
BELLOY	1.9.16		Conference at Office of D.D.M.S. X Corps. Visited 42 F.A. at ETREJUST.	[signature] Col. A.M.S.
St LEONARD	2.9.16		Made reconnaissance of FRESNEVILLE as site for F. Ambulance. Visited FLIXECOURT to arrange washing for Division.	[initials]
	3.9.16		Visited 43 F.A. at BOISRAULT. Visited SALEUX + SALOUEL for laundry accomodation.	[initials]
	4.9.16		Visited D.M.S. ARMY in reference to epidemic of diarrhoea and sanitation. Sanitary inspection 11/Liverpools.	[initials]
	5.9.16		Conference of regimental M.O's re sanitation in front line + billets.	[initials]
	6.9.16		Visited 43 F Ambulance.	[initials]
	7.9.16		Sanitary inspection of units of 41 Brigade: This was on the whole satisfactory	[initials]
	8.9.16		Sanitary inspection of units of 42 Brigade. Generally satisfactory	[initials]
	9.9.16		Sanitary inspection of units 43 Brigade. Generally satisfactory	[initials]
	10.9.16		41 Brigade with 44 F.A. to DERNANCOURT CAMP.	[initials]
	11.9.16		44 F.A. to FRICOURT CAMP. 42 F.A. to DERNANCOURT CAMP. D.H.Q. + SANITARY SECTION to BUIRE-SUR-ANCRE.	[initials]
BUIRE SUR ANCRE	12.9.16		42 F.A. to FRICOURT CAMP. 43 F.A. to DERNANCOURT CAMP. 42 F.A. took over Advanced Dressing Station at S.22 d.8.0., ~~and~~ (BERNAFAY WOOD) + Relay Post (Crucifix Corner) S23. a.6.8 from 55 Div	[initials]

1875 Wt. W593/826 1,000,000 4/15 J.B.C. & A. A.D.S.S./Forms/C. 2118.

Instructions regarding War Diaries and Intelligence Summaries are contained in F. S. Regs., Part II. and the Staff Manual respectively. Title Pages will be prepared in manuscript.

WAR DIARY
or
~~INTELLIGENCE SUMMARY~~
(Erase heading not required.)

Army Form C. 2118

Place	Date	Hour	Summary of Events and Information Map reference ALBERT 1/40000	Remarks and references to Appendices
FRICOURT CHATEAU. F.36.	13.9.16.		D.H.Q. to FRICOURT CHATEAU.	T.R.P.
	14.9.16.		42 F.A. opened Divl. Collecting Station at A2.6 8.0.	T.R.P.
	15.9.16.		Active operations. Visited Divl. Collecting Station, Advanced Dressing Station, Bearer Relay Post, and site for new A.D.S. in DELVILLE WOOD. S18 C.6.4. Operation orders as by Appendix I	T.R.P.
	16.9.16.		Active operations. Horse + motor transport advanced to BERNAFAY WOOD + DELVILLE WOOD.	T.R.P.
	17.9.16.		D.H.Q. to BUIRE CAMP. 42 F.A. to D18.a. 44 F.A. to billets at DERNANCOURT. 43 F.A. took over Corps Rest Station from 55 Divn. (D.23 c.)	T.R.P.
BUIRE CAMP. D29.a.3.0.	18.9.16.		Visited Corps Rest Station, CORPS troops R.E. + D.D.M.S.	T.R.P.
	19.9.16.		Visited Corps Rest Station, + British Red Cross Depot re stores.	T.R.P.
	20.9.16.		Visited Corps Rest Station + 36 C.C.S.	T.R.P.
	21.9.16.		Visited Corps Main Dressing Station, + Corps Collecting Station for lightly wounded.	

1875 Wt. W593/826 1,000,000 4/15 J.B.C. & A. A.D.S.S./Forms/C. 2118.

Army Form C. 2118

Instructions regarding War Diaries and Intelligence Summaries are contained in F. S. Regs., Part II. and the Staff Manual respectively. Title Pages will be prepared in manuscript.

WAR DIARY

or

~~INTELLIGENCE SUMMARY~~

(Erase heading not required.)

Map reference ALBERT 1/40000
LENS. 1/100,000.

Place	Date	Hour	Summary of Events and Information	Remarks and references to Appendices
BOIRE CAMP. D29.a.30.	22.9.16.		D.H.Q. to LECAUROY. 42 F.A. to GRANDE RULLECOURT. 43 F.A. to SUS St LEGER. 44 F.A. to GROUCHES. SAN. SEC. to LE CAUROY.	[illegible]
LE CAUROY	23.9.16.		Visited A.D.M.S. 12 Division to arrange reliefs of medical units. Visited 42, 43 & 44 F.A.	[illegible]
	24.9.16		Visited Advanced Dressing Station, RIVIERE, (R.25 d.9.6) Collecting Post LE FERMONT (R.27 a 2.7), Collecting Post at BRASSERIE (Q21 d.9.1) & Regimental Aid posts. F Sector	[illegible]
	25.9.16.		Collection from G & H. sectors, Advanced Dressing Station, St SACREMENT ARRAS (G27 a.3.10.), Collecting Post ACHICOURT (M2. 6.4.10) taken over by 43 F.A. from 36 F.A. Collection from F. sector, Advanced Dressing Station at RIVIERE, Collecting Posts at BRASSERIE & LE FERMONT taken over by 42 F.A from 38 F.A.	[illegible]
	26.9.16.		42 F.A. took over from 38 F.A. at GOUY (Q.19 a.7.8) 44 F.A. relieved 37 F.A. & took over D.R.S at CHATEAU, BARLY (P.15) D.H.Q to CHATEAU, GOUY.	[illegible]

1875 Wt. W593/826 1,000,000 4/15 J.B.C. & A. A.D.S.S./Forms/C. 2118.

Instructions regarding War Diaries and Intelligence Summaries are contained in F. S. Regs., Part II. and the Staff Manual respectively. Title Pages will be prepared in manuscript.

WAR DIARY

or

~~INTELLIGENCE SUMMARY~~

(Erase heading not required.)

Army Form C. 2118

Place	Date	Hour	Summary of Events and Information Map reference LENS 1/100,000.	Remarks and references to Appendices
GOUY	27.9.16.		43 F.A. relieved 36 F.A. at WANQUETIN (K.32.C.2.4.)	T.r.P.
	28.9.16.		D.H.Q. to CHATEAU, WARLUS. Selected site for F.A. at K.36.a.C.9.7.	T.r.P.
WARLUS	29.9.16.		Visited DOULLENS re laundry	T.r.P.
	30.9.16.		Visited 42, 43 & 44 F. Ambulances	T.r.P.

1875 Wt. W593/826 1,000,000 4/15 J.B.C. & A. A.D.S.S./Forms/C. 2118.

APPENDIX I

R.A.M.C. Operation Order No. 44 by Colonel H.V. Prynne. A.M.S. Commanding R.A.M. Corps. 14th Light Division
14th Sept 1916.

Reference Maps. Albert 1,40,000. and Trench Maps.

---

1. The 14th Division will attack enemy's lines at Zero on "Z" day. Zero and "Z" day to be notified later.

2. O.C. 42nd F. Ambulance will be in charge of collection of wounded and will post himself at Divisional Collecting Station (A 2 B 8.0) two hours before Zero.

3. Liaison Officers each with a runner will be attached as under two hours before Zero:–

   41st Infantry Brigade. (S 23 B 2.8) 42nd Field Amb.
   42nd Infantry Brigade (S 28 A 4.0) 44th Field Amb.

4. Two runners will be attached to each battalion Medical Officer as under, to proceed forthwith:–

   41st Infantry Brigade : 42nd Field Ambulance.
   42nd Infantry Brigade : 44th Field Ambulance.

5. All wheeled stretchers will be immediately placed at disposal of O.C. 42nd Field Ambulance at Divisional Collecting Station.

6. Bearers will be disposed as follows, inclusive of those at present attached to Aid Posts, and will report forthwith to Brigade Headquarters as under. All will carry double equipment of stretchers.

<u>42nd Field Ambulance.</u> One bearer subdivision under an officer to report to 41st Brigade Headquarters at S. 23. B. 2.8. This bearer subdivision will follow behind Infantry to SWITCH trench under orders of Brigadier General Commanding and will clear from there back to existing Aid Posts.

<u>44th Field Ambulance.</u> Bearer division under two officers to report to 42nd. Infantry Brigade Headquarter at S 28 A 4.0. These will follow Infantry under order of Brigadier General Commanding, two subdivisions under one officer, halting on line of road N 33 C 0.1 – N 31 B 4.0, and will clear from the area between that and SWITCH trench; remaining subdivision and officer will follow to final objective and clear back to line N 33. C ~~0.1~~ 0.1 – N 31 B 4.0.

43rd Field Ambulance. Bearer division under an officer will proceed to MONTAUBAN ALLEY (portion to west of BERNAFAY WOOD) so as to arrive at six hours after Zero and will remain there in reserve, under the orders of O.C. 42nd Field Ambulance.

7. One tent subdivision 43rd Field Ambulance will park at S 26 D 6·70 at Zero.

8 All motor ambulances will be immediately placed under the orders of O.C. 42nd Field Ambulance and will be parked at F 10 B 90·35. at Zero All horsed ambulances and G. S. Wagons, except those parked with one tent subdivision in each Field Ambulance will park at 44th Field Ambulance forthwith.

9. O.C. 43rd Field Ambulance will detail an officer with an orderly and motor cyclist to form "Loading Point" at Divisional Collecting Station.

10 All "walking wounded" will be directed to Divisional Collecting Station.

11. In the event of the attack reaching the final objective (GUEUDECOURT) the tent subdivision 43rd Field Ambulance will immediately move up and open an advanced Dressing Station in dug outs about S 18 central, with a collecting post in SUNKEN ROAD about T 1 A 9·3. The existing advanced Dressing Station and bearer relay post will be closed. Motor ambulances will then work up to the CRUCIFIX (S 23 A 6·9) or further if the road permits. Loading Point for "Walking Wounded" will be advanced to N.W. corner BERNAFAY WOOD (S 22 D 85·10) and cases transferred to motor ambulances at Divisional Collecting Station.

12. Please acknowledge.

[signature]

Captain.
D. A. D. M. S.
14th Division.

Copies to:—
14 Div "G."
" " "A"
D.D.M.S. XV Corps
A.D.M.S. Guards Div.
" 41st "
42nd Inf Bde
41st " "
43rd " "
42nd F amb.
43rd "
44th "
A.P.M.

Confidential

War Diary

of

Colonel H V Prynne ADMS

ADMS 14th (Light) Division.

for

Month of October 1916.

COMMITTEE FOR THE MEDICAL HISTORY OF THE WAR
Date 9 DEC. 1916

Instructions regarding War Diaries and Intelligence Summaries are contained in F. S. Regs., Part II. and the Staff Manual respectively. Title Pages will be prepared in manuscript.

WAR DIARY
or
~~INTELLIGENCE SUMMARY~~
(Erase heading not required.)

Army Form C. 2118

Place	Date	Hour	Summary of Events and Information	Remarks and references to Appendices
WARLUS	1916. October 2nd	8 pm	To day took over duties of A.D.M.S.	W.J. Vaughan Lt Col RAMC
" "	3rd	8 pm	Visited proposed site for laundry at AUESNES.	WJV.
" "	4th	8 pm	Visited A.D.S. at ARRAS. Inspected proposed site for M.D.S at WANQUETIN.	WJV
" "	5th	8 pm	Met D.M.S. III Army at WANQUETIN. — Hd Qrs 42nd F.A. moved from GOUY to IZEL les HAMEAU today, they still run A.D.S. at RIVIERE and BEAUMETZ	WJV
" "	6th	8 pm	Visited 43rd F.A. at WANQUETIN. Wounded from "F" sector are now conveyed by 42nd F.A. motor ambulances to 2nd N.M.F.A. at GOUY and sick to 43rd F.A at WANQUETIN.	WJV
" "	8th	8 pm	Visited 41 C.C.S. to try to arrange for them to take over scabies patients unsuccessful	WJV
" "	9th	8 pm	Attended D.M.S. Conference at ST POL.	WJV
" "	10th	8 pm	Held medical board on 5 cases at survey school BEAUMETZ	WJV
" "	11th	5 pm	Handed over duties to A.D.M.S. W.J. Vaughan Lt Col RAMC	

1875 Wt. W593/826 1,000,000 4/15 J.B.C. & A. A.D.S.S./Forms/C. 2118.

Army Form C. 2118

Instructions regarding War Diaries and Intelligence Summaries are contained in F. S. Regs., Part II. and the Staff Manual respectively. Title Pages will be prepared in manuscript.

WAR DIARY
or
~~INTELLIGENCE SUMMARY~~

(Erase heading not required.)

Map reference. France Sheet 51c

Place	Date	Hour	Summary of Events and Information	Remarks and references to Appendices
WARLUS	12.10.16		Visited baths & A.D.S. ARRAS. Visited new site for F. Ambulance K.32.d.9.5. Visited Divisional Laundry, AVESNES, & 42. F.A. IZEL-LEZ-HAMEAU.	[signature] Col. A.M.S.
	13.10.16		Visited Collecting Post & Baths, ACHICOURT, and posts of G & H. sectors & Baths, AGNY & RONVILLE. Visited Officers' Rest Station, MARIN & Div.l Laundry.	[signature]
	14.10.16		Visited baths BERNEVILLE, & SIMENCOURT, and 44 F.A. BARLY. Visited baths & Collecting Post, BEAUMETZ, Collecting Posts at LE FERMONT and BRASSERIE, A.D.S. at G ROSVILLE, baths at LE FERMONT, and aid posts F. Sector.	[signature]
	15.10.16		Visited 43 F.A. Visited Prisoners' of War Camp, FOSSEUX Visited Div.l Laundry.	[signature]
	16.10.16		Inspected sanitation, BERNEVILLE. Visited A.D.M.S. 35 Div.l & visited their Div.l Laundry.	[signature]
	17.10.16		Visited 43 & 44 F.A., Div.l Laundry & Officers' Rest Station with D.D.M.S. VI Corps. Operation orders issued as in Appendix I	[signature]
	18.10.16		Visited SCHOOLS, DAINVILLE to be used as Div.l Collecting Station Visited Chateau, FREVENT re use of stables for a Div.l Laundry	[signature]
	19.10.16		Visited Div.l Laundry, Town Major, AVESNES for rebilleting of Laundry party. Visited 37 C.C.S. re A.F. B117	[signature]

1875 Wt. W593/826 1,000,000 4/15 J.B.C. & A. A.D.S.S./Forms/C. 2118.

Instructions regarding War Diaries and Intelligence Summaries are contained in F. S. Regs., Part II. and the Staff Manual respectively. Title Pages will be prepared in manuscript.

WAR DIARY

or

~~INTELLIGENCE SUMMARY~~

(Erase heading not required.)

Army Form C. 2118

Map reference France Sheet 51C.

Place	Date	Hour	Summary of Events and Information	Remarks and references to Appendices
WARLUS	20.10.16.		Inspected sanitation WARLUS; visited Div! Laundry.	J.D.P.
	21.10.16.		Visited 43 F.A. + Div! Laundry. Conference at D.D.M.S. VI Corps. Visited Officers' Rest Station.	J.D.P.
	22.10.16.		Inspected sanitation BEAUMETZ, FOSSEUX and BARLY. Visited 44 F.A.	J.D.P.
	23.10.16.		Inspected sanitation SIMENCOURT. Visited Div! Laundry.	J.D.P.
	24.10.16.		Visited A.D.M.S. 12 Division to arrange relief of duties	J.D.P.
	25.10.16.		Collection of wounded, and Advanced Dressing Station, with Collecting Posts belonging to "F" sector handed over to 38 F. Ambulance. Collection of wounded, Advanced Dressing Station + Collecting Post belonging to "G + H" sectors handed over to 36 F. Ambulance	J.D.P.
	26.10.16.		F. Ambulance camp at K.32.d.9.5 handed over by 43 F.A. to 36 F.A. Officers' Rest Station handed over to 37 F.A. 43 F.A. to IZEL-LEZ-HAMEAU.	J.D.P.
LE CAUROY	27.10.16.		Div! H.Q. and SAN. SEC. to LE CAUROY. 43 F.A. to GIVENCHY-LE-NOBLE. (I.17.b.2.3) D.R.S. BARLY handed over by 44 F.A. to 37. F.A. 44. F.A. to SOMBRIN. (O.23.b.0.4.)	J.D.P.
	28.10.16		Visited 43 F.A. at GIVENCHY-LE-NOBLE CHATEAU.	J.D.P.
	29.10.16.		Visited FREVENT CHATEAU re Div! Laundry. Visited 105 F.A. re Corps School of Instruction for R.A.M.C. which D.D.M.S. VI Corps requires formed. Conference of Regimental M.O's, + O's. Comd'g F.A's at LE CAUROY.	J.D.P.
	30.10.16.		Visit by O.C. 105 F. Ambulance re Corps School.	J.D.P.
	31.10.16		Visited D.D.M.S. VI Corps re Corps School, + also Divisional Laundry.	

J. D. [illegible] Col. A.M.S.

1875 Wt. W593/826 1,000,000 4/15 J.B.C. & A. A.D.S.S./Forms/C. 2118.

R.A.M.C. Operation Order No 47 by Colonel H.V. Prynne A.M.S.

Commanding R.A.M. Corps, 14th Division.

17th October 1916.

The 14th Division will assist at Zero on 'Z' day an attack to be made further south.

O.C. 42nd F. Amb. will be in charge of collection from 'F' sector and will post himself at the Advanced Dressing Station, GROSVILLE. He will detail 2 additional bearers for each Regimental Aid Post to be held in reserve at the Brasserie, under an officer, one hour before 'Zero'. This officer will post the men, whenever required, at the Regimental Aid Posts and will himself act as liaison officer between the Regimental Aid Posts and the Advanced Dressing Station and collecting Posts.

The party at the A.D.S. will be reinforced by 12 O.R. and 1 motor cyclist, and that at BEAUMETZ made up to 1 officer and 7 O.R. This will be a Collecting Post for walking cases and necessary arrangements will be made for provision of necessary dressings hot drinks etc. 8 men will be detailed to report at Brasserie 1 hour before Zero. 3 G.S. Wagons and 3 Horsed ambulances will report to A.D.M.S., WARLUS 1 hour before 'Zero' ready to proceed to BEAUMETZ on receipt of message from O/c Collecting Post.

The party at LE FERMONT will report at A.D.S. 1 hour before Zero. All available wheeled stretchers, oxygen cylinders and inhalers will be sent to A.D.S.

All requests for extra bearers for 'F' sector will be made to O.C. 42nd F.amb. at A.D.S. GROSVILLE.

O.C. 43rd F amb. will be responsible for collection from 'G and H' sectors, and will post himself at A.D.S. ARRAS.

He will detail 2 additional stretcher-bearers for each Regtl Aid Post, to be held in reserve, those for G and H.1 under an officer, will arrive at Collecting Post ACHICOURT 1 hour before 'Zero'. When required these bearers will be posted by the officer at the Regtl aid Posts, who will then himself act as liaison officer between Regtl aid Posts & Collecting Post ACHICOURT.

The reserve bearers for H.2 will report to M.O. of that Regtl aid Post an hour before 'Zero'.

O.C. 43rd F.A. will detail 1 officer, 2 N.C.Os, & 8 men & 1 cyclist with equipment for necessary dressings & provision of hot drinks to form a Collecting Post for walking cases at the Schools DAINVILLE 1 hour before 'Zero'. Walking cases will be conducted to loading point at L 28 C.1.2 (Sheet 51c) where they will be conveyed to 44th F amb BARLY. 1 N.C.O. and 3 men from this Collecting Post will be stationed at L 28 C.1.2. to direct traffic.

– to marked Mappe.

He will also arrange for 3 Horsed ambulances and 3 G.S. Wagons to report to A.D.M.S. WARLUS 1 hour before 'Zero' ready to proceed to DAINVILLE on receipt of message by cyclist from O/c Collecting Post there.

Motor ambulances, less 1 Ford, will park at ECOLE NORMALE ARRAS. 1 hour before 'Zero'.

All available wheeled Stretchers, oxygen cylinders and inhalers to be sent to A.D.S.

1 Bearer subdivision will be kept in reserve at A.D.S. ARRAS.

All requests for extra bearers for 'G & H' sectors will be made to O.C. 43rd F. Amb at A.D.S. ARRAS.

O.C. 44th F. Amb will be temporarily in charge of Main Dressing Station. He will send 1 bearer subdivision and 1 motor cyclist to A.D.S., BEAUMETZ, 1 hour before 'Zero'.

Also 3 wheeled stretchers, 7 oxygen cylinders will be sent to A.D.S., ARRAS & 3 wheeled stretchers and 7 oxygen cylinders to A.D.S. GROSVILLE.

Motor Ambulances less 1 Ford and 3 G.S. Wagons and 3 Horsed ambulances will report to A.D.M.S. WARLUS at 'Zero'.

(Please acknowledge.)

Copies to; –
D.D.M.S.
42 F. Amb
43 "
44 "
A.A. & Q.M.G.
G. 14 Div.
42 Inf Bde
43 "
44 "

Colonel.
A.D.M.S.
14th Division.

140/1062 14
Vol 16

Confidential

COMMITTEE FOR THE
MEDICAL HISTORY OF THE WAR
Date 3 JAN. 1917

War Diary
of
ADMS
14th
Division
for
month.
November 1916

Nov 1916

Army Form C. 2118.

WAR DIARY

or

~~INTELLIGENCE SUMMARY~~

(Erase heading not required.)

Instructions regarding War Diaries and Intelligence Summaries are contained in F. S. Regs., Part II. and the Staff Manual respectively. Title Pages will be prepared in manuscript.

Map reference Sheet 51 C. FRANCE 1/40,000.

Place	Date	Hour	Summary of Events and Information	Remarks and references to Appendices
LE CAUROY	1.11.16		Visited 42 F.A. to arrange accomodation for scabies cases. Visited 43 F.A. + 105 F.A. to arrange concerning Corps School of Instruction for R.A.M.C.	[illegible] Col. A.M.S.
	2.11.16		Visited 43 F.A, and inspected billets of personnel &c.	[illegible]
	3.11.16		Visited OPPY re washing machines. Visited 44 F.A.	[illegible]
	4.11.16		Visited CORPS SCHOOL, LIGNEREUIL and attended opening lectures.	[illegible]
	5.11.16		Captain L.H. GUEST (T.C.) reported from 87 F.A. to take over duties of D.A.D.M.S. in relief of Captain J. du P. LANGRISHE appointed to command of No 12 F.A.	[illegible]
	6.11.16		Captain LANGRISHE left. Visited Divisional Laundry at AVESNES, with D.A.D.M.S.	[illegible]
	7.11.16		42 F.A. to HAUTEVILLE. Visited PETIT HOUVIN, MONTJOIE FARM, and HAUTEVILLE re proposed sites for F.A's. Visited 43 F.A. and 44 F.A.	[illegible]
	8.11.16		Visited baths, BERLENCOURT, 43 Brigade H.Q, 43 + 44 F.A. Conference at D.D.M.S. VI Corps. Visited Divisional Laundry. Issued orders re move of 43 + 44 F.A.	[illegible]

2449 Wt. W14957/M90 750,000 1/16 J.B.C. & A. Forms/C.2118/12.

Army Form C. 2118.

Instructions regarding War Diaries and Intelligence Summaries are contained in F. S. Regs., Part II. and the Staff Manual respectively. Title Pages will be prepared in manuscript.

WAR DIARY
or
~~INTELLIGENCE SUMMARY~~
(Erase heading not required.)

Map reference Sheet 51C. FRANCE 1/40,000.

Place	Date	Hour	Summary of Events and Information	Remarks and references to Appendices
LE CAUROY	9.11.16.		Visited Divisional Laundry, AVESNES, and 42 F.A.	S.v.P.
	10.11.16.		43 F.A. moved to PETIT HOUVIN, 44 F.A. to LIENCOURT. Attended lectures at CORPS SCHOOL.	S.v.P.
	11.11.16.		Visited 42 and 44 F.A. (Divisional Rest Station)	S.v.P.
	12.11.16.		Visited 44 and 43 F.A.	S.v.P.
	13.11.16.		Visited FREVENT re establishment of Divisional Laundry at the CHATEAU.	S.v.P.
	14.11.16.		Visited FREVENT re laundry.	S.v.P.
	15.11.16.		Attended as President of Medical Board at WARLUS. Visited Divisional Laundry, FREVENT.	S.v.P.
	16.11.16.		Visited Divisional Rest Station (44 F.A.	S.v.P.
	17.11.16.		Attended lectures on GAS defence, and treatment of cases at CORPS SCHOOL.	S.v.P.
	18.11.16.		Attended conference D.D.M.S. VI Corps. Visited 42 F.A., who take scabies cases of the Division.	S.v.P.
	19.11.16.		Capt. GUEST proceeded on leave. Captain BROSTER reported for temporary duty as D.A.D.M.S.	S.v.P.

2449 Wt. W14957/M90 750,000 1/16 J.B.C. & A. Forms/C.2118/12.

Instructions regarding War Diaries and Intelligence Summaries are contained in F. S. Regs., Part II. and the Staff Manual respectively. Title Pages will be prepared in manuscript.

WAR DIARY
or
~~INTELLIGENCE SUMMARY~~
(Erase heading not required.)

Army Form C. 2118.

Map reference. Sheet 51 C. FRANCE. 1/40,000.

Place	Date	Hour	Summary of Events and Information	Remarks and references to Appendices
LE CAUROY	20.11.16.		Attended lecture by Surg. Gen. Macpherson at G.H.Q. Visited Laundry, FREVENT.	[signature] Col. AMS.
	21.11.16.		Visited 12 Division to arrange for medical arrangements of 14 Division Units in 12 Division area.	[initials]
	22.11.16.		Visited A.D.M.S. 12 Division, O.C. XV M.A.C., & O.C. 41 C.C.S. regarding evacuation of 14 Division sick. Visited 42 F.A., and Clean Clothing Store, AVESNES. Visited Laundry, FREVENT.	[initials]
	23.11.16.		Visited M.O's 7 K.R.R.C. and 7 R.B. 42nd Bde moved to Forward Area.	[initials]
	24.11.16.		Visited D.D.M.S. VI Corps. Inspected baths at SOMBRIN, OPPY, BERLENCOURT, HOUVIN, BUNEVILLE and SERICOURT. Visited 106 F.A., AGNEZ-LEZ DUISANS, & LOUEZ re 14 Division sick in 35 Division area. Visited A.D.M.S. 12 Division re 14 Division sick from transport lines in 12 Division area. Visited 42 Bde to report medical arrangements.	[initials]
	25.11.16.		Visited 43 F.A., and Laundry, FREVENT.	[initials]
	26.11.16.		Visited 42, 43 & 44 F.A. with D.D.M.S. VI Corps.	[initials]
	27.11.16.		Visited 42 F.A. re accomodation for Scabies, and billets of personnel.	[initials]

2449 Wt. W14957/M90 750,000 1/16 J.B.C. & A. Forms/C.2118/12.

Instructions regarding War Diaries and Intelligence Summaries are contained in F. S. Regs., Part II. and the Staff Manual respectively. Title Pages will be prepared in manuscript.

WAR DIARY
or
~~INTELLIGENCE SUMMARY~~
(Erase heading not required.)

Army Form C. 2118.

Map reference Sheet 57^c FRANCE 1/40,000.

Place	Date	Hour	Summary of Events and Information	Remarks and references to Appendices
LE CAUROY	28.11.16.		Inspected 43 F.A. — personnel in marching order, transport animals harnessed, transport ~~vehicles~~ vehicles + motor transport.	[illegible]
			Visited baths OPPY + BERLENCOURT.	
	29.11.16.		Inspected 44 F.A. — personnel in marching order, transport animals harnessed, transport vehicles + motor transport	[illegible]
	30.11.16.		Inspected 42 F.A. — personnel in marching order, transport animals harnessed, transport vehicles + motor transport	[illegible] Col. A.M.S.

2449 Wt. W14957/M90 750,000 1/16 J.B.C. & A. Forms/C.2118/12.

Dec 1916

1461/903

A. D. M. S. 14th (Light) Division. Vol 17

War Diary.

for period – December 1 to 31. 1916.

COMMITTEE FOR THE
MEDICAL HISTORY OF THE WAR
Date 31 JAN. 1917

Army Form C. 2118.

WAR DIARY
or
~~INTELLIGENCE SUMMARY~~ Map reference Sheet 51c FRANCE 1/40,000.

(Erase heading not required.)

Instructions regarding War Diaries and Intelligence Summaries are contained in F. S. Regs., Part II. and the Staff Manual respectively. Title Pages will be prepared in manuscript.

Place	Date	Hour	Summary of Events and Information	Remarks and references to Appendices
LE CAUROY	1.12.16.		Visited Divisional Laundry FREVENT. Visited Baths, D.R.S. Brigade Laundries, & F. Ambulances 9th Division.	[illegible] Col. A.M.S.
	2.12.16		Visited 44 F.A. Visited Divl. Laundry, and also MONCHEL, FILIEVRES and BOUBERS for site for Divl. Laundry.	[initials]
	3.12.16		Visited Divl. Laundry.	[initials]
	4.12.16		Visited ANVIN, MONCHY, GAUCHIN and HERNICOURT for site for Divl. Laundry. Visited 43 F.A. H.Q. PETIT HOUVIN and Tent subdivn. HOUVIN.	[initials]
	5.12.16.		Visited baths, OPPY.	[initials]
	6.12.16		Visited ANVIN, BLANGY, BLINGEL, ROLLENCOURT, AUCHY-LEZ-HESDIN, VAIL, ~~VEIL~~ HESDIN and GALAMETZ for laundry site.	[initials]
	7.12.16		Visited 42 F.A., and inspected arrangements of sick, & personnel. Visited Clothing Store, AVESNES. Visited BOUBERS, MONCHEL, CONCHY & FILIEVRES for laundry site. Visited Divl. Laundry.	[initials]
	8.12.16.		Visited 44 F.A. Conference of regimental M.O's at Divl. H.Q.	[initials]
	9.12.16.		Visit by A.D.M.S. & D.A.D.M.S. 12 Division to arrange relief.	[initials]
	10.12.16.		Visited 42 F.A. Visited sanitary exhibition of THIRD ARMY, at SAINT POL. Visited H.Q. 43 F.A., & detachment HOUVIN.	[initials]

2449 Wt. W14957/M90 750,000 1/16 J.B.C. & A. Forms/C.2118/12.

Instructions regarding War Diaries and Intelligence Summaries are contained in F. S. Regs., Part II. and the Staff Manual respectively. Title Pages will be prepared in manuscript.

WAR DIARY
or
~~INTELLIGENCE SUMMARY~~
(Erase heading not required.)

Army Form C. 2118.

Map reference. Sheet 51c FRANCE 1/40,000.

Place	Date	Hour	Summary of Events and Information	Remarks and references to Appendices
LE CAUROY	11.12.16.		Attended lectures at R.A.M.C. Corps School, LIGNEREUIL. D.A.D.M.S. Sanitation, THIRD ARMY inspected sanitation of Division	S.r.P.
	12.12.16.		D.A.D.M.S. 12 Division visited to arrange reliefs of F. Ambulances & duties. Visited baths OPPY.	S.r.P.
	13.12.16.		Visited A.D.M.S. 12 Division, and Brigade Laundry, ARRAS. Visited VI Corps re reliefs.	S.r.P.
	14.12.16.		Visited Corps Officers' Rest Station, MANIN.	S.r.P.
	15.12.16.		Visited 36, 37 and 38 F.A's of 12 Division. Visited 37 C.C.S. and A.D.M.S. 12 Division.	S.r.P.
	16.12.16.		Attended lecture on Collection of Wounded at R.A.M.C. Corps School. Visited 42 F.A. 43 F.A. to LIENCOURT	S.r.P.
	17.12.16.		Attended VI Corps Conference. 43 F.A. to GOUY in relief of 38 F.A.	S.r.P.
	18.12.16.		42 F.A. to BARLY in relief of 37 F.A. 44 F.A. to WANQUETIN in relief of 36 F.A.	S.r.P.
	19.12.16.		D.H.Q. to WARLUS. Visited A.D.S. ARRAS and Brigade Laundry & baths DAINVILLE.	S.r.P.
WARLUS	20.12.16.		Visited Collecting Post & Baths, BEAUMETZ, A.D.S. GROSVILLE, Collecting Post LE FERMONT & baths LE FERMONT.	S.r.P.

2449 Wt. W14957/M90 750,000 1/16 J.B.C. & A. Forms/C.2118/12.

Instructions regarding War Diaries and Intelligence Summaries are contained in F. S. Regs., Part II. and the Staff Manual respectively. Title Pages will be prepared in manuscript.

WAR DIARY
or
~~INTELLIGENCE SUMMARY~~
(Erase heading not required.)

Army Form C. 2118.

Map reference Sheet 51^C FRANCE 1/40,000.

Place	Date	Hour	Summary of Events and Information	Remarks and references to Appendices
WARLUS.	21.12.16.		Visited A.D.S. ARRAS, and Regimental Aid Post, RONVILLE.	S.T.P.
			Visited VI Corps re evacuation of wounded. Visited 44 F.A.	S.T.P.
	22.12.16.		Visited 43 F.A.	S.T.P.
	23.12.16.		Visited 43 F.A. re "shell shock" case.	S.T.P.
	24.12.16.		Visited medical arrangements Right battalion "F" Sector.	
			Visited BERNEVILLE, SIMENCOURT and GOUY with D.D.M.S.	S.T.P.
	25.12.16.		Christmas Day.	S.T.P.
	26.12.16		Visited Town Majors BERNEVILLE, SIMENCOURT, GOUY, FOSSEUX, and BARLY re sanitation. Visited 42 F.A.	S.T.P.
	27.12.16.		Visited Divisional Laundry, AVESNES, & D.S.C. WORKSHOP.	S.T.P.
			Visited Town Majors BEAUMETZ and MONCHIET re sanitation	
	28.12.16.		Visited VI Corps, re Defence Scheme. Visited Collecting Post, ACHICOURT Regimental Aid Posts, AGNY and H.R.; also Rest dugout GOWERS.	S.T.P.
	29.12.16.		Visited 41, 42 & 43 Brigade H.Q. re precautions against TRENCH FEET	S.T.P.
	30.12.16.		Visited Manure Dumps, WARLUS, BERNEVILLE & SIMENCOURT.	S.T.P.
	31.12.16.		Attended VI Corps Conference. Visited D.D.M.S. VII Corps.	S.T.P.

S. T. Pryme[?]
Col. A.M.S.

2449 Wt. W14957/M90 750,000 1/16 J.B.C. & A. Forms/C.2118/12.

14

140/943

Vol 18

Dupl

War Diary

of

Colonel H V Prynne DSO.

ADMS

14th

Division

January 1917.

COMMITTEE FOR THE
MEDICAL HISTORY OF THE WAR
Date 13 MAR. 1917

Jan 1917

Instructions regarding War Diaries and Intelligence Summaries are contained in F. S. Regs., Part II. and the Staff Manual respectively. Title Pages will be prepared in manuscript.

WAR DIARY
or
~~INTELLIGENCE SUMMARY~~
(Erase heading not required.)

Army Form C. 2118.

Map reference Sheet 51c FRANCE 1/40,000.

Place	Date	Hour	Summary of Events and Information	Remarks and references to Appendices
NARLUS	1.1.17		Handed over duties of A.D.M.S. to Lt Col. VAUGHAN, R.A.M.C. and proceeded on leave.	[signature] Col. A.M.S.
" "	1.1.17.		Taken over W.H. Vaughan Lt Col RAMC	
" "	2.1.17.		Visited A.D.S. at BEAUMETZ to ~~[illegible]~~ enquire into evacuation of sick & wounded –	W.H. Vaughan Lt Col RAMC
" "	3.1.17		D.D.M.S. VII Corps was conducted round villages in rest area by Captn PIKE.	W.H.V.
" "	4.1.17		Visited 43rd & 44th F.A.s Handed over to Lt Col Sneath RAMC W.H. Vaughan Lt Col RAMC	

2449 Wt. W14957/M90 750,000 1/16 J.B.C. & A. Forms/C.2118/12.

Instructions regarding War Diaries and Intelligence Summaries are contained in F. S. Regs., Part II. and the Staff Manual respectively. Title Pages will be prepared in manuscript.

WAR DIARY

or

~~INTELLIGENCE SUMMARY~~ Map reference Sheet 51C FRANCE 1/40,000

(Erase heading not required.)

Army Form C. 2118.

Place	Date	Hour	Summary of Events and Information	Remarks and references to Appendices
WARLUS	4.1.17		took over duties of A.D.M.S. H G Smeeth Lt. Col Ramc	H.G.S
"	5.1.17		visited 44th Fd. Amb. Lt Col. W VAUGHAN transferred for duty to 22 General Hospital ETAPLES	
			" BARNCOURT to see ADMS. 30th Div.	H.G.S.
"	6.1.17		visited 44th Fd. Amb.	
			" ADMS 30th Division + inspected site for 44th Fd Amb. a BAVINCOURT	H.G.S
			D.A.D.M.S. completed survey of Front line.	
			Lt. Col. EVES reported his arrival + took over command of 43rd Fd Amb from 7th	H.G.S.
"	7.1.17		visited 42nd Fd. Amb.	H.G.S
"	8.1.17		visited 43rd Fd. Amb.	H.G.S.
"	9.1.17		D.D.M.S. VII Corp called.	
			visited DAINVILLE with DDMS. VII Corps	
			" Baths at BERNEVILLE.	H.G.S.
"	10.1.17		visited RONVILLE. R.A.P., and Chalk Quarries in Rue St QUINTIN. ACHICOUR returning to DAINVILLE via Cowerst.	H.G.S
"	11.1.17		visited 42nd Fd. Amb.	H.G.S
"	12.1.17		attended meeting of A.Ds.M.S. at office of D.D.M.S. VII Corps.	
			visited 42 + 44 Fd. Ambs.	H.G.S.

Army Form C. 2118.

Instructions regarding War Diaries and Intelligence Summaries are contained in F. S. Regs., Part II. and the Staff Manual respectively. Title Pages will be prepared in manuscript.

WAR DIARY
or
~~INTELLIGENCE SUMMARY~~
(Erase heading not required.)

Map reference Sheet 57c FRANCE 1/40,000

Place	Date	Hour	Summary of Events and Information	Remarks and references to Appendices
WARLUS.	12.1.17.		Returned from leave of absence.	St. V. Byrne Col. A.M.S.
	13.1.17.		Took over duties of A.D.M.S. from Lt Col. Smeeth. R.A.M.C.	St. V. P.
	14.1.17		Visited 43 F.A. and Town Commandant, GOUY re sanitation.	St. V. P.
	15.1.17		Visited 44 F.A. Visited 42 F.A. and Town Commandant, BARLY re sanitation.	St. V. P.
	16.1.17		Visited baths ACHICOURT and AGNY, Collecting Post, ACHICOURT, & R.A.P. of G. Left. Reconnoitred tram line.	St. V. P.
	17.1.17.		Visited R.A.P. of H. Right, and inspected proposed site for R.A.P. of this sector.	St. V. P.
	18.1.17.		Accompanied D.D.M.S. who visited SCHOOLS, DAINVILLE, A.D.S. ARRAS, Collecting Post, ACHICOURT, and R.A. Posts of G. Right, left, and Reserve, and H. Right.	St. V. P.
	19.1.17.		Visited Battalion H.Q. of G. Right & G. Left re sites for R.A Posts. Visited F. Ambulance site, BAVINCOURT 42 and 43 F. Ambs.	St. V. P.
	20.1.17		Visited Collecting Post, ACHICOURT, Visited R.A.P's of H. Right, G. Right & G. Left, St. dug out with A.D.M.S. 30 Division. Chateau & GOWER ST.	St. V. P.
	21.1.17		Visited R.A.P. of H. Left, and White Chateau, RONVILLE. Inspected foot washing & massage rooms, & drying arrangements, RONVILLE.	St. V. P.
	22.1.17		Visited 44 F.A. Visited H.Q. 41 Bde, R.A.P's F. Right & F. Left. Inspected foot washing & massage rooms & drying arrangements, WAILLY.	St. V. P.

2449 Wt. W14957/M90 750,000 1/16 J.B.C. & A. Forms/C.2118/12.

Instructions regarding War Diaries and Intelligence Summaries are contained in F. S. Regs., Part II. and the Staff Manual respectively. Title Pages will be prepared in manuscript.

WAR DIARY
or
~~INTELLIGENCE SUMMARY~~
(Erase heading not required.)

Army Form C. 2118.

Map reference Sheet 51^{c} FRANCE 1/40,000.

Place	Date	Hour	Summary of Events and Information	Remarks and references to Appendices
WARLUS.	23.1.17		Visited baths and manure dumps BERNEVILLE & SIMENCOURT. Inspected sanitation, WARLUS.	S.v.P.
	24.1.17		Visited proposed sites for A.D.S., and Regimental Aid Posts, RONVILLE.	S.v.P.
	25.1.17		Visited Town Commandant, SIMENCOURT re manure dump. Visited O.C. 7 R.B. re sick rate of battalion. Visited D.D.M.S VII Corps.	S.v.P.
	26.1.17		Conference VII Corps D.D.M.S. Visited SIMENCOURT re huts.	S.v.P.
	27.1.17		Conference Divisional H.Q. Visited RONVILLE re sites for A. Dressing Station.	S.v.P.
	28.1.17		Visited A.D.S., GROSVILLE, and 41 Brigade H.Q. re medical arrangements.	S.v.P.
	29.1.17		Visited 43 F. Ambulance, and O.C. No 3 M.A.C. re evacuation	S.v.P.
	30.1.17		Visited 42 F. Ambulance. Attended Third Army Lectures, Avesnes	S.v.P.
	31.1.17		Visited 44 F. Ambulance. Visited proposed site for A.D.S., RONVILLE.	S.v.P.

S.v. Pryce [signature]
Col. A.M.S.

2449 Wt. W14957/M90 750,000 1/16 J.B.C. & A. Forms/C.2118/12.

14

Confidential

Vol 19

War Diary

of

Colonel H V Prynne DSO,

ADMS

14th

Division

for

month February 1917

140/901

COMMITTEE FOR THE
MEDICAL HISTORY OF THE WAR
Date 4 - APR. 1917

140/901

Instructions regarding War Diaries and Intelligence Summaries are contained in F. S. Regs., Part II. and the Staff Manual respectively. Title Pages will be prepared in manuscript.

WAR DIARY
or
INTELLIGENCE SUMMARY
(Erase heading not required.)

Army Form C. 2118.

Map reference Sheet FRANCE 51c 1/40,000.

Place	Date	Hour	Summary of Events and Information	Remarks and references to Appendices
WARLUS	1.2.17		Visited A.D.M.S. 49th Division and 43 F. Ambulance re taking over of collection of sick and wounded from F. Sector. Visited Laundry, AVESNES.	T.D.P. Visited Col. A.M.S
	2.2.17		Visited RONVILLE and reconnoitred railway and approaches.	T.D.P.
	3.2.17		Visited Laundry and baths, ARRAS and DAINVILLE. Attended Third Army Medical Officers' meeting. AVESNES. Collection of sick and wounded F. sector handed over to 49th Divn (1/1 West Riding F.A.)	T.D.P.
	4.2.17		Visited 44 F. Ambulance.	T.D.P.
	5.2.17		Visited schools + baths, BERNEVILLE. Visited 42 F. Ambulance	T.D.P.
	6.2.17		Visited 42, 43 + 44 F. Ambulances re relief of 44 F.A., for which orders had been received. Collection of sick and wounded from G. Sector handed over to 30th Division (98 F.A.)	T.D.P.
	7.2.17		Reconnoitred Railway embankment + cutting DAINVILLE for dug-outs for D.C.S., if required.	T.D.P.
	8.2.17		Visited baths, BERNEVILLE + SIMENCOURT. Visited RONVILLE. H.Q. 44 F.A. moved to Convent SAINT SACREMENT, ARRAS, + transport to BARLY.	T.D.P.

2449 Wt. W14957/M90 750,000 1/16 J.B.C. & A. Forms/C.2118/12.

Instructions regarding War Diaries and Intelligence Summaries are contained in F. S. Regs., Part II. and the Staff Manual respectively. Title Pages will be prepared in manuscript.

WAR DIARY
or
~~INTELLIGENCE SUMMARY~~
(Erase heading not required.)

Army Form C. 2118.

Map reference Sheet FRANCE 51c 1/40,000.

Place	Date	Hour	Summary of Events and Information	Remarks and references to Appendices
WARLUS	9.2.17		Capt. GUEST. R.A.M.C. proceeded on leave. Reconnoitred routes for motor ambulances and walking wounded from ACHICOURT to DAINVILLE, and dump for motor ambulances.	Tr. P.
	10.2.17		Visited BERNEVILLE re accomodation for Med. Inspection Room. Inspected sanitation, DAINVILLE.	Tr. P.
	11.2.17		Visited 43 F. Ambulance. Visited 42 Bde H.Q. & Advanced Dressing Station, RONVILLE.	Tr. P.
	12.2.17		Visited Divl School, and 41 Bde H.Q. Visited RONVILLE and proposed Regimental Aid Post for H. Left.	Tr. P.
	13.2.17		Visited RONVILLE. Reconnoitred H. sector for R.A.P. sites.	Tr. P.
	14.2.17		Visited 42 F. Ambulance.	Tr. P.
	15.2.17		Visited A.D.S. RONVILLE, 44 F.A. and ACHICOURT with D.D.M.S. VII Corps. Visited 43 F. Ambulance.	Tr. P.
	16.2.17		Conference at office of D.D.M.S. VII Corps.	Tr. P.
	17.2.17		Visited 44 F. Ambulance, A.D.S. RONVILLE and reconnoitred caves for R.A.P. sites.	Tr. P.
	18.2.17		Visited baths, BERNEVILLE, & route for walking wounded	Tr. P.
	19.2.17		Two officers evacuated, three arrived from Base.	Tr. P.

2449 Wt. W14957/M90 750,000 1/16 J.B.C. & A. Forms/C.2118/12.

Instructions regarding War Diaries and Intelligence Summaries are contained in F. S. Regs., Part II. and the Staff Manual respectively. Title Pages will be prepared in manuscript.

WAR DIARY
or
~~INTELLIGENCE SUMMARY~~
(Erase heading not required.)

Army Form C. 2118.

Map reference Sheet FRANCE 51C 1/40,000.

Place	Date	Hour	Summary of Events and Information	Remarks and references to Appendices
WARLUS.	20.2.17		Reconnoitred SCHOOLS, DAINVILLE for Corps Collecting Station for lightly wounded.	T.r.P.
	21.2.17		Visited 42 F. Ambulance and 43 F. Ambulance.	T.r.P.
	22.2.17		Visited SCHOOLS, DAINVILLE with O.C. 43 F. Ambulance	T.r.P.
	23.2.17		Visited Citadel A.D.S. RONVILLE and 44 F. Ambulance.	T.r.P.
	24.2.17		Visited 43 F. Ambulance	T.r.P.
	25.2.17		Inspected sanitation, BERNEVILLE. Visited 42 F. Ambulance	T.r.P.
	26.2.17		Visited baths SOMBRIN, and laundry, AVESNES. Visited 42 F.A. and D.D.M.S. VII Corps.	T.r.P.
	27.2.17		Visited sanitation, and laundry arrangements, DAINVILLE 43 F. Ambulance moved to BERNEVILLE. (R.1 a 6.5)	T.r.P.
	28.2.17		Visited A.D.S. RONVILLE, HUILERIE on ACHICOURT ROAD, and R.A.P's in Christchurch and Blenheim Caves.	T.r.P.

T. r. Payne
Col. A.M.S.
A.D.M.S. 14 Div.

2449 Wt. W14957/M90 750,000 1/16 J.B.C. & A. Forms/C.2118/12.

Confidential

War Diary of

Colonel H. V. Prynne DSO., ADMS.

ADMS 14th (Light) Division

for

month of March 1917.

Vol 20

140/2037

COMMITTEE FOR THE MEDICAL HISTORY OF THE WAR
Date 11 MAY. 1917

Mar. 20

51

Instructions regarding War Diaries and Intelligence Summaries are contained in F. S. Regs., Part II. and the Staff Manual respectively. Title Pages will be prepared in manuscript.

WAR DIARY
or
~~INTELLIGENCE SUMMARY~~
(Erase heading not required.)

Army Form C. 2118.

Map reference FRANCE 51^c 1/40,000.

Place	Date	Hour	Summary of Events and Information	Remarks and references to Appendices
WARLUS	1.3.17		Visited 43 Field Ambulance, BERNEVILLE. Visited R.A.P. being built in H ~~Left~~ Left and inspected sanitation of H. Left. Sector.	[illegible] Col. A.M.S.
	2.3.17		Visited White Chateau with a view to use for R.A.P., and reconnoitred trenches for use to and from it.	[illegible]
	3.3.17		Visited Town Majors at DAINVILLE, BERNEVILLE + SIMENCOURT with reference to supplying M.O. to each for sanitary duties only.	[illegible]
	4.3.17		Visited D.D.M.S. VII Corps. Visited Advanced Dressing Station, 12th Division	[illegible]
	5.3.17		Visited 43 Field Ambulance. Visited Advanced Dressing Station, 9th Division, A.D.S. RONVILLE, HUILERIE and 44 Field Ambulance. Reconnoitred part of ACHICOURT — BEAUMETZ Road.	[illegible]
	6.3.17		Visited M.I. Rooms of O.C.L.I., Durham L.I., Oxford + Bucks L.I. with reference to isolation of contacts from Inf. Disease, + latrine accom.	[illegible]
	7.3.17		Visited R.A.P. being built in H ~~Right~~ Left Sector, White Chateau, Christchurch Cave, and 44 Field Ambulance.	[illegible]
	8.3.17		Visited 43 Field Ambulance. Reconnoitred roads between ACHICOURT and BEAUMETZ for motor ambulance routes.	[illegible]
	9.3.17		Conference at office of D.D.M.S. VII Corps. Inspected sanitation of VIII Corps Caves, RONVILLE.	[illegible]
	10.3.17		Visited SCHOOLS, DAINVILLE with O.C. 43 F Ambulance. Visited R.A.P. in progress at H Left Sector. Reconnoitred Sunken Road H Left for motor ambulance, and wheeled stretcher traffic.	[illegible]

2449 Wt. W14957/M90 750,000 1/16 J.B.C. & A. Forms/C.2118/12.

Army Form C. 2118.

WAR DIARY
or
~~INTELLIGENCE SUMMARY~~
(Erase heading not required.)

Map reference FRANCE 57.c 1/40,000.

Instructions regarding War Diaries and Intelligence Summaries are contained in F. S. Regs., Part II. and the Staff Manual respectively. Title Pages will be prepared in manuscript.

Place	Date	Hour	Summary of Events and Information	Remarks and references to Appendices
WARLUS.	11.3.17.		Visited and inspected 42 Field Ambulance, Divisional Rest Station, and Officers' Convalescent Hospital.	S.R.P.
	12.3.17.		Visited Christchurch Cave, and inspected proposed site for R.A.P's, and sanitation with O.C. 25 Sanitary Section.	S.R.P.
	13.3.17.		Visited 44 Field Ambulance. Visited 42 Field Ambulance, and inspected Clayton Disinfector installation.	S.R.P.
	14.3.17.		Visited G.M.O. SIMENCOURT concerning Diphtheria cases. Visited laundry + Baths, ARRAS.	S.R.P.
	15.3.17.		Visited D.D.M.S. VII Corps. Visited A.D.M.S. 15th Division.	S.R.P.
	16.3.17.		Visited A.D.S., RONVILLE and HUILERIE.	S.R.P.
	17.3.17.		Visited baths, SOMBRIN.	S.R.P.
	18.3.17.		Visited D.D.M.S. VII Corps.	S.R.P.
	19.3.17.		Visited 43 Field Ambulance, and baths, BERNEVILLE. Visited 42 Field Ambulance, 44 Field Ambulance, and advanced R.A.P's of 43rd Brigade, who have advanced to maintain touch. R.A.P. of 6 D.C.L.I. is situated in crater at M.5 a.1.1, but dugout being cleared at M.4 d 8.0 9.5. R.A.P. of 6 Som. L.I. about G34 d.5.5 in cave cellar.	S.R.P.
	20.3.17.		Collecting Post established yesterday at Brewery, RONVILLE to which cases brought by wheeled stretchers via Sunken Road from G.35. d2.0 8.5 and G34 d.5.5. Visited 42 + 43 Inf. Brigades + M.O's front line re sanitation. Visited new R.A.P. 43rd Brigade (D.C.L.I.)	S.R.P.

Instructions regarding War Diaries and Intelligence Summaries are contained in F. S. Regs., Part II. and the Staff Manual respectively. Title Pages will be prepared in manuscript.

Army Form C. 2118.

WAR DIARY
or
~~INTELLIGENCE SUMMARY~~ Map reference FRANCE 51c 1/40,000.

(Erase heading not required.)

Place	Date	Hour	Summary of Events and Information	Remarks and references to Appendices
WARLUS	21.3.17		Visited HUILERIE, A.D.S. RONVILLE, and R.A.P. for H. Left with A.D.M.S. 21 Divn. Attended conference at D.D.M.S. office, VII Corps.	H.r.P.
	22.3.17		Concentration of Division.	H.r.P.
	23.3.17		Visited A.D.S. RONVILLE, R.A.P's and Battalion H.Q's. R+L. Sectors.	H.r.P.
	24.3.17		Visited 43 Field Ambulance.	H.r.P.
	25.3.17		Visited Corps Collecting Station for Lightly Wounded Cases with O.C. 43. F. Ambulance. Visited D.D.M.S. Corps.	H.r.P.
	26.3.17		Visited 44 F. Ambulance. Reconnoitred road for Walking Wounded from BEAURAINS to AGNY	H.r.P.
	27.3.17		Visited H. Sector, and selected R.A.P. for Right battalion	H.r.P.
	28.3.17		Visited AGNY with O.C. 43 Field Ambulance to meet A.D.M.S. 56th Division and select site for Corps Collecting Station for Lightly Wounded. Reconnoitred route for Walking Wounded from Left Brigade.	H.r.P.
	29.3.17		Visited 42 Field Ambulance and D.D.M.S. VII Corps. Visited H.Q and R.A.P. of Right battalion. Visited Battn H.Q. 9 Rifle Brigade re change of M.O.	H.r.P.
	30.3.17		Conference at D.D.M.S. VII Corps.	H.r.P.
	31.3.17		Sanitary section details recalled preliminary to passing out of Divisional control into that of Corps.	H.r.P.

2449 Wt. W14957/M90 750,000 1/16 J.B.C. & A. Forms/C.2118/12.

War Diary

of

Colonel H. V. Prynne D.S.O.

A.D.M.S. 14th (Light) Division

for

month of April 1917.

COMMITTEE FOR THE
MEDICAL HISTORY OF THE WAR
Date -6 JUN. 1917

Summary now with Diary
Vol 21
14/5023

April 1917
S

Instructions regarding War Diaries and Intelligence Summaries are contained in F. S. Regs., Part II. and the Staff Manual respectively. Title Pages will be prepared in manuscript.

WAR DIARY
or
~~INTELLIGENCE SUMMARY~~
(Erase heading not required.)

Army Form C. 2118.

Map reference. FRANCE 57B + 57C 1/40,000.

Place	Date	Hour	Summary of Events and Information	Remarks and references to Appendices
WARLUS	1.4.17		Inspection of men proposed for P.B. Visited O.C. 10. Durham L.I. concerning use of band as stretcher bearers.	Str. Bynne Col. A.M.S. A.D.M.S. 14 Div.
	2.4.17		Visited 42 Field Ambulance. Visited Corps Walking Wounded Post, and 44 Field Ambulance.	Str. P.
	3.4.17		Visited 43 Field Ambulance.	Str. P.
	4.4.17		Issued Operation orders, as in Appendix.	Str. P.
	5.4.17		Visited 42 Field Ambulance + D.D.M.S. Corps. Visited R.A.P's in KRIEGER STELLUNG (M.5 C.60.90) + BROWN DUMP (M11.a.60.95.), + A.D.S. RONVILLE.	Str. P.
	6.4.17		Conference at D.D.M.S. VII Corps. Visited R.A.P. at G35.d.20.90 + proposed R.A.P in GALWAY TRENCH (M.5.b80.80). Visited A.D.S, RONVILLE 42 Brigade H.Q., + 44 F. Ambulance.	Str. P.
	7.4.17		Visited R.A.P (G.35. d.20.90), 41 + 43 Inf. Brigade H.Q, + A.D.S. RONVILLE + SAN SACREMENT.	Str. P.
	8.4.17		Visited Corps Walking Wounded Collecting at AGNY (M8.b.65.40.)	Str. P.
	9.4.17		Active operations. Proceeded to my Advanced H.Q at A.D.S RONVILLE, at 8 A.M. Visited Regimental Aid Posts of 42nd + 43rd Inf. Brigades, in action. Visited Corps Walking Wounded Collecting Post. R.A.P's 42 Bde advanced to M.12.C.80,80 – N7. a.20.50., + those of 43 Bde advanced to N7.C.10.50, N.7.C.20.40, + N.8.C.80.20. Horsed ambulances + Ford cars run to M.11 a 70.40	Str. P.

2449 Wt. W14957/M90 750,000 1/16 J.B.C. & A. Forms/C.2118/12.

Instructions regarding War Diaries and Intelligence Summaries are contained in F. S. Regs., Part II. and the Staff Manual respectively. Title Pages will be prepared in manuscript.

WAR DIARY

or

~~INTELLIGENCE SUMMARY~~

(Erase heading not required.)

Army Form C. 2118.

Map reference FRANCE 51^B + 51^C 1/40,000.

Place	Date	Hour	Summary of Events and Information	Remarks and references to Appendices
NARLUS.	10.4.17.		Visited Corps Walking Wounded Collecting Post. Visited R.A.P.s of 43rd Bde in action. 42nd Bde relieved. 43rd Bde relieved by 41 Bde.	S.V.P.
	11.4.17.		41st Bde in action. Visited Collecting Post at N 8. c. 80.20. + R.A.P (7RB). R.A.P.s of 41 Bde established at N.14 b. 90.80., + N. 15. d. 40.40. Reconnoitred BEAURAINS — NEUVILLE ROAD for horsed and motor ambulances. Relay Bearer Posts established at N 8. c. 80.20, M. 12. c. 4.5 and M. 11 a. 70.40.	S.V.P.
	12.4.17.		Visited Collecting and Relay Posts, also Walking Wounded Collecting Post. Reconnoitred BEAURAINS — NEUVILLE VITASSE ROAD. Horsed ambulances sent forward as far as N 19. c. 80.80. A.D.S. + collection from front area taken over by 1/1 NORTHUMBRIAN Field Ambulance. Corps Walking Wounded Collecting Post handed over to 2/2 NORTHUMBRIAN Field Ambulance. Tent subdivision of 43rd F. Ambulance detailed to proceed to MANIN, + tent subdivision of 44 F. Ambulance to HABARCQ. Returned to Div. H.Q. WARLUS.	S.V.P.
	13.4.17.		Visited 43 F. Ambulance, AGNY, + detachments BERNEVILLE + MANIN. Detachment 43 F.A. handed over BERNEVILLE to 1/1 Northumbrian F.A. Visited ~~Detachment~~ 44 F.A. at HABARCQ, D.D.M.S. XVIII Corps, and Corps Rest Station.	S.V.P.

2449 Wt. W14957/M90 750,000 1/16 J.B.C. & A. Forms/C.2118/12.

Instructions regarding War Diaries and Intelligence Summaries are contained in F. S. Regs., Part II. and the Staff Manual respectively. Title Pages will be prepared in manuscript.

WAR DIARY
or
~~INTELLIGENCE SUMMARY~~
(Erase heading not required.)

Army Form C. 2118.

Map reference FRANCE 57^B + 51^C 1/40,000.

Place	Date	Hour	Summary of Events and Information	Remarks and references to Appendices
WARLUS.	14.4.17		43 F. Ambulance moved to SUS-S^T-LEGER. (N24. d. 40.80.) Visited 42 F Ambulance. Corps Rest Station handed over by 42 F. Amb. to 1/3 Northumbrian Field Ambulance. 42 F.A. remained at BARLY	[illegible]
	15.4.17		Visited 42 F. Ambulance, which moved to LE CAUROY to-day. Visited D.D.M.S. XVIII Corps. 44 F. Ambulance to BERNEVILLE.	[illegible]
	16.4.17		Visited D.D.M.S. XVIII Corps. Visited 42 F. Ambulance & held conference of R.M.O's & bearer officers from F. Ambulances.	[illegible]
	17.4.17		Visited laundry, AVESNES. Visited 42 and 44 Field Ambulance	[illegible]
	18.4.17		Visited Baths at SUS-S^T-LEGER, SOMBRIN, GRAND RULLECOURT, OPPY & BERLENCOURT, laundry AVESNES, 42 & 43 F. Ambulances.	[illegible]
	19.4.17		Handed over baths & laundries to Officer appointed by "A" Branch.	[illegible]
	20.4.17		Visited A.D.S. 30th Division & Advanced C. Post of 50th Divisional NEUVILLE VITASSE.	[illegible]
	21.4.17		Recommendations for immediate awards prepared & forwarded to "A" branch.	[illegible]
	22.4.17		Visited VI Corps Rest Station re Shell shock cases of 14th Division	[illegible]
	23.4.17		42 F.A. to BIENVILLERS. 43 F.A. to BAVINCOURT 44 F.A. to BARLY.	

2449 Wt. W14957/M90 750,000 1/16 J.B.C. & A. Forms/C.2118/12.

Instructions regarding War Diaries and Intelligence Summaries are contained in F. S. Regs., Part II. and the Staff Manual respectively. Title Pages will be prepared in manuscript.

WAR DIARY

or

~~INTELLIGENCE SUMMARY~~

(Erase heading not required.)

Army Form C. 2118

Map reference FRANCE 51B 1/20.000 + LENS. 11. 1/100.000

Place	Date	Hour	Summary of Events and Information	Remarks and references to Appendices
BAILLEULMONT	24.4.17		Divisional H.Q. to BAILLEULMONT. 42 F.A. to RANSART. 43 F.A. to BAILLEULVAL. 44 F.A. to BELLACOURT.	S.R.P.
	25.4.17		Visited A.D.S., NEUVILLE VITASSE (M 24 d. 60.60) and Walking Wounded Collecting Station, MERCATEL (M. 29. d. 60.60) to arrange taking over.	S.R.P.
ARRAS	26.4.17		D.H.Q. to ARRAS (No 12 BOULEVARD CARNOT). 42 F.A. took over A.D.S. from 1/1 Northumbrian F.A., 44 F.A. took over W.W.C Station from 2/2 Northumbrian F.A., + 43 F.A. took over Convent of St SACREMENT (G 21 c. 40.00) as accomodation for sick of Division neighbourhood	S.R.P.
	27.4.17		Visited W.W.C. Station, A.D.S., Advanced Dressing Post (N 23 b. 50.10) Relay Posts at N 22 d. 60.60 + N. 15. d. 80.20, + loading point for Horsed ambulances + Ford Motor Ambulances at N. 21. b. 90.90. Visited Regimental Aid Posts of 3 battalions in line at O. 19 a. 30.60 + N 23 d. 80.70.	S.R.P.
	28.4.17		Visited W.W.C Sn, A.D.S, 42 Inf. Bde, A.D. Post + Relay Posts. Visited Corps Main Dressing Station at S 2 b. 90.40.	S.R.P.
	29.4.17		Visited W.W.C.Sn A.D.S., Relay Posts, 41 Bde H.Q., A. Dressing Post, + 47 Bde R.F.A. Reconnoitred sites for R.A.P.S. Visited 7 R.B.	S.R.P.
	30.4.17		Visited 6 K.O.Y.L.I. Visited 20, 32, + 43 C.C. Stations re wounded.	S.R.P.

S. R. Pye [illegible] Col. A.M.S.
A.D.M.S. 14 Div.

1875 Wt. W593/826 1,000,000 4/15 J.B.C. & A. A.D.S.S./Forms/C. 2118.

B.E.F.

4

SUMMARY OF MEDICAL WAR DIARIES FOR 14th Divn. 7th Corps, 3rd Army.

WESTERN FRONT April- May. '17.

A.D.M.S. Col. H.V. Prynne

D.A.D.M.S. Capt. W.H. Shephard.

SUMMARISED UNDER THE FOLLOWING HEADINGS.

<u>Phase "B" Battle of Arras- April- May. '17.</u>

1st Period Attack on Vimy Ridge April.

2nd Period Capture of Siegfried Line May.

14th Divn. 7th Corps, 3rd.Army. WESTERN FRONT.

A.D.M.S. Col. H.V. Prynne. April. '17.

Phase "B" Battle of Arras April- May. '17.

1st Period Attack on Vimy Ridge April.

1917 Headquarters. at Warlus

April. 5th. Medical Arrangements: R.A.Ps. Krieger Stellung M.5.c.60.90.

Browndump M.11.a.60.95., G.35.d.20.90.

A.D.S. Ronville- 44th Field Ambulance.

C.W.W. Coll. P. Agny M.8.b.65.40. - 43rd Field Ambulance.

C.R.S. 42nd Field Ambulance. (Sheets 51B and 51C)

9th. Operations. Active operations commenced.

Medical Arrangements: R.A.Ps. 42nd Bgde advanced to M.12.c.80.80., N.7.a.20.20.

R.A.Ps. 43rd Bgde advanced to N.7.c.10.50., N.7.C.20.40. and N.8.c.80.20.

Evacuation: H. Ambulances and Ford Cars went up as far as M.11.a.70.40.

10th. Military Situation: 42nd Bgde relieved.

43rd Bgde relieved by 41st Bde.

11th. Operations. 41st Bde. went into action.

Medical Arrangements: R.A.Ps. 41st Bde. established at N.14.b.90.80. and N.15. d.40.40.

Relay Br. Posts established at N.8.c.80.20. M.12.c.4.5., M.11.a.70.40.

12th. H. Ambulances sent forward as far as N.19.c.80.80.

A.D.S and collection from front area taken over by 1/1st Northumbrian Field Ambulance.

C.W.W. Coll. P. taken over by 2/2nd Northumbrian Field Ambulance.

14th Divn. 7th Corps, 3rd Army. WESTERN FRONT

A.D.M.S. Col. H.V. Prynne. April. '17.

Phase "B" cont.

1st Period cont.

1917. April. 12th. cont.	Moves Field Ambulance Det.
	T.S.D. 43rd F.A. to Manin.
	T.S.D. 44th " " Harbarcq.
13th.	Medical Arrangements: Det. 43rd Field Ambulance handed over Berneville to 1/1st Northumbrian Field Ambulance.
14th.	Moves Field Ambulance. 43rd Field Ambulance to Sus St. Leger (N.24.d.40.80.)
	Medical Arrangements: C.R.S. handed over to 1/3rd N.F.A
15th.	Moves Field Ambulances. 42nd Field Ambulance to Le Cauroy.
	44th Field Ambulance to Berneville.
23rd/24th.	Moves Field Ambulances.
	42nd Field Ambulance to Ransart.
	43rd " " " Bailleul.
	44th " " " Bellacourt.
	Moves: To Bailleulmont.
26th.	" To Arras.
26th/ 27th.	Medical Arrangements: A.D.S. Neuville Vitasse (M.24. D.60.60.) taken over by 42nd Field Ambulance.
	W.W.Coll. S.. Mercatel (M.29.d.60.60.) taken over by 44th Field Ambulance.
	Convent of St. Sacremont. (G.21.c.40.00) taken over by 43rd Field Ambulance as accommodation for sick of Divn. and neighbourhood.
	Adv. Br.Ps. at N.23.b.50.10.

Phase "B" cont.

1st Period cont.

1917.

April. 26th-27th. Medical Arrangements:cont.
cont.

Relay Posts. at N. 22.d.60.60. and N.15.d.80.20.

Loading Posts. for H. Ambulances and Ford Ambulances, at N.21.b.90.90.

R.A.Ps. at O.19.a.30.60. and N.23.d.80.70.

C.M.D.S. at S.2.b.90.40. (Sheets 51B and Lens 11.)

Appendices. Nil.

14th Divn. 7th Corps, 3rd.Army. WESTERN FRONT.

A.D.M.S. Col. H.V. Prynne. April. '17.

Phase "B" Battle of Arras April- May. '17.

1st Period Attack on Vimy Ridge April.

1917 Headquarters. at Warlus

April. 5th. Medical Arrangements: R.A.Ps. Krieger Stellung M.5.c.60.90.

Browndump M.11.a.60.95., G.35.d.20.90.

A.D.S. Ronville- 44th Field Ambulance.

C.W.W. Coll. P. Agny M.8.b.65.40. - 43rd Field Ambulances.

C.R.S. 42nd Field Ambulance. (Sheets 51B and 51C)

9th. Operations. Active operations commenced.

Medical Arrangements: R.A.Ps. 42nd Bgde advanced to M.12.c.80.80., N.7.a.20.20.

R.A.Ps. 43rd Bgde advanced to N.7.c.10.50., N.7.C.20.40. and N.8.c.80.20.

Evacuation: H. Ambulances and Ford Cars went up as far as M.11.a.70.40.

10th. Military Situation: 42nd Bgde relieved.

43rd Bgde relieved by 41st Bde.

11th. Operations. 41st Bde. went into action.

Medical Arrangements: R.A.Ps. 41st Bde. established at N.14.b.90.80. and N.15. d.40.40.

Relay Br. Posts established at N.8.c.80.20. M.12.c.4.5., M.11.a.70.40.

12th. H. Ambulances sent forward as far as N.19.c.80.80.

A.D.S and collection from front area taken over by 1/1st Northumbrian Field Ambulance.

C.W.W. Coll. P. taken over by 2/2nd Northumbrian Field Ambulance.

14th Divn. 7th Corps, 3rd Army. WESTERN FRONT

A.D.M.S. Col. H.V. Prynne. April. '17.

Phase "B" cont.

1st Period cont.

1917.
April. 12th. cont. Moves Field Ambulance Det.

T.S.D. 43rd F.A. to Manin.

T.S.D. 44th " " Harbarcq.

13th. Medical Arrangements: Det. 43rd Field Ambulance handed over Berneville to 1/1st Northumbrian Field Ambulance.

14th. Moves Field Ambulance. 43rd Field Ambulance to Sus St. Leger (N.24.d.40.80.)

Medical Arrangements: C.R.S. handed over to 1/3rd N.F.A.

15th. Moves Field Ambulance. 42nd Field Ambulance to Le Cauroy.

44th Field Ambulance to Berneville.

23rd/24th. Moves Field Ambulances.

42nd Field Ambulance to Ransart.

43rd " " " Bailleul.

44th " " " Bellacourt.

Moves: To Bailleulmont.

26th. " To Arras.

26th/ 27th. Medical Arrangements: A.D.S. Neuville Vitasse (M.24. D.60.60.) taken over by 42nd Field Ambulance.

W.W.Coll. S.. Mercatel (M.29.d.60.60.) taken over by 44th Field Ambulance.

Convent of St. Sacremont. (G.21.c.40.00) taken over by 43rd Field Ambulance as accommodation for sick of Divn. and neighbourhood.

Adv. Br.Ps. at N.23.b.50.10.

Phase "B" cont.

1st Period cont.

1917.

April. 26th-27th. Medical Arrangements:cont.
cont.

Relay Posts. at N. 22.d.60.60. and N.15.d.80.20.

Loading Posts. for H. Ambulances and Ford Ambulances. at N.21.b.90.90.

R.A.Ps. at O.19.a.30.60. and N.23.d.80.70.

C.M.D.S. at S.2.b.90.40. (Sheets 51B and Lens 11.)

Appendices. Nil.

War Diary

of

Colonel H V Prynne DSO AMS

ADMS

14 Division

for

month of

May 1917

Vol 22

Summary now with Diary

COMMITTEE FOR THE
MEDICAL HISTORY OF THE WAR
Date 10 JUL. 1917

5

Instructions regarding War Diaries and Intelligence Summaries are contained in F. S. Regs., Part II. and the Staff Manual respectively. Title Pages will be prepared in manuscript.

WAR DIARY
or
~~INTELLIGENCE SUMMARY~~
(Erase heading not required.)

Army Form C. 2118

Map reference FRANCE 51C 1/40,000 + 57 B.L. 20.000

Place	Date	Hour	Summary of Events and Information	Remarks and references to Appendices
ARRAS.	1.5.17		Proceeded to Advanced H.Q. at A.D. Station (N24 d. 60. 60) Visited W.W.C. Station.	T.V.P
	2.5.17		Visited W.W.C. Station, A.D. Post at N22 d. 60. 60, A.B.P. at N23d.50.10 Bde H.Q., & R.A.P's at O.19c. 0.5.90, N24a.90.20, & N.23. d.90.30. Visited Corps Main Dressing Station at S.2.b.90.40.	T.V.P
	3.5.17		Active operations. Visited W.W.C. Station, & R.A.P's now at O.19.a.30.60, & O.19.c.0.5.95. A.B.P, A.D.P & loading Post for Horsed & motor ambulances N22d.60.60. Visited Brigade H.Q. Reconnoitred WANCOURT, and NEUVILLE VITASSE — WANCOURT ROAD.	T.V.P
	4.5.17		Visited R.A.P's, A.B.P, A.D.P. & Bde H.Q. Transferred A.B.P. from N23 d.50.10. to WANCOURT (N23 b.30.50) Cases brought by stretcher to N.24 a.50.00, thence by wheeled stretcher to A.B.P. and from there by Ford ambulance to Loading point (N.22 a.0.5.0.5) for horsed ambulances to convey to A.D.S. Regimental Aid Posts are now situated as follows:— R. Brigade O.19.c.10.80, & O.25b.95.20. Left Brigade O.19c. 0.5.90. Visited W.W.C. Station. Later R.A.P's of R & L Sector withdrawn to O.19 a 10.20.	T.V.P
	5.5.17		A.B.P. at WANCOURT evacuated owing to heavy shelling. Cases conveyed by wheeled stretcher through Relay Posts at N24 a.50.00, N.23 d.20.30, & N.23 c.90.30 to A.D.P. & Loading Point for Ford & Horsed ambulances at N22d.60.60. Visited R.A.P's, A.D.P. & Relay Posts	T.V.P

1875 Wt. W593/826 1,000,000 4/15 J.B.C. & A. A.D.S.S./Forms/C. 2118.

Instructions regarding War Diaries and Intelligence Summaries are contained in F. S. Regs., Part II. and the Staff Manual respectively. Title Pages will be prepared in manuscript.

WAR DIARY
or
~~INTELLIGENCE~~ SUMMARY

(Erase heading not required.)

Army Form C. 2118

Map reference FRANCE 57c $\frac{1}{40.000}$ & 57 b $\frac{1}{20.000}$

Place	Date	Hour	Summary of Events and Information	Remarks and references to Appendices
ARRAS	6.5.17		Visited A.O.P and Loading Post, R.A.P's, & Relay Posts	S.r.P.
	7.5.17		Reduced the number of R.A.M.C. at all posts on account of casualties due to deficient shelter. Arranged for R.E to build splinter proof Relay Post. Visited D.H.Q. ARRAS re shell shock case.	S.r.P.
	8.5.17		Visited R.A.P's, Relay Posts, A.B.P. and A.D. Post.	S.r.P.
	9.5.17		Visited A.D.P. Consulted O.C. 6/Som. L.I., & O.C. 6 K.O.Y.L.I. re selection of sites for R.A.P's	S.r.P.
	10.5.17		Visited A.D.P. Returned to Divl H.Q.	S.r.P.
	11.5.17		Visited No 6 Stationary Hospital & inspected cases of "shell shock"	S.r.P.
	12.5.17		Visited A.D Station (42 F.A.) & W.W.C. Station (44 F.A.) Reconnoitred AGNY for sites for F. Ambulance. Visited 43 F.A.	S.r.P.
	13.5.17		Reconnoitred AGNY with O.C 43 F.A. Visited Corps Rest Station.	
	14.5.17		Visited W.W. Collecting Station & A.D. Station	S.r.P.
	15.5.17		Visited Advanced Dressing Station	S.r.P.
	16.5.17		Visited AGNY and selected site for F. Ambulance at M.9.c.30.70.	S.r.P.
			Visited Advanced Dressing Post (N22.d.60.60) R.A.P's at O.19.a.10.30, O.25.c.20.50, N30.a.05.45 & N.23.d.90.30, Relay Posts at N23.d.90.30 & N24 b.60.40, & Loading Post N.29.a.90.55.	S.r.P.

1875 Wt. W593/826 1,000,000 4/15 J.B.C. & A. A.D.S.S./Forms/C. 2118.

Instructions regarding War Diaries and Intelligence Summaries are contained in F. S. Regs., Part II. and the Staff Manual respectively. Title Pages will be prepared in manuscript.

WAR DIARY
or
~~INTELLIGENCE SUMMARY~~
(Erase heading not required.)

Army Form C. 2118

Map reference FRANCE 51^c 1/40,000. & 57^B 1/20,000.

Place	Date	Hour	Summary of Events and Information	Remarks and references to Appendices
ARRAS	17.5.17		Visited 43 Field Ambulance.	S.R.P.
	18.5.17		Divisional H.Q. moved to M23.a.60.50.	S.R.P.
M.25a60.50	19.5.17		Inspected sanitation of units of 43rd Bde. M.10.d.00.50.	S.R.P.
	20.5.17		Active operations 33rd Division. Visited W.W. Collecting Station	S.R.P.
	21.5.17		Visited A.D.S., A. Dressing Post, W. Stretcher Relay Post, and R.A.P's of two battalions in support	S.R.P.
	22.5.17		Visited H.Q. of Divisional H.Q. Company re medical inspection of men temporarily unfit. Visited A.D.S. with Captain C. HELM R.A.M.C., who reported to take over command of 42 F. Ambulance.	S.R.P.
	23.5.17		Visited Advanced Dressing Post and R.A.P's Left Sector.	S.R.P.
	24.5.17		Visited O.C. 70 Sanitary Section re latrines for front area. Visited Corps Main Dressing Station. Inspected sanitation of 2 battalions holding R. sector. D.A.D.M.S. inspected sanitation of 2 battalions holding L. sector.	S.R.P.
	25.5.17		Attended conference VII Corps. Visited Corps Rest Station	S.R.P.
	26.5.17		Visited Advanced Dressing Station. 43 F.A. to AGNY. (M.9.c.40.60.)	S.R.P.
	27.5.17		Visited 43 F. Ambulance. Visited O.C. 70 SAN. SECTION concerning sanitation Front Area.	S.R.P.

1875 Wt. W593/826 1,000,000 4/15 J.B.C. & A. A.D.S.S./Forms/C. 2118.

Army Form C. 2118

WAR DIARY
or
~~INTELLIGENCE SUMMARY~~
(Erase heading not required.)

Instructions regarding War Diaries and Intelligence Summaries are contained in F. S. Regs., Part II. and the Staff Manual respectively. Title Pages will be prepared in manuscript.

Map reference. FRANCE 57.C 1/40,000 + 57 B 1/20,000.

Place	Date	Hour	Summary of Events and Information	Remarks and references to Appendices
M.25.a.6o.5o	28.5.17		Visited Corps Main Dressing Station and 44 F. Ambulance.	
			Inspected sanitation 42 Inf. Brigade with O.C. 70. SAN. SECTION	/H.P.
	29.5.17		Inspected sanitation 11/King's (Liverpool Regt.)	/H.P.
	30.5.17		Inspected sanitation + visited R.A.P's of two battalions holding R. Sector	
	31.5.17		Visited 43 and 44 F. Ambulances. Inspected sanitation of Divl. Train, Divl. Ammunition Column and Mobile Veterinary Section. Reconnoitred site for 44 F. Ambulance.	/H.P.

H. P[illegible]
Col. A.M.S.
A.D.M.S. 14 Divn.

1875 Wt. W593/826 1,000,000 4/15 J.B.C. & A. A.D.S.S./Forms/C. 2118.

B.E.F.

SUMMARY OF MEDICAL WAR DIARIES FOR 14th Divn. 7th Corps, 3rd Army.

WESTERN FRONT April- May. '17.

A.D.M.S. Col. H.V. Prynne

D.A.D.M.S. Capt. W.H. Shephard.

SUMMARISED UNDER THE FOLLOWING HEADINGS.

Phase "B" Battle of Arras- April- May. '17.

1st Period Attack on Vimy Ridge April.

2nd Period Capture of Siegfried Line May.

14th Divn. 7th Corps, 3rd Army. WESTERN FRONT.

A.D.M.S. Col. H.V. Prynne. May.'17.

Phase "B" Battle of Arras April- May. '17.

2nd Period Capture of Siegfried Line May.

1917.

May. 3rd. Operations. Active Operations commenced.

Medical Arrangements: R.A.P. moved from N.23.d.80.70 to O.19.c.05.95. Loading Post for H. and M. Ambulances moved to N.22. a.60.60.

4th. A.Br. p. moved to Wancourt N.23.b.30.50.

Evacuation: Cases brought by stretcher to N.24.a.50.00. thence by wheeled stretcher to A. Br. P.

Thence by Ford Ambulance to loading P.

Thence by Horse Ambulance to A.D.S.

Medical Arrangements: R.A.Ps. now at O.19.c.10.80 and O.25.b.95.20. Right Bde. O.19.c.05.90. Left Bde.

Later all withdrawn to O.19.a.10.20.

5th. Operations Enemy. Heavy shelling around A.Br. P.

Medical Arrangements: A.Br. P. evacuated.

Evacuation: Cases conveyed by wheeled stretcher through Relay Posts at N.24.a.50.00 - N.23.d.80.30- N.23.C.90.30. to loading Post.

18th. Moves: To M. 23.a.60.50(sheet 51B)

20th. Operations. Active operations by 33rd Divn. commenced.

26th. Moves Field Ambulance. 43rd Field Ambulance to Agny M.19.C.40.60. (Sheet 51B)

Appendices. Nil.

14th Divn. 7th Corps, 3rd Army. WESTERN FRONT.

A.D.M.S. Col. H.V. Prynne. May.'17.

Phase "B" Battle of Arras, April- May. '17.

2nd Period Capture of Siegfried Line May.

1917.

May. 3rd. Operations. Active Operations commenced.

Medical Arrangements: R.A.P. moved from N.23.d.80.70 to O.19.c.05.95. Loading Post for H. and M. Ambulances moved to N.22. a.60.60.

4th. A.Br. p. moved to Wancourt N.23.b.30.50.

Evacuation: Cases brought by stretcher to N.24.a.50.00. thence by wheeled stretcher to A. Br. P.

Thence by Ford Ambulance to loading P.

Thence by Horse Ambulance to A.D.S.

Medical Arrangements: R.A.Ps. now at O.19.c.10.80 and O.25.b.95.20. Right Bde. O.19.c.05.90. Left Bde.

Later all withdrawn to O.19.a.10.20.

5th. Operations Enemy. Heavy shelling around A.Br. P.

Medical Arrangements: A.Br. P. evacuated.

Evacuation: Cases conveyed by wheeled stretcher through Relay Posts at N.24.a.50.00 - N.23.d.80.30- N.23.C.90.30. to loading Post.

18th. Moves: To M. 23.a.60.50 sheet 51B

20th. Operations. Active operations by 33rd Divn. commenced.

26th. Moves Field Ambulance. 43rd Field Ambulance to Agny M.19.C.40.60. (Sheet 51B)

Appendices. Nil.

Vol 23

Confidential

War Diary

A.D.M.S.

14th. (Light) Division

June

1917

COMMITTEE FOR THE
MEDICAL HISTORY OF THE WAR
Date -7 AUG. 1917

Instructions regarding War Diaries and Intelligence Summaries are contained in F. S. Regs., Part II. and the Staff Manual respectively. Title Pages will be prepared in manuscript.

WAR DIARY
or
~~INTELLIGENCE SUMMARY~~
(Erase heading not required.)

Army Form C. 2118

Map reference FRANCE 51.c 1/40.000.

Place	Date	Hour	Summary of Events and Information	Remarks and references to Appendices
M.23a6.5	1.6.17		Visited Advanced Dressing Station (42 F. Ambulance)	[illegible] Col. A.M.S.
	2.6.17		Visited R.A. Rest Camp, HENDECOURT & inspected sanitation.	[illegible]
	3.6.17		Inspected sanitation of two battalions in L. sector of front line.	[illegible]
			Visited No. 6. Stationary Hospital re cases of "shell-shock"	[illegible]
	4.6.17		Visited 43 & 44 F. Ambulances. Visited Officers' Hospital (6. Stationary) re "shell shock" case	[illegible]
	5.6.17		Visited A.D.S. and Div! Salvage Company.	[illegible]
	6.6.17		Visited D.D.M.S. VII Corps.	[illegible]
	7.6.17		Visited A.D.S. with D.D.M.S. VI Corps re relief. Visited by D.A.D.M.S. 56 Divn. re relief.	[illegible]
	8.6.17		Visited 5. K.S.L.I. re change of Medical Officer	[illegible]
	9.6.17		Visited Rest Area & sites for Field Ambulances. 43 F.A. to BEAUMETZ	[illegible]
MARIEUX	10.6.17		D.H.Q. to Chateau, MARIEUX. 43 F.A. to SAULTY.	[illegible]
	11.6.17		43 F.A. to RAINCHEVAL. 44 F.A. to MONCHIET.	[illegible]
	12.6.17		44 F.A. to SAULTY. Visited 43 F.A.	[illegible]
	13.6.17		Proceeded on leave. Lt Col. T.S. EVES. R.A.M.C. assumed duties of A.D.M.S.	[illegible]

Instructions regarding War Diaries and Intelligence Summaries are contained in F. S. Regs., Part II. and the Staff Manual respectively. Title Pages will be prepared in manuscript.

WAR DIARY
or
INTELLIGENCE SUMMARY
(Erase heading not required.)

Army Form C. 2118

Place	Date	Hour	Summary of Events and Information	Remarks and references to Appendices
MARIEUX	13.6.17		Acting for ADMS T.S. Eccles. Lt.Col. RAMC.	TSE.
			42nd F.Amb to MONCHIET. 44th F.Amb. to VAUCHELLES	
	14.6.17		42nd F.Amb. to LARBRET. Visited 44th F.Amb.	TSE
	15.6.17		42nd F.Amb to BUS-en-ARTOIS	TSE
	16.6.17		Visited 42nd Infantry Brigade	TSE
	17.6.17		Inspected sanitation of 8th KRRC	TSE
	21.6.17		Visited 43rd F.Amb.	TSE
	23.6.17		COLONEL H.V.PRYNNE returned from leave.	TSE
	24.6.17		Resumed duties as ADMS.	H.V. Prynne Col. ADMS
	25.6.17		Visited 42 F. Ambulance. Visited 44 F. Ambulance Sports.	H.V.P.
	27.6.17		Conference [illegible] Corps.	H.V.P.
	28.6.17		Visited 43 F. Ambulance & their Sports.	H.V.P.
	29.6.17		Visited 43 F. Ambulance Sports.	H.V.P.
	30.6.17		D.A.D.M.S. inspected sanitation of Div. H.Q.	H.V.P.

1875 Wt. W593/826 1,000,000 4/15 J.B.C. & A. A.D.S.S./Forms/C. 2118.

Vol 24

140/2292

Confidential

War Diary of

ADMS 14 Division

for

July 1917

COMMITTEE FOR THE
MEDICAL HISTORY OF THE WAR
Date 10 SEP. 1917

S

July 1917

Instructions regarding War Diaries and Intelligence Summaries are contained in F. S. Regs., Part II. and the Staff Manual respectively. Title Pages will be prepared in manuscript.

WAR DIARY
or
~~INTELLIGENCE SUMMARY~~
(Erase heading not required.)

Army Form C. 2118

Map reference FRANCE 57D
FRANCE 27
FRANCE 28.

Place	Date	Hour	Summary of Events and Information	Remarks and references to Appendices
MARIEUX	1.7.17		Visited 42 F. Ambulance.	S.T.P.
	4.7.17		Conference of Regimental M.O.'s at Div. H.Q	S.T.P.
	6.7.17		Capt. A.T. TODD. R.A.M.C. to C.C.S. for permanent duty.	S.T.P.
	7.7.17		Visited D.D.M.S. IX Corps at MONT NOIR.	S.T.P.
	10.7.17		Visited D.D.M.S. IX Corps.	S.T.P.
	11.7.17		A.D.M.S. Office to ST JANS CAPPEL (Sheet 27)	S.T.P.
	12.7.17		D.H.Q. to ST JANS CAPPEL 42 F.A. to RUE DE METEREN, BAILLEUL. 43 F.A. to METEREN 44 F.A. to MONT KOKEREELE (R.17 b 50.30.)	S.T.P.
ST JANS CAPPEL	13.7.17		Visited 42 and 43 F. Ambulances.	S.T.P.
	14.7.17		Visited 44 F. Ambulance.	S.T.P.
	16.7.17		Visited 42 and 43. F. Ambulances. Visited No 2 & No 1 Australian C.C.S. to select site for 42 F.A.	S.T.P.
	17.7.17		Visited 43 F.A.	S.T.P.
	18.7.17		Visited 42 F.A.	S.T.P.
	19.7.17		Visited site for 43 F.A. at X 12 a. 8.8. Conference of A.D.M.S. at IX Corps H.Q.	S.T.P.

1875 Wt. W593/826 1,000,000 4/15 J.B.C. & A. A.D.S.S./Forms/C. 2118.

Instructions regarding War Diaries and Intelligence Summaries are contained in F. S. Regs., Part II. and the Staff Manual respectively. Title Pages will be prepared in manuscript.

WAR DIARY

or

~~INTELLIGENCE SUMMARY~~

(Erase heading not required.)

Army Form C. 2118

Map reference. Sheets FRANCE 27 + 28

Place	Date	Hour	Summary of Events and Information	Remarks and references to Appendices
ST JANS CAPPEL	20.7.17		Inspected sanitation of four battalions of 42nd Inf. Brigade and Brigade H.Q.	S.R.P.
	21.7.17		Inspected sanitation of battalions of 43rd Inf. Brigade.	S.R.P.
	23.7.17		Inspected sanitation 8 K.R.R.C., 8. Rifle Brigade + Divisional Train.	S.R.P.
	24.7.17		Inspected sanitation 7 Rifle Brigade + 7 K.R.R.C.	S.R.P.
	25.7.17		Visited A.D.M.S. 47 Divn with reference to relief.	S.R.P.
	26.7.17		Visited 42 and 44 F.A. 42 F.A. to S14 C.20.50.	S.R.P.
	27.7.17		Visited R.A.P. Advanced Dressing Station, and Lightly Wounded Collecting Post of 19th Divn with D.A.D.M.S. 19 Divn.	S.R.P.
	28.7.17		Visited 43 F.A.	S.R.P.
	29.7.17		Visited Baths + Laundry re disposal of sullage water.	S.R.P.
	30.7.17		Visited 42 F.A.	S.R.P.
	31.7.17		Visited A.D.M.S. 41 Divn, also M.D.S. 19th Divn, 19th Divn Lightly Wounded Collecting Station, + IX Corps L.W.C. Station. Visited Collecting Posts NORFOLK LODGE + SHELLEY DUMP, + A.D.S. 41st Divn VOORMEZEELE with D.A.D.M.S. 41 Divn.	S.R.P.

S.R. Byrne Col. AMS
A.D.M.S. 14 Divn

1875 Wt. W593/826 1,000,000 4/15 J.B.C. & A. A.D.S.S./Forms/C. 2118.

B.E.F.

Summary of Medical War Diaries for

14th Divn. 9th Corps, 2nd Army.

2nd Corps, 5th Army from 15/8/17.

WESTERN FRONT. July- ~~Aug.~~ '17.

A.D.M.S. Lt. Col. H.V. Prynne.

D.A.D.M.S. ?

Summarised under the following headings.

Phase "D"1. PASSCHENDAELE OPERATIONS July- Nov. 1917.

(a) Operations commencing 1/7/17.

B.E.F.

14th Divn. 9th Corps 2nd Army. WESTERN FRONT.

A.D.M.S. Lt. Col. H.V. Prynne. July- ~~Aug.~~ 1917.

2nd Corps, 5th Army from 15/8/17.

Phase "D"1. Passchendaele Operations, July- Nov. 1917.

(a) Operations commencing 1/7/17.

1917.	Head quarters. at MARIEUX.
July 13th.	Moves and Transfer. To St. Jans Cappel 2nd Army.
14th- 31st.	Operations R.A.M.C. Nothing of note.
	Appendices. Nil.

B.E.F.

14th Divn. 9th Corps nd Army. WESTERN FRONT.

A.D.M.S. Lt. Col. H.V. Prynne. July- Aug. 1917.

2nd Corps, 5th Army from 15/8/17.

Phase "D"1. Passchendaele Operations, July- Nov. 1917.

(a) Operations commencing 1/7/17.

1917. Head quarters. at MARIEUX.

July 13th. Moves and Transfer. To St. Jans Cappel 2nd Army.

14th- 31st. Operations R.A.M.C. Nothing of note.

Appendices. Nil.

Confidential

WAR DIARY

of

ADMS 14 Division

for month of

August 1917

COMMITTEE FOR THE MEDICAL HISTORY OF THE WAR
Date -1 OCT. 1917

Vol 25

14/2262

Instructions regarding War Diaries and Intelligence Summaries are contained in F. S. Regs., Part II. and the Staff Manual respectively. Title Pages will be prepared in manuscript.

WAR DIARY
or
~~INTELLIGENCE SUMMARY~~
(Erase heading not required.)

Army Form C. 2118

Map reference FRANCE Sheets 27 + 28.

Place	Date	Hour	Summary of Events and Information	Remarks and references to Appendices
ST. JANS	1.8.17		Visited D.D.M.S. IX Corps.	[illegible signature]
CAPPEL	2.8.17		Visited 42 + 44 F. Ambulances.	[initials]
	3.8.17		Visited LA CLYTTE site for Field Ambulance	[initials]
	4.8.17		Visited 8 Rifle Brigade. Visited D.M.S. Second Army	[initials]
	5.8.17		Visited 42 F. Ambulance	[initials]
CAESTRE	6.8.17		D.H.Q. to CAESTRE. 42 Field Ambulance to P32. d.5.5. 43 Field Ambulance to V.3 Central. 44 Field Ambulance to V2. b.3.7.	[initials]
	7.8.17		Inspected sanitation of units + H.Q. 42 Inf. Brigade.	[initials]
	8.8.17		Conference of R.M.O.'s at D.H.Q.	[initials]
	9.8.17		Visited 4 Coy. Div. Train.	[initials]
	10.8.17		Visited 43 and 44 F. Ambulances.	[initials]
	14.8.17		Visited 42, 43 and 44 F. Ambulances.	[initials]
RENINGHELST	15.8.17		D.H.Q. to RENINGHELST. 42 F.A. to G.26. c.40.30. (Sheet 28) 43 F.A. to 27K. 36. d.5.5. 44 F.A. to 28 L. 23. d.9.4. Visited II Corps	[initials]
	16.8.17		Visited D.R.S. at WARATAH CAMP (28 G15. c.0.8) + A.D.M.S. 8 Divn. at 28 G 23. a. 9.6.	[initials]
	17.8.17		43 F. Ambulance to 28 G30 a.5.1. 44 F. Ambulance to 28 G15.c.0.8. Visited D.D.M.S. II Corps, + A.D.M.S. 56 Division	[initials]

1875 Wt. W593/826 1,000,000 4/15 J.B.C. & A. A.D.S.S./Forms/C. 2118.

Instructions regarding War Diaries and Intelligence Summaries are contained in F. S. Regs., Part II. and the Staff Manual respectively. Title Pages will be prepared in manuscript.

WAR DIARY
or
~~INTELLIGENCE SUMMARY~~
(Erase heading not required.)

Map reference Sheet France 28.

Army Form C. 2118

Place	Date	Hour	Summary of Events and Information	Remarks and references to Appendices
H27.b.6.8	18.8.17		Visited D.M.S. Fifth Army. D.H.Q. moved to H27 b.6.8. Visited A.D.S. at MENIN ROAD + WOODCOTE HOUSE, Advanced Dressing Post at HOOGE TUNNEL. 43 F. Ambulance took over A.D. Stations, A.D. Post + Relay Posts, and collection from front line. 42 F.A. took over Corps Main Dressing Station at H.27 c.1.9.	J.v.P.
	19.8.17		Visited D.R.S. at G15 c.0.8. (44 F. Ambulance), and Corps Main Dressing Station (42 F. Ambulance)	J.v.P.
	20.8.17		Visited A.D.S. MENIN ROAD, CAR LOADING POINT at I19 c.9.6, at J17 a.8.8, Advanced Dressing Post at HOOGE TUNNEL (J.13 a 6.3), R.A.Ps at J13 d.8.8 and J13 d.4.0. Visited Nos 44, 32 and 3 Australian C.C.S. to arrange exchange of splints &c. Visited Corps Main Dressing Station.	J.v.P.
	21.8.17		Visited A.D.S. MENIN ROAD. R.A.P. at I.18 b.4.8, Advanced Dressing Post, 43rd + 42nd Bde H.Q. at DORMY + HALFWAY HOUSE. R.A.Ps at HALFWAY HOUSE (I17 c.4.6), Collecting Post at COW FARM (I22 b.6.4.) A.D. Station at WOODCOTE HOUSE (I20 c.4.2) and L.W. Collecting Station at I9 c.6.5. Conference at D.D.M.S. II Corps.	J.v.P.
	22.8.17		Active operations. Visited A.D.S, MENIN Rd, RELAY POST at CULVERT (I18 a 5.7) + A.D. Post. Visited L.W. Collecting Station and A.D.S. at WOODCOTE HOUSE. Visited 42nd Bde H.Q.	J.v.P.
	23.8.17		Visited A.D.S. MENIN ROAD, RELAY POST, A.D. Post, R.A.Ps at J13.d.88 + J.13.d.40. L.W. Collecting Station, 43 Bde H.Q, Collecting Post at I22 b.6.4 + A.D.S at WOODCOTE HOUSE	J.v.P.

1875 Wt. W593/826 1,000,000 4/15 J.B.C. & A. A.D.S.S./Forms/C. 2118.

Army Form C. 2118

WAR DIARY
or
~~INTELLIGENCE SUMMARY~~
(Erase heading not required.)

Instructions regarding War Diaries and Intelligence Summaries are contained in F. S. Regs., Part II. and the Staff Manual respectively. Title Pages will be prepared in manuscript.

Map reference. FRANCE
Sheets 27 and 28.

Place	Date	Hour	Summary of Events and Information	Remarks and references to Appendices
28H.27 + 6.8.	24.8.17		Visited Corps Main Dressing Station. Visited Advanced Dressing Station, MENIN ROAD.	T.P.
	25.8.17		Visited A.D.S. MENIN ROAD, RELAY POST at I 18.a.5.7, A.D. Post, and A.D.S. WOODCOTE HOUSE. Visited L.W. Collecting Post.	T.P.
RENINGHELST	26.8.17		D.H.Q. to RENINGHELST. 43 F. Ambulance handed over A.D.S at MENIN ROAD + WOODCOTE HOUSE, A.D. Post and collection from front line to 71 Field Ambulance (23rd Division). 43 F. Amb. moved to 27K 29.b.9.9.	T.P.
	27.8.17		Visited O.C. 75 SAN. SECTION re sanitation of 14 Divn. Camps in WIPPONHOEK area. Visited 43 F. Ambulance at 27K.29.b.9.9	T.P.
	28.8.17		Visited Baths + Laundries. RENINGHELST	T.P.
BERTHEN	29.8.17		D.H.Q. to BERTHEN. 43 F.A. to 27 W 5.c.3.5. Visited 3 F.A. sites + II ANZAC CORPS.	T.P.
	30.8.17		Visited II Corps, II ANZAC CORPS, + 43 F. Ambulance. 43 F. Ambulance to X 16.d.8.9. Advance party 44 F.A. to RUE DE MUSÉE BAILLEUL	T.P.
	31.8.17		Visited A.D.M.S. 4 Australian Division, + saw M.D. Station at WESTHOF (28T (9.d.4.5) + A.D.S. at KANDAHAR (T10 b.7.7.) Advance party to KANDAHAR.	T.P.

T. P. Kyme [?] Col. A.M.S.
A.D.M.S. 14th Divn

B.E.F.

Summary of Medical War Diaries for

14th Divn. 9th Corps, 2nd Army.

2nd Corps, 5th Army from 15/8/17.

WESTERN FRONT. ~~July~~- Aug. '17.

A.D.M.S. Lt. Col. H.V. Prynne.

D.A.D.M.S. ?

Summarised under the following headings.

Phase "D"1. PASSCHENDAELE OPERATIONS July- Nov. 1917.

(a) Operations commencing 1/7/17.

Aug. 1st-5th. Operations R.A.M.C. Nothing of note.

6th. Moves: To Caestre.

Moves Field Ambulances:-

42nd F.A. to P.32.d.5.5.

43rd " " V.3. central (Sheet 27)

44th " " V.2.b.3.7.

15th. Moves and Transfer. To 2nd Corps 5th Army and moved to RENINGHELST.

5

B.E.F.

SUMMARY OF MEDICAL WAR DIARIES of

14th Division,

2nd Corps, 5th Army, from 15.8.17.
To 2nd Anzac Corps, 2nd Army, 29.8.17.

WESTERN FRONT, AUGUST 1917.

A.D.M.S. Col. H.V. Prynne.

D.A.D.M.S.

Summarised under the following headings:-

PHASE "D1". PASSCHENDAELE OPERATIONS, "JULY-DECEMBER 1917.

(a). Operations commencing 1st July.

14th Division, WESTERN FRONT,

2nd Corps, 5th Army. AUGUST 1917.
2nd Anzac Corps, 2nd Army, from 29.8.17.

A.D.M.S. Col. H.V. Prynne.

PHASE "D1". Passchendaele Operations, "July_Dec. 1917."

(a). Operations commencing 1st July.

August. H.Q. at RENINGHELST.

15th Moves & Transfer. Divn. transferred from 9th Corps, 2nd Army to 2nd Corps, 5th Army, and moved to RENINGHELST

Moves F.A. 42nd F.A. to G.26.c.4.3. (Sheet 28).
43rd F.A. to K.36.d.5.5. (Sheet 27).
44th F.A. to L.23.d.9.4. (Sheet 27).

17th Moves F.A. 43rd F.A. to G.30.a.5.1. } Sheet 28.
44th F.A. to G.15.c.0.8. }

Med. Arr. 44th F.A. took over D.R.S.

18th Moves. To H.27.b.6.8. (Sheet 28).

Med. Arr. 43rd F.A. took over A.D.S's at Menin Rd. I.9.c.9.6. & Woodcote House, I.20.c.4.2.

A.D.P. at Hooge Tunnel, J.13.a.6.3. & Relay P's and collection of Wd. from Front line.

42nd F.A. took over C.M.D.S. at H.27.c.1.9.

22nd Operations. Active operations commenced.

26th Med. Arr. 43rd F.A. handed over all P's to 71st F.A., 23rd Divn.

Moves. To RENINGHELST.

Moves F.A. 43rd F.A. to K.29.b.9.9.(SHeet 27)

29th Moves & Transfer. 14th Divn. transferred to 2nd Anzac Corps, 2nd Army and moved to BERTHEN.

B.E.F.

SUMMARY OF MEDICAL WAR DIARIES of

14th Division,

2nd Corps, 5th Army, from 15.8.17.
To 2nd Anzac Corps, 2nd Army, 29.8.17.

WESTERN FRONT, AUGUST 1917.

A.D.M.S. Col. H.V. Prynne.

D.A.D.M.S.

Summarised under the following headings:-

PHASE "D1". PASSCHENDAELE OPERATIONS, "JULY-DECEMBER 1917.

(a). Operations commencing 1st July.

Aug.	1st-5th.	Operations R.A.M.C. Nothing of note.
	6th.	Moves: To Caestre.
		Moves Field Ambulances:-
		42nd F.A. to P.32.d.5.5.
		43rd " " V.3. central (Sheet 27)
		44th " " V.2.b.3.7.
	15th.	Moves and Transfer. To 2nd Corps 5th Army and moved to RENINGHELST.

~~N.B:- Diaries for Aug. with 5th Army.~~

14th Division, WESTERN FRONT,

2nd Corps, 5th Army. AUGUST 1917.
2nd Anzac Corps, 2nd Army, from 29.8.17.

A.D.M.S. Col. H.V. Prynne.

PHASE "D1". Passchendaele Operations, "July_Dec. 1917."

(a). Operations commencing 1st July.

August. H.Q. at RENINGHELST.

15th Moves & Transfer. Divn. transferred from 9th Corps, 2nd Army to 2nd Corps, 5th Army, and moved to RENINGHELST

Moves F.A. 42nd F.A. to G.26.c.4.3. (Sheet 28).
43rd F.A. to K.36.d.5.5. (Sheet 27).
44th F.A. to L.23.d.9.4. (Sheet 27).

17th Moves F.A. 43rd F.A. to G.30.a.5.1.
44th F.A. to G.15.c.0.8. Sheet 28.

Med. Arr. 44th F.A. took over D.R.S.

18th Moves. To H.27.b.6.8. (Sheet 28).

Med. Arr. 43rd F.A. took over A.D.S's at Menin Rd. I.9.c.9.6. & Woodcote House, I.20.c.4.2.

A.D.P. at Hooge Tunnel, J.13.a.6.3. & Relay P's and collection of Wd. from Front line.

42nd F.A. took over C.M.D.S. at H.27.c.1.9.

22nd Operations. Active operations commenced.

26th Med. Arr. 43rd F.A. handed over all P's to 71st F.A., 23rd Divn.

Moves. To RENINGHELST.

Moves F.A. 43rd F.A. to K.29.b.9.9.(SHeet 27)

29th Moves & Transfer. 14th Divn. transferred to 2nd Anzac Corps, 2nd Army and moved to BERTHEN.

WAR DIARY.

of

A.D.M.S., 14th. DIVISION.

for

month of SEPTEMBER 1917.

****

COMMITTEE FOR THE
MEDICAL HISTORY OF THE WAR
Date -5 NOV.1917

Instructions regarding War Diaries and Intelligence Summaries are contained in F. S. Regs., Part II. and the Staff Manual respectively. Title Pages will be prepared in manuscript.

WAR DIARY

or

~~INTELLIGENCE SUMMARY~~

(Erase heading not required.)

Army Form C. 2118

Map reference Sheets 28 + 36. FRANCE. 1/40.000.

Place	Date	Hour	Summary of Events and Information	Remarks and references to Appendices
28 S. 17. b. 5. 2.	1.9.17		D.H.Q. to RAVELSBERG (28 S. 17. b. 52). 43 F. Ambulance took over Main Dressing Station at WESTHOF (28 T. 19 B 5. 3) from 4th Australian F. Ambulance.	J.R.P.
	2.9.17.		Conference at office of D.D.M.S. VIII Corps. Visited 43 Field Ambulance.	J.R.P.
	3.9.17		Visited R.A.P.'s of L. battalion in line at 28 O.34 a.9.2, support battalion at 28 O.32 central, + R.A.P. of R. battalion in line at 28 U. d.4.5: also Relay Posts at SWAYNE'S POST (28 O.32 b.3.3.) + BOYLE'S FARM (28 U.1.a.3.1), and Advanced Dressing Post at GOOSEBERRY FARM (28 U.7. b.4.8) and Advanced Dressing Station at KANDAHAR FARM (28 T.10. b.7.7). 44 F. Ambulance took over D.R.S. at 28 S.16. c.3.4 from 12 Australian Field Ambulance. 42 F. Ambulance took over M.D.S. at 28 T. 19. b. 5. 3. from 43 F. Ambulance, whose H.Q. remained at same location. Visited D.R.S. (44 F. Ambulance), and detachment 44 Field Ambulance at RUE DE MUSÉE, BAILLEUL.	J.R.P.

1875 Wt. W593/826 1,000,000 4/15 J.B.C. & A. A.D.S.S./Forms/C. 2118.

Instructions regarding War Diaries and Intelligence Summaries are contained in F. S. Regs., Part II. and the Staff Manual respectively. Title Pages will be prepared in manuscript.

WAR DIARY

or

~~INTELLIGENCE SUMMARY~~

(Erase heading not required.)

Army Form C. 2118

Map reference. FRANCE
Sheets 28 + 36. 1/40.000

Place	Date	Hour	Summary of Events and Information	Remarks and references to Appendices
28 S.17 6.5.2	4.9.17		Visited 42 + 43 Field Ambulances at T19.b.5.3.)	S.r.P.
	5.9.17		Visited Advanced Dressing Station, Advanced Dressing Post, R.A.P. of Reserve Battalion at BRISTOL CASTLE (28 T.d.6.4.) Relay post at 28 U.1 a 3.7. + reconnoitred tracks from A.D.P. and BRISTOL CASTLE to this Relay post. Visited 42 Inf. Brigade.	S.r.P.
	6.9.17		Visited O.C. 4 Australian Sanitary Section.	S.r.P.
	7.9.17		Visited 42 + 43 Field Ambulances.	S.r.P.
	8.9.17		Visited DDMS VIII Corps.	S.r.P.
	9.9.17		Visited Divisional Rest Station (44 F. Ambulance)	S.r.P.
	10.9.17		Visited 42 + 43 F. Ambulances.	S.r.P.
	11.9.17		Visited A.D.S., Relay Posts at Boyle's Farm, Swanne's Post + Fanny's Post (28 O.33 c 4.4.) + R.A.P's of L. battalion in line, + R support battalion. Visited Div. Baths + laundries.	S.r.P.
	12.9.17		Visited A.D.P. (Gooseberry Farm), R.A.P. of R. battalion in line + proposed R.A.P. for this battalion, R.A.P. of Reserve battalion + Relay Post at Boyle's Farm.	S.r.P.

1875 Wt. W593/826 1,000,000 4/15 J.B.C. & A. A.D.S.S./Forms/C. 2118.

Instructions regarding War Diaries and Intelligence Summaries are contained in F. S. Regs., Part II. and the Staff Manual respectively. Title Pages will be prepared in manuscript.

WAR DIARY
or
~~INTELLIGENCE SUMMARY~~
(Erase heading not required.)

Army Form C. 2118

Map reference FRANCE Sheets 28 + 36. 1/40.000.

Place	Date	Hour	Summary of Events and Information	Remarks and references to Appendices
28S.17 b.5.2	13.9.17		Held a conference of F.A. Commanders on sanitation of Brigades.	S.T.P.
	14.9.17		Inspected sanitation of Reserve Battalion.	S.T.P.
	15.9.17		Visited Detachment 44 F. Ambulance at BAILLEUL	S.T.P.
	16.9.17		Conference at D.D.M.S. office.	S.T.P.
	17.9.17		Visited 42, 43 + 44 Field Ambulances.	S.T.P.
	18.9.17		Visited 42, 43 + 44 F. Ambulances + inspected medical arrangements, billets of personnel &c. Inspected sanitation of 43 Inf Brigade H.Q., T.M. Battery + M.G. Coy + 6 Som: L. Inf.	S.T.P.
	19.9.17		Visited Advanced Dressing Station + 41 Inf. Bde. H.Q. Inspected sanitation of 6 D.C.L.I., 6. K.O.Y.L.I., + 10 D.L.I.	S.T.P.
	20.9.17		Inspected sanitation of Divl Police + P. of W. Cage, 47 Bde R.F.A. H.Q., H.Q. of 47. A. Battery + 3 Coys. Divl Train	S.T.P.
	21.9.17		Visited Divl Rest Station (44 F. Ambulance). Visited wagon lines of A, B + D batteries 46 Bde R.F.A. + inspected sanitation	S.T.P.
	22.9.17		Inspected sanitn H.Q. 42 Inf. Bde, 42 T.M. Battery + M.G. Coy, 9 R.B., 9 K.R.R.C. and 5 Ox + Bucks L.I.	S.T.P.

1875 Wt. W593/826 1,000,000 4/15 J.B.C. & A. A.D.S.S./Forms/C. 2118.

Army Form C. 2118

Instructions regarding War Diaries and Intelligence Summaries are contained in F. S. Regs., Part II. and the Staff Manual respectively. Title Pages will be prepared in manuscript.

WAR DIARY
or
INTELLIGENCE SUMMARY
(Erase heading not required.)

Map reference. FRANCE
Sheets 28 & 36. 1/40.000.

Place	Date	Hour	Summary of Events and Information	Remarks and references to Appendices
28. 5. 17	23.9.17		Conference at D.D.M.S. Office. Visited 44 F. Ambulance	[initials]
L. 5. 2	24.9.17		Visited Advanced Dressing Station & 3 F. Ambulances.	[initials]
	25.9.17		Visited R.A.P. of Reserve Battalion. Inspected medical arrange-ments of 42, 43 & 44 F. Ambulances.	[initials]
	26.9.17		Proceeded on leave — Lt Col. T.S. EVES. RAMC. assumed duties of A.D.M.S.	[initials]
			VIII Corps "Q" and DDMS inspected the DRS (44th F.A) the MDS (42nd F.A) & the ADS (43rd F.A) in the morning.	
			In the afternoon the G.O.C. 14th Division inspected the DRS. MDS. and ADS. T.S. Eves Lt Col. RAMC	
	27.9.17		Visited ADS. Most of the constructional work completed.	T.S.E.
	28.9.17		Inspected sanitation of 116 Battery R.F.A.	
			New Right RAP. taken into use.	T.S.E.
	29.9.17		Visited 42nd and 44th F. Ambulances.	T.S.E.
	30.9.17		Visited 43rd and 44th F Ambulances.	T.S.E.

T.S. Eves, Lt Col. RAMC
for ADMS 14 Div.

1875 Wt. W593/826 1,000,000 4/15 J.B.C. & A. A.D.S.S./Forms/C. 2118.

B.E.F.

SUMMARY OF MEDICAL WAR DIARIES of

14th Division,

2nd Anzac Corps, 2nd Army, till 2.9.17.
8th Corps, from 2.9.17.

WESTERN FRONT, SEPTEMBER, 1917.

A.D.M.S. Col. H.V. Prylle.

Summarised under the following headings:-

PHASE "D"1. PASSCHENDAELE OPERATIONS, "JULY-NOVEMBER, 1917."

(a). Operations commencing 1st July.

14th Division, WESTERN FRONT,

2nd Anzac Corps, 2nd Army, till 2.9.17. SEPTEMBER, 1917.
8th Corps, from 2.9.17.
A.D.M.S. Col. H.V. Prylle

PHASE "D"1. Passchendaele Operations, "July-Nov. 1917."

(a). Operations commencing 1st July.

September. H.Q. at BERTHEN.

1st Moves. To RAVELSBERG, 17.b.5.2. (28).

2nd Transfer. To 8th Corps.

14th Division, WESTERN FRONT,

8th Corps, 2nd Army. SEPTEMBER 1917.

A.D.M.S. Col. H.V. Prylle.

PHASE "D"1. Passchendaele Operations, "July-Nov. 1918."

(a). Operations commencing 1st July.

September. H.Q. at RAVELSBERG.

2nd Transfer. To 8th Corps.

3rd Med. Arr. R.A.P.s. L. Btln.

O.34.a.9.2. (28).

Support Btln.

O.32.Central.

R. Btln.

U.d.4.5.

Reserve Btln.

T.6.d.4.

Relay Posts. Swaynes P. O.32.b.3.3.

Boyles Farm, U.1.a.3.1.

Adv. D.P. Gooseberry Farm, U.7.b.4.8.

A.D.S. Kandahar Farm, T.10.b.7.7.

D.R.S. S.16.c.3.4.

M.D.S. T.19.b.5.3.

4th-30th Operations R.A.M.C. Routine.

Appendices. Nil.

B.E.F.

SUMMARY OF MEDICAL WAR DIARIES of

14th Division,

2nd Anzac Corps, 2nd Army, till 2.9.17.
8th Corps, from 2.9.17.

WESTERN FRONT, SEPTEMBER, 1917.

A.D.M.S. Col. H.V. Prylle.

Summarised under the following headings:-

PHASE "D"1. PASSCHENDAELE OPERATIONS, "JULY-NOVEMBER, 1917."

(a). Operations commencing 1st July.

14th Division, WESTERN FRONT,

2nd Anzac Corps, 2nd Army, till 2.9.17. SEPTEMBER, 1917.
8th Corps, from 2.9.17.
A.D.M.S. Col. H.V. Prylle

PHASE "D"1. Passchendaele Operations, "July-Nov. 1917."

(a). Operations commencing 1st July.

September. H.Q. at BERTHEN.

1st Moves. To RAVELSBERG, 17.b.5.2. (28).

2nd Transfer. To 8th Corps.

14th Division, WESTERN FRONT,

8th Corps, 2nd Army. SEPTEMBER 1917.

A.D.M.S. Col. H.V. Prvlle.

PHASE "D"1. Passchendaele Operations, "July-Nov. 1917."

(a). Operations commencing 1st July.

September. H.Q. at RAVELSBERG.

2nd Transfer. To 8th Corps.

3rd Med. Arr. R.A.P.s. L. Btln.

O.34.a.9.2. (28).

Support Btln.

O.32.Central.

R. Btln.

U.d.4.5.

Reserve Btln.

T.6.d.4.

Relay Posts. Swaynes P. O.32.b.3.3.

Boyles Farm, U.1.a.3.1.

Adv. D.P. Gooseberry Farm, U.7.b.4.8.

A.D.S. Kandahar Farm, T.10.b.7.7.

D.R.S. S.16.c.3.4.

M.D.S. T.19.b.5.3.

4th-30th Operations R.A.M.C. Routine.

Appendices. Nil.

Confidential.

WAR DIARY

of

A.D.M.S., 14th. DIVISION.

for month of

OCTOBER 1917.

COMMITTEE FOR THE MEDICAL HISTORY OF THE W...
Date -5 JAN. 1918

Instructions regarding War Diaries and Intelligence Summaries are contained in F. S. Regs., Part II. and the Staff Manual respectively. Title Pages will be prepared in manuscript.

WAR DIARY
or
~~INTELLIGENCE SUMMARY~~
(Erase heading not required.)

Army Form C. 2118

Map Ref. Sheets 27, 28 and 36 FRANCE 1/40,000.

Place	Date 1917	Hour	Summary of Events and Information	Remarks and references to Appendices
28.S.17 b.2.2.	Oct. 1		The work on the bunking at the ADS. held up for want of timber. Saw CRE and got permission to draw material from KURRIE DUMP.	TSE
	2.		Visited ADS and MDS.	TSE
	3.		Visited ADS. Work on bunking has been resumed.	TSE
	4.		Visited 42nd and 44th F. Ambs.	
	5.		Received Warning Order that the 42nd and 44th F. Ambs were to be prepared to march with the 41st and 43rd Brigades respectively.	TSE
	6.		44th Field Ambulance handed over DRS. to 101st F. Ambulance and 42nd Field Ambulance handed over MDS. to 99th F. Amb. 44th Field Ambulance less handing over party marched to camp at 28 M d. 8.0. 42nd Field Ambulance less handing over party marched to camp at 28. G. 34. d. 9.5. Assumed duties of A.D.M.S.	[illegible] Col. A.D.M.S.
	7.10.17		Conference D.D.M.S. VIII Corps.	[illegible]
	8.10.17		Visited 42 + 44 F. Ambulances.	[illegible]
WESTOUTRE	9.10.17		D.H.Q. to WESTOUTRE. 44 F. Ambulance to 28 M. 6. a. 4.7	[illegible]
	10.10.17		Visited D.D.M.S. X Corps. Visited 42 + 44 F. Ambulances + A.D.M.S. 5th Divn. re reliefs. 43 F. Amb to 27 R. 10 a 3.8	[illegible]

1875 Wt. W593/826 1,000,000 4/15 J.B.C. & A. A.D.S.S./Forms/C. 2118.

Instructions regarding War Diaries and Intelligence Summaries are contained in F. S. Regs., Part II. and the Staff Manual respectively. Title Pages will be prepared in manuscript.

WAR DIARY
or
INTELLIGENCE SUMMARY
(Erase heading not required.)

Army Form C. 2118

Map reference FRANCE
Sheets 27/28 — 1/40.000

Place	Date	Hour	Summary of Events and Information	Remarks and references to Appendices
28 M.6 d.5.8. LA CLYTTE CAMP	11.10.17		Advanced Divisional Head Quarters to 28 H.34 a 3.7. Rear Divisional Head Quarters to 28 M.6. d.5.8. Visited F. Ambulance site LA CLYTTE. 42 F. Ambulance to LA CLYTTE (28 N7 c.3.5.)	T.P.
	12.10.17		Visited 42 F. Ambulance, and A.D.S. for Walking Wounded at WOODCOTE HOUSE (28 I 20 c.4.2) Visited O.C. Sanitary Section re sanitary appliances.	T.P.
	13.10.17		Visited sanitation of Reserve Brigade, RIDGEWOOD + BEDFORD HOUSE. Visited Area Commandant re sanitary appliances + A.D.S. WOODCOTE HOUSE.	T.P.
	14.10.17		Visited R.A.P's. Right Brigade, Posts at CLAPHAM JUNCTION, HOOGE TUNNEL, + ECOLE DE BIENFAISANCE, MENIN ROAD. Visited 23rd Division + 43 F. Ambulance.	T.P.
	15.10.17		Visited Water Tank Company + Sterilisor. Visited 23rd Division + D.R.S.	T.P.
	16.10.17		Visited 42 F. Ambulance + D.D.M.S. X Corps.	T.P.
	17.10.17		Visited D.D.M.S. X Corps	T.P.
	18.10.17		Visited Battalions of Reserve Brigade re sanitation. Visited A.D.S. WOODCOTE HOUSE + ECOLE	T.P.

1875 Wt. W593/826 1,000,000 4/15 J.B.C. & A. A.D.S.S./Forms/C. 2118.

Instructions regarding War Diaries and Intelligence Summaries are contained in F. S. Regs., Part II. and the Staff Manual respectively. Title Pages will be prepared in manuscript.

WAR DIARY
or
~~INTELLIGENCE SUMMARY~~
(Erase heading not required.)

Army Form C. 2118

Map reference FRANCE.
Sheets 27 + 28 1/40,000.

Place	Date 1917 Oct	Hour	Summary of Events and Information	Remarks and references to Appendices
28 M6.d.5.8	19th		Visited 42 F. Ambulance.	S.R.P.
	20th		Visited D.R.S (43 F.A.) + D.R.S. 23rd Divn.	S.R.P.
	21st		Visited 42 F. Ambulance, + Area Commandant, BERTHEN AREA	S.R.P.
	22nd		Conference at D.D.M.S. Office X Corps.	S.R.P.
	23rd		42 F Ambulance handed over F.A. site LA CLYTTE to 13 F.A. + proceeded to 27 R32 d.7.2	S.R.P.
BERTHEN	24th		D.H.Q. to BERTHEN. Visited 42 F.A. at 27 R.32.d.7.2. 44 F.A. handed over Collection of wounded + WOODCOTE HOUSE to 14 F.A. (5th Divn) + proceeded to 27 Q 23.c.6.5.	S.R.P.
	25th		Visited 44 F Ambulance.	S.R.P.
	26th		Visited 43 F. Ambulance (D.R.S) at BOESCHEPE.	S.R.P.
	27th		Visited 43 F Ambulance + Divisional Baths.	S.R.P.
	28		Conference of Regimental M.O's at Divl H.Q.	S.R.P.
	29th		Visited 44th F. Ambulance. Detail of 42 F.A. to X Corps Entraining Centre	S.R.P.
	30th		Visited X Corps Entraining Centre at H27 c.3.7. Visited 43 F. Ambulance.	S.R.P.
	31st		Visited 42 F. Ambulance.	S.R.P.

S.R. Pryme Col. AMS
A.D.M.S. 14 Divn

B.E.F.

SUMMARY OF MEDICAL WAR DIARY FOR
14th Divn. 8th Corps, 2nd Army.
10th Corps from 9/10/17.
8th Corps from 12/11/17.
4th Army 2 0/12/17.

WESTERN FRONT. Oct.- Dec. 1917.

A.D.M.S.

D.A.D.M.S.

SUMMARISED UNDER THE FOLLOWING HEADINGS.

Phase "D" 1. Passchendaele Operations July-Dec. 1917.

(b) Operations commencing 1/10/17.
Canadians attacked Passchendaele Oct. 30th.
Canadians took Passchendaele Nov. 6th.

14th Divn. 8th Corps, 2nd Army. WESTERN FRONT.

A.D.M.S. Oct. 1917.

10th Corps from 9/10/17.

Phase "D" 1. Passchendaele Operations July-Dec. 1917.

(b) Operations commencing 1/10/17.
Canadians attacked Passchendaele Oct. 30th.
Canadians took Passchendaele Nov. 6th.

1917.	Headquarters. At 17.b.2.2.(28)
Oct. 1st-8th.	Operations R.A.M.C. Routine.
Oct. 9th.	Moves and Transfer. To Westoutre 10th Corps.

14th Divn. 10th Corps, 2nd Army. WESTERN FRONT.

A.D.M.S. Oct.- Dec. 1917.

4th Army from 20/12/17.

8th Corps from 12/11/17.

Phase "D" 1. Passchendaele Operations July-Dec. 1917.

(b) Operations commencing 1/10/17.
Canadians attacked Passchendaele Oct. 30th.
Canadians took Passchendaele Nov. 6th.

1917.

Oct. 9th. Moves and Transfer. To Westoutre 10th Corps.

Medical Arrangements: A.D.S. Woodcote House I.20.c.4.2. (28)

Posts. Clapham Junction.

Hooge Tunnel.

Ecole De Bien Faisance.

Menin Road.

11th. Moves. To M.6.d.5.8. (28) La Clytte Camp.

24th. " To Berthen.

Nov. 12th. Moves and Transfer. To Wizernes 8th Corps.

14th Divn. 8th Corps, 2nd Army. WESTERN FRONT.

A.D.M.S. Oct. 1917.

10th Corps from 9/10/17.

Phase "D" 1. Passchendaele Operations July-Dec. 1917.

(b) Operations commencing 1/10/17.
Canadians attacked Passchendaele Oct. 30th.
Canadians took Passchendaele Nov. 6th.

1917.

Oct. 1st-8th. Headquarters. At 17.b.2.2.(28)

Operations R.A.M.C. Routine.

Oct. 9th. Moves and Transfer. To Westoutre 10th Corps.

14th Divn. 10th Corps, 2nd Army. WESTERN FRONT.

A.D.M.S. Oct.- Dec. 1917.

4th Army from 20/12/17.

8th Corps from 12/11/17.

Phase "D" 1. Passchendaele Operations July-Dec. 1917.

(b) Operations commencing 1/10/17.
Canadians attacked Passchendaele Oct. 30th.
Canadia s took Passchendaele Nov. 6th.

1917.

Oct. 9th. Moves and Transfer. To Westoutre 10th Corps.

Medical Arrangements: A.D.S. Woodcote House I.20.c.4.2. (28)

Posts. Clapham Junction.

Hooge Tunnel.

Ecole De Bien Faisance.

Menin Road.

11th. Moves. To M.6.d.5.8. (28) La Clytte Camp.

24th. " To Borthen.

Nov. 12th. Moves and Transfer. To Wizernes 8th Corps.

Nov. 1917

14-0/2579

9/M 28

War Diary

of

Colonel H. V. Prynne D.S.O. ADMS.

ADMS 14th Division

for

month of November 1917.

COMMITTEE FOR THE
MEDICAL HISTORY OF THE WAR
Date 17 JAN. 1918

Army Form C. 2118

WAR DIARY
or
~~INTELLIGENCE SUMMARY~~
(Erase heading not required.)

Instructions regarding War Diaries and Intelligence Summaries are contained in F. S. Regs., Part II. and the Staff Manual respectively. Title Pages will be prepared in manuscript.

Map reference FRANCE. Sheets 27 & 28. 1/40.000
BELGIUM HAZEBROUCK 5A.

Place	Date	Hour	Summary of Events and Information	Remarks and references to Appendices
	1917 Nov.		X Corps.	
BERTHEN	1st		Visited D.Q.M.S. re additional tentage for D.R.S.	Col. AMS.
	2nd		Details returned from X Corps Entraining Centre.	T.P.
	3rd		Visited D.D.M.S. X Corps.	T.P.
	4th		Inspection of men proposed for P.B.	T.P.
	5th		Visited D.R.S. 23rd Division at HALLINES.	T.P.
	6th		Visited 43. F. Ambulance & D.D.M.S. VIII Corps.	T.P.
	7th		Capt. J.M. Crawford & H.M. Gilbertson reported for duty	T.P.
	8th		Visited 42 & 44 F. Ambulances.	T.P.
	9th		Visited D.D.M.S. X Corps.	T.P.
	10th		Visited F. Ambulance sites at LA WATTINE & CORMETTE in area W. of St. OMER.	T.P.
	11th		Visited D.D.M.S. VIII Corps. 42 F. Ambulance to CORMETTE	T.P.
WIZERNES	12th		D.H.Q. to WIZERNES. 44 F. Ambulance to HALLINES as D.R.S.	T.P.
			Visited 44 F. Ambulance.	T.P.
	13th		Visited 42 F. Ambulance at CORMETTE.	T.P.
	14th		Visited 43 F. Ambulance at LA WATTINE	T.P.
	15th		Visited 42 & 43 F. Ambulances.	T.P.
	16th		Visited D.R.S.	T.P.

1875 Wt. W593/826 1,000,000 4/15 J.B.C. & A. A.D.S.S./Forms/C. 2118.

Army Form C. 2118.

Instructions regarding War Diaries and Intelligence Summaries are contained in F. S. Regs., Part II. and the Staff Manual respectively. Title Pages will be prepared in manuscript.

WAR DIARY
or
~~INTELLIGENCE SUMMARY~~

(Erase heading not required.)

Map reference. Sheets. FRANCE 36ᴰ N.E + 27ᴬ S.E.

Place	Date 1917 Nov.	Hour	Summary of Events and Information	Remarks and references to Appendices
WIZERNES	18th		Visited N.Z. Stationary Hospital to arrange for treatment of Dental cases from the Division.	S.R.P.
	22nd		Visited 42 F. Ambulance.	S.R.P.
	23rd		Visited ~~O.C.~~ M.O. i/c 6. D.C.L.I. re relations with O.C. 6. D.C.L.I.	S.R.P.
	26th		Visited D.R.S.	S.R.P.
	27th		Visited A.D.M.S. 8 Div^n, H.Q. of F.A. collecting from Front Area, + D.R.S. at RED FARM (28 G 5 d. 7.3)	S.R.P.
	29th		Three reinforcement M.O's from SALONIKA reported for duty.	S.R.P.
	30th		42 F.A. proceeded by train to WIELTJE to relieve 25th F.A.	

S.R. Rynne[?]
Col. A.M.S.
A.D.M.S. 14 Div^n

2449 Wt. W14957/M90 750,000 1/16 J.B.C. & A. Forms/C.2118/12.

14th Divn. 8th Corps, 2nd Army. WESTERN FRONT.

A.D.M.S. Nov.-Dec. 1917.

4th Army, 20/12/17.

Phase "D" 1. Passchendaele Operations July-Dec. 1917.

(b) Operations commencing 1/10/17.
Canadians attacked Passchendaele Oct. 30th.
Canadians took Passchendaele Nov. 6th.

1917.	
Nov. 12th.	Moves and Transfer. To Wizernes 8th Corps.
13th- 30th.	Operations R.A.M.C. Nothing of note.
Dec. 3rd.	Moves. To Canal Bank Ypres I.1.b.7.8.(28)
20th.	Designation. 2nd Army became 4th Army.

14th Divn. 8th Corps, 2nd Army. WESTERN FRONT.

A.D.M.S. Nov.- Dec. 1917.

4th Army, 20/12/17.

Phase "D" 1. Passchendaele Operations July-Dec. 1917.

(b) Operations commencing 1/10/17.
Canadians attacked Passchendaele Oct. 30th.
Canadians took Passchendaele Nov. 6th.

1917.		
Nov. 12th.	Moves and Transfer.	To Wizernes 8th Corps.
13th- 30th.	Operations R.A.M.C.	Nothing of note.
Dec. 3rd.	Moves.	To Canal Bank Ypres I.1.b.7.8.(28)
20th.	Designation.	2nd Army became 4th Army.

Confidential.

War Diary

of

A. D. M. S.

14th (Light) Division

for

December 1917

COMMITTEE FOR THE MEDICAL HISTORY OF THE WAR
Date 29 JAN. 1918

9/C 29
140267

Instructions regarding War Diaries and Intelligence Summaries are contained in F. S. Regs., Part II. and the Staff Manual respectively. Title Pages will be prepared in manuscript.

WAR DIARY

or

~~INTELLIGENCE SUMMARY~~

(Erase heading not required.)

Army Form C. 2118.

Map reference — Sheets BELGIUM — 5A. FRANCE — 28.

Place	Date 1917 December	Hour	Summary of Events and Information	Remarks and references to Appendices
WIZERNES	1st		44 F.A. took over D.R.S. at RED FARM, BRANDHOEK (G.5 d.7.3) from 26th F.A.	H.N. Byrne Col. A.M.S.
	2nd		42 F.A. to WIELTJE (C.28. b. 3.7) & took over forward collection from 25th F.A.	H.N.B.
CANAL BANK YPRES. I.1.b 7.8.	3rd		43 F.A. to MOATED FARM, VLAMERTINGHE (H2 d.8.2) which was taken over by advanced party from 24th F.A. on 30.11.17 Div. H.Q. to I.1.b.7.8	H.N.B.
	4th		Visited 43 & 44 F. Ambulances. Visited H.Q. 42 F.A. and Collecting Post, St JEAN. (C.27. d. 2.2.)	H.N.B.
	5th		Visited Corps Main Dressing Station (PRISON, YPRES) Entraining Point (I.7.c.), Corps Rest Station (17 C.C.S.) & D.R.S. (44 F.A.)	H.N.B.
	6th		Visited A.D.S. at SOMME REDOUBT (D.13. d.6.6.) & Collecting Post at Bridge House (C.24 a. 3.6.)	H.N.B.
	7th		Visited sanitation of transport camps, 41 Inf. Bde. Visited 43 & 44 F.A's.	H.N.B.
	8th		Visited WIELTJE & St JEAN Collecting Post.	H.N.B.
	9th		Visited 43 & 44 F.A's & Delousing Station, POPERINGHE	H.N.B.
	10th		Visited WIELTJE & BRIDGE HOUSE. A.D.S. badly shelled.	H.N.B.

2449 Wt. W14957/M90 750,000 1/16 J.B.C. & A. Forms/C.2118/12.

Instructions regarding War Diaries and Intelligence Summaries are contained in F. S. Regs., Part II. and the Staff Manual respectively. Title Pages will be prepared in manuscript.

WAR DIARY
or
~~INTELLIGENCE SUMMARY~~
(Erase heading not required.)

Army Form C. 2118.

Map reference Sheets FRANCE – 28

Place	Date	Hour	Summary of Events and Information	Remarks and references to Appendices
	1917 DECEMBER			
CANAL BANK YPRES. I.1.b.7.8	11th		Visited 14 Divisional Salvage Company. Advanced Dressing Station at SOMME REDOUBT shelled and partly demolished. Personnel withdrawn + A.D.S. opened at BRIDGE HOUSE (28 C.24 a.3.6.) + Relay Post and Motor Ambulance Loading Post established at SOMME Redoubt (28 D.13. d.6.6)	T.N.P.
	12th		Visited D.D.M.S. VIII Corps, + Delousing Station	T.N.P.
			Visited M.O.s of 42nd Inf. Brigade re prevention of Trench Foot.	T.N.P.
	13th		Visited A.D.S., Relay Posts at SOMME REDOUBT + WATERLOO, and R.A.P's of 4 battalions in the line. Visited 43 + 44 F. Ambulances	T.N.P.
	14th		Met D.D.M.S. + A.D.M.S. 50 Division at C.M.D.S. by appointment	T.N.P.
	15th		Visited 44 F.A. with A.A. + Q.M.G. to arrange preventive treatment of Trench Foot. Arrangement to carry out treatment of each Brigade on day of relief at baths CANAL BANK completed	T.N.P.
	16th		Visited H.Q. 42 F. Ambulance, WIELTJE + Collecting Post ST JEAN	T.N.P.
	17th		Inspected sanitation 7 + 8 Rifle Brigade	T.N.P.
	18th		Conference at D.D.M.S. II Corps. Visited 43 + 44 Field Ambulances.	T.N.P.

2449 Wt. W14957/M90 750,000 1/16 J.B.C. & A. Forms/C.2118/12.

Army Form C. 2118.

Instructions regarding War Diaries and Intelligence Summaries are contained in F. S. Regs., Part II. and the Staff Manual respectively. Title Pages will be prepared in manuscript.

WAR DIARY
or
~~INTELLIGENCE SUMMARY~~
(Erase heading not required.)

Map reference — Sheets. FRANCE — 28 1/40.000 BELGIUM 5A

Place	Date 1917 DECEMBER	Hour	Summary of Events and Information	Remarks and references to Appendices
CANAL BANK YPRES I 16 7.8	19th		Visited 43 F Ambulance & inspected work completed	
	20th		Visited 42 F. Ambulance H.Q. WIELTJE & Collecting Post ST JEAN.	
	21st		Visit by A.D.M.S. 8th Division to arrange relief.	
	22nd		Visited Relay Post at SOMME REDOUBT & A.D.S. BRIDGE HOUSE	
	23rd		Visited 43 & 44 Field Ambulances.	
	24th		Visited 43 F.A. 44 F.A. handed over to 26 F.A.	
	25th		44 F.A. to HALLINES. 43 F.A. handed over to 25 F.A.	
	26th		43 F.A. to LA WATTINE. 42 F.A. handed over to 24 F.A.	
WIZERNES	27th		42 F.A. to LONGUENESSE. D.H.Q. to WIZERNES.	
	28th		Visited D.R.S. HALLINES (44 F Ambulance)	
	29th		Visited 42 F.A. at LONGUENESSE.	
	30th		42 F.A. to CORMETTE. Visited 44 F.A.	
	31st		Visited 42 F Ambulance.	

[illegible signature]
Col. A.M.S.
A.D.M.S. 14 Divn

2449 Wt. W14957/M90 750,000 1/16 J.B.C. & A. Forms/C.2118/12.

B.E.F.

SUMMARY OF MEDICAL WAR DIARY FOR
14th Divn. 8th Corps, 2nd Army.

10th Corps from 9/10/17.

8th Corps from 12/11/17.

4th Army 2 0/12/17.

WESTERN FRONT. Oct.- Dec. 1917.

A.D.M.S.

D.A.D.M.S.

SUMMARISED UNDER THE FOLLOWING HEADINGS.

Phase "D" 1. Passchendaele Operations July-Dec. 1917.

(b) Operations commencing 1/10/17.
Canadians attacked Passchendaele Oct. 30th.
Canadians took Passchendaele Nov. 6th.

14th Divn. 8th Corps, 4th Army. WESTERN FRONT.

A.D.M.S. Dec. 1917.

Phase "D" 1. Passchendaele Operations July-Dec. 1917.

(b) Operations commencing 1/10/17.
Canadians attacked Passchendaele Oct. 30th,
Canadians took Passchendaele Nov. 6th.

1917.

Dec. 20th. Headquarters. At Canal Bank Ypres I.1.b.7.8. (28)

Designation. 2nd Army became 4th Army.

27th. Moves. To Wizernes.

Appendices:- Nil.

14th Divn. 8th Corps, 4th Army. WESTERN FRONT.

A.D.M.S. Dec. 1917.

Phase "D" 1. Passchendaele Operations July-Dec. 1917.

(b) Operations commencing 1/10/17.
Canadians attacked Passchendaele Oct. 30th.
Canadians took Passchendaele Nov. 6th.

1917. H.Q. at Canal Bank Ypres I.1.b.7.8. (28)

Dec. 20th. Designation. 2nd Army became 4th Army.

27th. Moves. To Wizernes.

Appendizes:- Nil.

CONFIDENTIAL.

WAR DIARY OF

A.D.M.S., 14th. DIVISION,

for month

of JANUARY 1918.

COMMITTEE FOR THE
MEDICAL HISTORY OF THE W
Date -4 MAR. 1918

Army Form C. 2118.

Instructions regarding War Diaries and Intelligence Summaries are contained in F. S. Regs., Part II. and the Staff Manual respectively. Title Pages will be prepared in manuscript.

WAR DIARY
or
~~INTELLIGENCE SUMMARY~~

(Erase heading not required.)

Map reference. Sheets BELGIUM 5A. – FRANCE AMIENS.

Place	Date 1916 JANUARY	Hour	Summary of Events and Information	Remarks and references to Appendices
WIZERNES	1st		Routine duties	
	2nd		42 F Ambulance to SUZANNE, + 43 F Ambulance to BRAY-SUR-SOMME	
	3rd		DHQ. to MERICOURT-SUR-SOMME. 44 F. Ambulance to SAILLY LE SEC.	
MERICOURT sur SOMME	4th		Visited D.D.M.S. XVIII Corps, 42 + 43 F Ambulances.	
	5th		Visited 44 F Ambulance.	
	6th		Proceeded on leave. Lieut Col. Eves. D.S.O assumed duties.	[signature] Col. A.M.S.
	7th		Acting for ADMS Visited 42nd F.A.	TSE
	8th		Routine duties	TSE
	9th		Visited DADMS (San) V Army.	TSE
	10th		Routine duties.	
	11th		Visited 7 KRRC. Saw CAPTAIN WATSON about renewal of his contract. Visited 43rd FA	TSE
	12th		Conference VII Corps.	TSE

Eves Lt. Col. RAMC

2449 Wt. W14957/M90 750,000 1/16 J.B.C. & A. Forms/C.2118/12.

Army Form C. 2118.

WAR DIARY
or
~~INTELLIGENCE~~ SUMMARY
(Erase heading not required.)

Map reference. Sheets — FRANCE. AMIENS & ST QUENTIN

Instructions regarding War Diaries and Intelligence Summaries are contained in F. S. Regs., Part II. and the Staff Manual respectively. Title Pages will be prepared in manuscript.

Place	1918 Date	Hour	Summary of Events and Information	Remarks and references to Appendices
MERICOURT S. SOMME	JAN 13th		Routine duties. CAPTAIN COAD posted to 6th K.O.Y.L.I.	TSB
	14th		Visited 42nd and 43rd F.A.	TSB
	15th		Attended DDMS Conference at DMS V Army.	TSB
	16th		Routine duties.	TSB
	17th		Visited 42nd and 43rd F.Ambs. DADMS III Corps visited Division	TSB
	18th		Visited 44th F.A.	TSB
	19th		Visited 43rd F.A.	TSB
	20th		Routine duties.	TSB
	21st		CAPTAIN D.C. HANSON reported for duty - Detailed for duty with 9th K.R.R.C. CAPTAIN BATCHELOR from 9 K.R.R.C. to 43rd F.A.	TSB
	22nd		42nd F.A. moved to LE QUESNIL 43rd F.A. to HARBONNIERES 44th F.A. to FRESNOY EN CHAUSSEE.	TSB
	23rd		Assumed duties of A.D.M.S. 42 F.A. to DAVENESCOURT. 43 F.A. to LIANCOURT FOSSE. 44 F.A. to ARVILLERS.	H. [illegible] Col A.M.S.
GUISCARD	24th		D.H.Q. to GUISCARD. 43 F.A. to QUESNY. 44 F.A. to TIRLANCOURT. Visited A.D's M.S. 164 & 62 French Divisions to arrange details of relief.	[illegible]

2449 Wt. W14957/M90 750,000 1/16 J.B.C. & A. Forms/C.2118/12.

Army Form C. 2118.

WAR DIARY
or
~~INTELLIGENCE SUMMARY~~
(Erase heading not required.)

Instructions regarding War Diaries and Intelligence Summaries are contained in F. S. Regs., Part II. and the Staff Manual respectively. Title Pages will be prepared in manuscript.

Map reference Sheets
FRANCE — AMIENS + St. QUENTIN.
Sheet 66C.

Place	Date	Hour	Summary of Events and Information	Remarks and references to Appendices
	1918 JANUARY			
GUISCARD	25th		42 F Ambulance to BEINES. 43 F.A. to FLAVY-LE-MARTEL 44 F.A. to JUSSY.	T.P.
	26th		Visited 43 + 44 F. Ambulances.	T.P.
	27th		Visited 61 C.C.S. re trestles for D.R.S.	T.P.
JUSSY.	28th		Visited CLASTRES for site for scabies camp. D.H.Q. to CLASTRES + Rear Div. H.Q. to JUSSY (M.9 d.7.1)	T.P.
M9.d.7.1.	29th		Visited 44 F. Ambulance + selected site for scabies camp. Visited 43 F. Ambulance.	T.P.
	30th		Visited 44 F. Ambulance. Selected sites for First Aid Posts in case of air attacks at FLAVY-LE-MARTEL + JUSSY — MONTESCOURT ROAD.	T.P.
	31st		Attended Medical Board 41 Stationary Hospital. Visited D.R.S. (42 F. Ambulance)	T.P.

T. P. Byrne
Col. A.M.S.
A.D.M.S. 14 Div.

2449 Wt. W14957/M90 750,000 1/16 J.B.C. & A. Forms/C.2118/12.

CONFIDENTIAL.

WAR DIARY.

of

A.D.M.S., 14th. Division.

for month

of

FEBRUARY 1918.

WM 31

140/2782

COMMITTEE FOR THE
MEDICAL HISTORY OF THE WAR
Date -8 APR 1918

20.10.18

Army Form C. 2118.

Instructions regarding War Diaries and Intelligence Summaries are contained in F. S. Regs., Part II. and the Staff Manual respectively. Title Pages will be prepared in manuscript.

WAR DIARY
or
~~INTELLIGENCE SUMMARY~~

(Erase heading not required.)

Map reference. Sheet 66. FRANCE. 66c + 66d.

Place	Date	Hour	Summary of Events and Information	Remarks and references to Appendices
	1918 FEBRUARY			
JUSSY M9.d7.1.	1st		D.D.M.S. III Corps visited 42, 43 + 44 F. Ambulances, and Motor Ambulance Loading Posts at REMIGNY (N14.c.1.7) and BENAY (H21c.9.3.)	T.W. Byrne Col. AMS
	2nd		Visited R.A.P's of six battalions in line at I25.b.2.1, H24c.1.5, H12 a 3.3, H5 c 1.4, H4 b. 3.7, + B27 d 1.9. Also Bearer Relay Posts at CERISY (H23 a 4.4), CHARLOTTE POST (H16 d 5.9), URVILLERS N. (B27 d 2.3) + URVILLERS. S. (H3. b 8.0) + Motor Ambulance Loading Posts at BENAY (H21.c.9.3) + LA SABLIERE Fm. at ESSIGNY (H8.a.5.5)	T.W.B
	3rd		Visited D.D.M.S. III Corps + A.D.M.S. 30th Div.	T.W.B
	4th		Visited 43 F.A., 42 F.A (D.R.S.) + Bomb Casualty Aid Posts at R.E. Park, MONTESCOURT (M4 b.9.0) + MAIRIE, FLAVY-LE-MARTEL (R23 a 8.0 — Sheet 66d)	T.W.B
	5th		Visited Chateau de TIRLANCOURT re Corps Rest Station.	T.W.B
	6th		Visited 43 + 44 F. Ambulances.	T.W.B
	7th		Visited Chateau de TIRLANCOURT. Visited AREA COMMANDANT, JUSSY re site for 43 F.A transport.	T.W.B
	8th		Visited D.R.S. + 44 F.A. re Gas Centre. Visited D.D.M.S. XVIII Corps.	T.W.B
	9th		Sanitary Conference of Q. Masters at D.H.Q. Visited DDMS XVIII Corps	T.W.B

2449 Wt. W14957/M90 750,000 1/16 J.B.C. & A. Forms/C.2118/12.

Instructions regarding War Diaries and Intelligence Summaries are contained in F. S. Regs., Part II. and the Staff Manual respectively. Title Pages will be prepared in manuscript.

WAR DIARY
or
INTELLIGENCE SUMMARY
(Erase heading not required.)

Army Form C. 2118.

Map reference. FRANCE. Sheets 66c + 66d.

Place	Date 1918 FEBRUARY	Hour	Summary of Events and Information	Remarks and references to Appendices
JUSSY. M.9.d.7.1	10th		Conference of A.D's.M.S. at office of D.D.M.S. III Corps.	[illegible]
	11th		D.M.S. Fifth Army visited 43 F. Ambulance at A.D.S. and 44 F. Ambulance. Orders received to proceed as D.D.M.S. XVIII Corps. Visited D.D.M.S. XVIII Corps to arrange taking over.	[illegible]
	12th		Col. H.V. Prynne D.S.O. A.M.S. proceeded to XVIIIth Corps H.Q. to take over duties of D.D.M.S. Routine work in office. Visited 44th F. Amb. to see Lt. Col. Egan ref. Gas Centre:	W. H. [illegible] Capt. D.A.D.M.S. 14th Div
	13th		Wire received that Col. J. Hay Campbell D.S.O. A.M.S. would arrive on 14th to take over duties of A.D.M.S. 14th Div. Routine work in office. Visited Lt. Col. W. Egan. To arrange some details of Defence Scheme	W.H.S.
	14th		Visited 43rd F. Amb. in morning – saw new work in progress. Visited D.A.A.G. ref. billet for 43rd F. Amb. in SUCRERIE, MONTESCOURT. Routine duties in office. Col. J. Hay Campbell D.S.O. A.M.S. arrived to take over duties of A.D.M.S. 14th Div. at 4.30 p.m.	W.H.S.
	15th		A.D.M.S. visited D.Ds.M.S. III rd & XVIIIth Corps – formally taking over from late A.D.M.S. Visited 44th F. Amb. Visited 43rd F.A. & LA SABLIERE FM. Post.	W.H.S.
	16th		~~Visited 44th F.A.~~ A.D.M.S. visited 44 F.A. & inspected site & arrangements for new Gas Centre. A.D.M.S. visited (with) F.A. post at BENAY & CERIZY. A.D.M.S. called on & reported his arrival to G.O.C. [illegible]	W.H.S.

2449 Wt. W14957/M90 750,000 1/16 J.B.C. & A. Forms/C.2118/12.

Instructions regarding War Diaries and Intelligence Summaries are contained in F. S. Regs., Part II. and the Staff Manual respectively. Title Pages will be prepared in manuscript.

WAR DIARY
or
INTELLIGENCE SUMMARY
(Erase heading not required.)

Army Form C. 2118.

Place	Date	Hour	Summary of Events and Information	Remarks and references to Appendices
JUSSY.	February 17th		Routine duties in office, including inspection of men by ADMS for recommendation for P.B. ADMS visited 42nd F. Amb.	W Hepburn Capt for ADMS
	18th		Routine duties in office. Visit from ADMS 58th Div. ref. taking over of F.A. Post at REMIGNY by 43rd F.A. ADMS visited ADV. Div. HQ. to discuss defence scheme with G.S.O. 1.	WHS
	19th		Routine duties in office. ADMS visited F.A. Post at REMIGNY.	
	20th		ADMS attended Conference at DDMS office IIIrd Corps. Central Record Office started. Temp. Gas Centre instituted at JUSSY (44 F.A.)	WHS
	21st		Routine duties. ADMS visited 42nd F.A.	WHS
	22nd		ADMS visited F. Amb. posts & R.A.Ps. in left sector of Divnl. front. Four officers surplus to establishment left to report to ADMS. 24th Div.	WHS
	23rd		Routine duties. ADMS 18th Div. visited ADMS. to arrange taking over of posts on rearrangement of areas. ADMS visited AA & QMG & discussed question of delousing arrangements at baths.	WHS WHS
	24th		Routine duties.	WHS
	25th		DADMS. visited posts in left sector of Divnl. front. ADMS visited & inspected Baths at FLAVY LE MARTEL & 44th. F.A.	WHS
	26th		Routine duties. ADMS visited left sectors of front. ADMS visited 44 F.A. Construction of Gas Centre at 44 F.A. started by REs. 43rd F.A. transport moved from MONTESCOURT to JUSSY. F.A. posts at REMIGNY, LY FONTAINE, CERIZY, MOY & LA GOINGETTE FM taken over by 18th Div.	WHS
	27th		ADMS attended Conference at DDMS IIIrd Corps. ADMS visited DDMS XVIII th Corps & 42nd F. Amb.	WHS
	28th		Routine duties in office. OC 42nd F.A. proceeded on leave. "Battle Zone take precautns. action" message received 1.15 pm. All medical arrangements completed by 5.20 pm. Precautionary message cancelled at 11.15 pm.	WHS WHS.

W Hepburn Capt
for ADMS 14th Div.

2449 Wt. W14957/M90 750,000 1/16 J.B.C. & A. Forms/C.2118/12.

March 18

A.D.M.S. 14 Div.

140/2845

From March 21st 1918

COMMITTEE FOR THE
MEDICAL HISTORY OF THE WAR
Date 12 MAY 1918

4

Instructions regarding War Diaries and Intelligence Summaries are contained in F. S. Regs., Part II, and the Staff Manual respectively. Title pages will be prepared in manuscript.

WAR DIARY
or
INTELLIGENCE SUMMARY.
(Erase heading not required.)

ADMS 14 D

Army Form C. 2118.

Vol 32

Place	Date	Hour	Summary of Events and Information	Remarks and references to Appendices
Jussy	March 21st	12 Noon	All Diary destroyed up to 21st March. The bombardment opened at 4.45 am. The office of A.D.M.S. destroyed by a direct hit from a shell and set on fire, and inconsequence all documents destroyed. The A.D.M.S. moved at 12 noon to Petit ~~De Troit~~. The A.D.S. Montescourt (43rd F.A) / Gas centre (44th F.A) Jussy / D.R.S. (42nd FA) Petit Detroit	
		2 pm	44th F.A. evacuated Jussy and moved to Beaumont en Beine.	
		4 pm	A.D.M.S moved to Beaumont en Beine. The 42nd F.A moved to Beaumont en Beine and opened Main Dressing Station.	
		10.30 pm	43rd F.A vacated Montescourt and moved to Beaumont en Beine leaving a party at Flavy to act as Adv. Dressing Post.	
			Casualties. Capt. R.R. Duncan 43rd F.A. missing. O.R. missing 55. Wounded 5.	
			Abel Thomson Capt. for A.D.M.S 14th Division	
Beaumont en Beine	22.	10 am	44th F.A. sent part to relieve party of 43rd F.A. at Adv. (Dressing) Post - Flavy	
			43rd F.A and 44th F.A moved to Guivry.	
		2 pm	Adv. (Dressing) Post moved back to Cugny.	

D. D. & L., London, E.C. (A7883) Wt. W809/M1672 350,000 4/17 Sch. 52a Forms/C/2118/14

Instructions regarding War Diaries and Intelligence Summaries are contained in F. S. Regs., Part II. and the Staff Manual respectively. Title pages will be prepared in manuscript.

WAR DIARY
or
INTELLIGENCE SUMMARY.
(*Erase heading not required.*)

Army Form C. 2118.

Place	Date	Hour	Summary of Events and Information	Remarks and references to Appendices
	March			
Beaumont-sur-Beine	22nd	2 pm	42nd FA sent up 20 bearers to Adv. Dressing post.	
			Casualties approx. 2 wounded (O.R) NJ	
Beaumont sur Beine	23rd		ADMS moved to Guivry. 43rd F.A. moved to Crisolles. The 42nd and 44th F. Ambces moved to Tirlancourt.	
			44th F.A. opened Adv. Dressing Stn at Tirlancourt. Chateau.	
			Adv. Dressing Post moved to Villeselve. NJ	
Guivry	24th		The A.D.M.S moved to Quesmy; later to Crissoles and at 10 p.m moved back to Lassigny.	
		3 p.m	A.D Stn Tirlancourt, evacuated cases being sent direct to C.C.S. Noyon.	
			A.D. Post. moved to Bouchoir which was evacuated about 6 pm the Infantry of the Division being withdrawn to hold Canal line at Beaurains.	
			42nd — / 43rd Fd Ambulances / 44th — } moved to cavalry barracks Noyon. At 5 p.m all three ambulances moved to Lassigny. The following casualties occurred at Cavalry Barracks Noyon, (all wounded by) Bombs from enemy Aeroplanes. Capt. H.W. Batchelor R.A.M.C. Killed. Lt. F.V. Frazier R.A.M.C. Wounded. 17 O.R. (Killed) 6 O.R. (Wounded) Q.M.S. Beatton R.A.M.C. A.D.M.S. Office Killed. NJ	

D. D. & L., London, E.C. (A7853) Wt W809/M1672 350,000 4/17 Sch. 52a Forms/C/2118/14

Army Form C. 2118.

Instructions regarding War Diaries and Intelligence Summaries are contained in F. S. Regs., Part II, and the Staff Manual respectively. Title pages will be prepared in manuscript.

WAR DIARY
or
INTELLIGENCE SUMMARY.
(Erase heading not required.)

Place	Date	Hour	Summary of Events and Information	Remarks and references to Appendices
Lassigny	25	4am	ADMS arrived at Lassigny.	
		12 noon	ADMS moved to Chiry.	
			42nd F.A } 43rd F.A } moved to Ressons sur Matz. 44th F.A }	
			The O.C. 42nd F.A. detailed small party of 1 Officer and 12. O.R. to open Adv Dressing Post at Beauvains at 12 noon. The wounded evacuated to Roye.	
			Casualties — nil.	
			NS	
Chiry.	26th	3.30 a.m	A.D.M.S. moved to Ribecourt and at 12 noon to Villers sur Coudon. The Infantry of Division held heights around Thiescourt Wood. 44th FA opened Dressing post at Elincourt. wounded evacuated to 16 Hospt. Evacuation Compiegne.	
			42nd } 43rd } F.As moved to road between Coudon and Clairoix 44th }	
			Casualties. Capt. A.W. Webster R.A.M.C. 43rd FA wounded by bomb on way to 53rd F.A. Compiegne	
			NS	

D. D. & L., London, E.C.
(A7883) Wt. W809/M1672 350,000 4/17 Sch. 52a Forms/C/2118/14

Instructions regarding War Diaries and Intelligence Summaries are contained in F. S. Regs., Part II, and the Staff Manual respectively. Title pages will be prepared in manuscript.

WAR DIARY
or
INTELLIGENCE SUMMARY.
(Erase heading not required.)

Army Form C. 2118.

Place	Date	Hour	Summary of Events and Information	Remarks and references to Appendices
	March			
Villers sur Coudon	27	2pm	A.D.M.S. moved to Estrées St. Denis	
			Infantry withdrawn.	
			A.D. Post withdraw at 2pm	
			42nd F.A. to R.E.M.Y	
			43rd F.A. to Estrées St. Denis	
			44th F.A. to Beaupuits. NY.	
Estrées St Denis.	28th	1pm	A.D.M.S moved at 1pm. to Sarron.	
			42nd F.A to Sarron	
			43rd F.A Rieux	
			44th F.A Cinqueux.	
			NY	
Sarron	29th		A.D.M.S moved to Nogent – preparatory to moving elsewhere. Returned to Sarron at 11pm for night.	
			42nd, 43rd, 44th F.A. to Nogent.	
			NY.	

D. D. & L., London, E.C.
(A7883) Wt W809/M1672 350,000 4/17 Sch. 52a Forms/C/2118/14

Army Form C. 2118.

Instructions regarding War Diaries and Intelligence Summaries are contained in F. S. Regs., Part II. and the Staff Manual respectively. Title pages will be prepared in manuscript.

WAR DIARY
or
INTELLIGENCE SUMMARY.
(Erase heading not required.)

Place	Date	Hour	Summary of Events and Information	Remarks and references to Appendices
Sarron	March 30th	10am	A.D.M.S. moved to Hebécourt	
			42nd / 43rd / 44th F.A's commenced to moved by march route to new area South of Amiens	
			M.	
Hebécourt	31st	2pm	Office routine duties.	
			All cases have been evacuated successfuly ~~all along~~ up to date from Field Ambulances.	
			Capt. W. H. Shepherd (D.A.D.M.S.) left for England this morning	

R. Thomson
Capt RAMC
for A.D.M.S.
14th Division

D. D. & L., London, E.C.
(A7883) Wt W809/M1672 350,000 4/17 Sch. 52a. Forms/C/2118/14

April 1/18 7

Vol 33

WAR DIARY of A.D.M.S., 14th (Light) Division.

From. 1/4/18. To. 30/4/18.

****

140/2906.

COMMITTEE FOR THE MEDICAL HISTORY OF THE WAR
Date 6 JUN. 1918

Instructions regarding War Diaries and Intelligence Summaries are contained in F. S. Regs., Part II. and the Staff Manual respectively. Title pages will be prepared in manuscript.

WAR DIARY
or
INTELLIGENCE SUMMARY.
(Erase heading not required.)

Army Form C. 2118.

Place	Date	Hour	Summary of Events and Information	Remarks and references to Appendices
HEBECOURT	1/4/18		ADMS office moved to BOVES (Sheet AMIENS 17 1/100.000)	
			42nd, 43rd and 44th F Ambs moved to HARDEVILLERS. Three M.O. reinforcements arrived	APS
BOVES	2/4/18		ADMS arranged with ADMS 61st Division for evacuation of wounded of 14th Division from the GENTILLE — DOMART line. Car loading posts (14th Division) established at HOURGES and BERTEAUCOURT to assist in evacuation of wounded of 61st Division. 40 Cases were Successfully evacuated from these posts during night 2nd/3rd.	
			42nd and 44th F Ambs moved to FOSSEMANANT. 43rd F Amb moved to BUYON.	APS
"	3/4/18		ADMS office moved to AUBIGNY arriving at 7. p.m.	
			Infantry of 14th Division relieved 1st Cavalry Div. and 16th Div in SAILLY-LE-SEC-WARFUSÉE line. ADMS arranged with ADMS 1st Cav. Div. to take over ADStn at VAIRE-SOUS-CORBIE and RAPs at HAMEL, BOIS DE VAIRE and the W in WARFUSEE. 44th F. Amb took over these posts during the night 3rd/4th. T/Capt A.P. SAINT. M.C. RAMC. took over duties of DADMS vice Capt. W. H. SHEPHARD RAMC (to England)	APS
AUBIGNY	4/4/18		44th F Amb took over M.D. Stn and W.W.C.P. at FOUILLOY from 3rd Cav. F. Amb, relief Completed by 7. a.m. ADMS visited M D Stn at 7.30. a.m.	
		11am	Owing to heavy Shelling RAPs were withdrawn and Concentrated at P.13.b.9.6. (Sheet 62D 1/40,000)	

D. D. & L., London, E.C. (A7883) Wt. W809/M1672 350,000 4/17 Sch. 52a Forms/C/2118/14

Army Form C. 2118.

Instructions regarding War Diaries and Intelligence Summaries are contained in F. S. Regs., Part II. and the Staff Manual respectively. Title pages will be prepared in manuscript.

WAR DIARY
or
INTELLIGENCE SUMMARY.
(Erase heading not required.)

Place	Date	Hour	Summary of Events and Information	Remarks and references to Appendices
AUBIGNY	4/4/18	11 am	A.D.Stn moved to HAMELET. M.D.Stn moved to AUBIGNY. Tent subdivision of 42nd F Amb sent to assist	
			44th F Amb. Three American M.O. (reinforcements) arrived. During night 4th/5th 14th Divn relieved	
			by 3rd Cav. Divn and 5th Australian Inf Bde	
		11 pm	ADMS office moved to GLISY.	
			43rd F Amb took over M.D.Stn at St Acheul (AMIENS) from 7th Cav. F. Amb.	APS
GLISY	5/4/18		All posts operated by 44th F Amb. relieved by 7th Cav F. Amb. Relief complete by 5 am. 44th F Amb on	
			relief moved to GLISY and were placed in charge of Sick Collection from 14th Div. Troops	
			in the BOIS L'ABBE – AUBIGNY reserve line. 44th F. Amb established an A.D.Stn at	
			BLANGY-TRONVILLE in connection with this reserve line. DDMS XIX Corps visited ADMS	APS
GLISY	6/4/18		ADMS visited 43rd F Amb at St ACHEUL and 42nd F Amb at the S in AMIENS. DADMS visited	
			AD.Stn at BLANGY and RAPs at 0.7 a. central, 0 13 d 3.8, and 0.19 b.8.8 (Sheet 62D).	
			T/Capt S.A FORBES RAMC attd 9th R.B. missing (Believed P. of W).	
			Wounded of 14th Division admitted to F Ambs of 14th Divn from noon 20/3/18 to noon 6/4/18. Offs. 44. ORs 1,031.	APS
GLISY	7/4/18		ADMS visited ADStn at BLANGY. ADMS office moved to ST FUSCIEN on relief of 14th Div by	
			5th Australian Inf Bde. 44th F. Amb moved to St ACHEUL. 43rd F Amb handed over M.D.Stn	
			at ST ACHEUL to 55th F Amb.	

D. D. & L., London, E.C.
(A7883) Wt. W809/M1672 350,000 4/17 Sch. 52a Forms/C/2118/14

Instructions regarding War Diaries and Intelligence Summaries are contained in F. S. Regs., Part II. and the Staff Manual respectively. Title pages will be prepared in manuscript.

WAR DIARY
or
INTELLIGENCE SUMMARY.
(*Erase heading not required.*)

Army Form C. 2118.

Place	Date	Hour	Summary of Events and Information	Remarks and references to Appendices
ST. FUSCIEN	8/4/18	11.55am	Transport of all F. Ambs less 3 vehicles per F. Amb moved to FRESNOY DADMS visited all F. Ambs.	APS
"	9/4/18	10.am	Remaining transport of all F Ambs moved to vicinity of AIRAINES (Sheets AMIENS 17 and DIEPPE 16)	APS
"	10/4/18		F. Ambs entrained at SALEUX for GAMACHES area. ADMS office moved to FEUQUIERES (Sheet ABBEVILLE 14)	APS
FEUQUIERES	11/4/18		42nd F. Amb located at BOUVAINCOURT, 43rd F. Amb at OUST-MAREST, 44th F Amb at DARGNIES	
			43rd F Amb entrained at EU, 42nd and 44th F Ambs at FEUQUIERES for FRUGES area (Sheet LENS 11)	
			ADMS office moved to HUCQUELIERS	APS
HUCQUELIERS	12/4/18		42nd F Amb arrived at MANINGHEM, 43rd F Amb at RUMILLY and 44th F Amb CREQUY	
			DADMS visited 42nd F Amb	APS
"	13/4/18		DADMS visited 44th F. Amb	APS
"	14/4/18		43rd F Amb moved to BOYAVAL, 44th F Amb moved to CREPY. 1 MO (reinforcement) arrived.	
			ADMS visited 42nd F. Amb.	APS
"	15/4/18		ADMS office moved to ECQUERDECQUES. 43rd and 44th F. Ambs moved to L'OBLOIS Wood.	
			Lt F.O. TAYLOR. RAMC, 44th F Amb evacuated sick to CCS. 30. ORs (reinforcements) arrived.	
			42nd F Amb detailed to collect sick from 41st Inf Bde details at LISBOURG and 42nd Inf Bde details	
			at LAIRES. 43rd F Amb to collect from re-organised 43rd Inf Bde at MOLINGHEM area	
			and 44th F Amb to collect from Div. HQ and from 2nd Portuguese Inf Bde attached to the Division	APS

D. D. & L., London, E.C.
(A7883) Wt. W809/M1672 350,000 4/17 Sch. 52a Forms/C/2118/14

Instructions regarding War Diaries and Intelligence Summaries are contained in F. S. Regs., Part II. and the Staff Manual respectively. Title pages will be prepared in manuscript.

WAR DIARY
or
INTELLIGENCE SUMMARY.
(Erase heading not required.)

Army Form C. 2118.

Place	Date	Hour	Summary of Events and Information	Remarks and references to Appendices
ECQUERDECQUES	16/4/18		ADMS attended Conference at office DDMS XIIIth Corps	APS
"	17/4/18		ADMS visited 43rd and 44th F. Ambs.	APS
"	18/4/18		DADMS visited 9th R.B. and 43rd F. Amb. Portuguese M.O. att^{d} 44th F. Amb.	APS
"	19/4/18		DDMS XIIIth Corps visited ADMS. ADMS reconnoitred MOLINGHEM—LILLERS Defence line and fixes (provisionally) sites for F. Amb posts and dressing stations. 42nd F Amb moved to CAVRON-ST-MARTIN.	APS
"	20/4/18		ADMS attended Conference at office DMS First Army	APS
"	21/4/18		ADMS office moved to COYECQUE. 44th F Amb moved to ECQUERDECQUES. ADMS reconnoitred WESTREHEM and fixed site for M.D.S/S in event of above defence line having to be occupied.	
COYECQUE	22/4/18		ADMS visited ~~42nd~~ C.R.A at DELETTE	APS
"	23/4/18		ADMS visited 42nd F. Amb	APS
"	24/4/18		ADMS reconnoitred positions for RAPs in connection with Defence Line.	APS
"	25/4/18		ADMS attended Conference at office DMS First Army	APS
"	26/4/18		ADMS inspected Sanitary Condition of ~~[illegible]~~ Camps of Portuguese troops attached. All motor ambulances of 44th F Amb sent to S.M.T.O. XI Corps and struck off strength.	APS
"	27/4/18		4 MOs rendered surplus by formation of skeleton battalion training staffs and despatch of remaining infantry to the Base	APS
"	28/4/18		43rd F. Amb moved to RANNEVILLE	
"	29/4/18		43rd F Amb moved to ROYON. ADMS office moved to TORCY	APS
TORCY	30/4/18		ADMS visited 43rd F. Amb	APS

A P Sargent Capt RAMC
for ADMS

A7092). Wt. W12839/M1293 750,000. 1/17. D. D & L. Ltd. Forms/C2118/14.

4

May 1918.

Vol 34

140/2973.

A.D.M.S.,
14th (Light) Division.
****

WAR DIARY.

From 1st May, 1918.
To, 31st " , 1918.

****

COMMITTEE ... MEDICAL HI...
Date 9 JUL 1918

1/6/18.

Army Form C. 2118.

Instructions regarding War Diaries and Intelligence Summaries are contained in F. S. Regs., Part II. and the Staff Manual respectively. Title pages will be prepared in manuscript.

WAR DIARY
or
INTELLIGENCE SUMMARY.
(Erase heading not required.)

Place	Date	Hour	Summary of Events and Information	Remarks and references to Appendices
TORCY	1/5/18		ADMS visited 43rd F Amb at ROYON. All RMOs except those attached to 14th D.A and R.E. withdrawn to F. Ambs.	APS
"	2/5/18		42nd F Amb moved to BOUBERS (Sheet ABBEVILLE 14) and 43rd F Amb to RIMBOVAL (Sheet CALAIS 13) 4 MOs sent to 11th Division, 4 to 20th Division and 1 to 55th Division	APS
"	3/5/18		DADMS visited 42nd and 43rd F. Ambs	APS
"	4/5/18		2 motor ambulance Cars sent to DMS. L of C and struck off strength	APS
"	5/5/18		ADMS reconnoitred MORBECQUE — LILLERS defence line and arranged scheme of RAPs, Dressing Stations etc. also visited 44th F. Amb	APS.
"	6/5/18		ADMS attended Conference at DDMS office XIth Corps.	APS.
"	7/5/18		Routine duties	APS
"	8/5/18		DADMS visited 42nd F. Amb. Lieut E.M. GRACE RAMC 42nd F. Amb evacuated sick and struck off Strength.	APS
"	9/5/18		ADMS inspected Water Carts of units in the 41st Inf Bde	APS
"	10/5/18	2 a.m.	Orders received (under 14th Div No. A. 829/21) for Training Staff and transport of 42nd F. Amb to report to 77th American Division at NORTKERQUE (Sheet HAZEBROUCK 5A). Sick Collection from 42nd Inf Bde was taken over from 42nd F. Amb by 43rd F. Amb.	
"	"	1.30 p.m.	Party started for NORTKERQUE	
"	"	4. p.m.	Orders received for recall of party. The column was located at BOURTHES (Sheet CALAIS 13) and returned to previous location at BOUBERS the same day, having marched 25 miles.	APS
"	11/5/18		Capt + QM. B.G. BROOK RAMC proceeded to report to DDMS ETAPLES for duty and struck off strength.	APS
"	12/5/18		Routine duties	APS

A7092. Wt. W12839/M1293 750,000. 1/17. D. D & L. Ltd. Forms/C2118/14.

Instructions regarding War Diaries and Intelligence Summaries are contained in F. S. Regs., Part II. and the Staff Manual respectively. Title pages will be prepared in manuscript.

WAR DIARY

or

INTELLIGENCE SUMMARY.

(Erase heading not required.)

Army Form C. 2118.

Place	Date	Hour	Summary of Events and Information	Remarks and references to Appendices
TORCY	13/5/18		Capt + Qr Mr C W HOOK RAMC reported for duty with 42nd F Amb	APS
"	14/5/18		ADMS visited 42nd F Amb	APS
"	15/5/18		ADMS visited ADMS of 16th Division at AIRE re relief of 16th Division by 14th Division	APS
"	16/5/18		43rd F Amb (less advanced party which proceeded direct to AIRE to take over from 111th F Amb) moved to DELETTE.	APS
"	17/5/18		43rd F Amb moved to AIRE (HQ and one section) and LES CISEAUX (two sections).	
"	"	6	ADMS moved to ~~AIRE~~ MOULIN LE COMTE. 6 pm. 42nd F Amb ordered to proceed to 82nd American Division at FRIVILLE-ESCARBOTIN (sheet ABBEVILLE 14) 10 pm. ~~[illegible]~~ move of 42nd F Amb postponed to 19th inst. Detachment of 44th F Amb moved to BOUBERS to take over medical charge of 42nd and 43rd Inf Bdes from 42nd F Amb.	APS
MOULIN-LE-COMTE	18/5/18		ADMS visited 43rd F Amb, 44th F Amb, 14th MT Coy and DDMS XIth Corps.	APS
"	19/5/18		42nd F Amb left BOUBERS at 6 am en route for 82nd American Div at FRIVILLE-ESCARBOTIN 43rd F Amb ~~[illegible]~~ concentrated whole unit at LES CISEAUX ADMS visited 44th F Amb and GSO I Portuguese Inf Div. MOs from 43rd F Amb temporarily attached to 8th KRRC and 8th RB 44th F Amb handed over to Portuguese F Amb at ECQUERDECQUES	APS APS.
"	20/5/18		ADMS visited British Mission att'd 2nd Port Inf Bde	APS
"	21/5/18		ADMS visited 43rd F Amb.	APS
"	22/5/18		ADMS reconnoitred posts & submitted scheme of medical arrangements for ~~the~~ emergency defence of LILLERS – STEENBECQUE line. Also visited 43rd F Amb, 41st Inf Bde HQ and DDMS XIth Corps	APS
"	23/5/18			
"	24/5/18		ADMS visited No 1 ADM Stores	APS
"	25/5/18		ADMS visited 43rd + 44th F Ambs, British Mission to Portuguese, GSO1 Port Inf Division (1st) and DDMS XIth Corps	APS
"	26/5/18		Routine duties.	APS
"	27/5/18		ADMS visited DDMS XIth Corps	APS

A7092. Wt. W12839/M1293 750,000. 1/17. D. D & L Ltd. Forms/C2118/14.

Army Form C. 2118.

WAR DIARY
or
INTELLIGENCE SUMMARY.

(*Erase heading not required.*)

Instructions regarding War Diaries and Intelligence Summaries are contained in F. S. Regs., Part II. and the Staff Manual respectively. Title pages will be prepared in manuscript.

Place	Date	Hour	Summary of Events and Information	Remarks and references to Appendices
MOULIN-LE-COMTE	28/5/18		43rd F Amb (with equipment and transport complete and with training staff) left LES CISEAUX en route for 35th U.S.A. Division at EU. (Sheet ABBEVILLE 14). The duties of this F Amb were transferred to Surplus personnel remaining.	
			44th F Amb (with equipment and transport complete and with training staff) left ECQUERDECQUES and TORCY en route for NIELLES-BLEQUIN (Sheet HAZEBROUCK 5A) and 28th USA Division.	APS.
			ADMS attended Conference on Sanitation at office of DDMS XIth Corps	APS
"	29/5/18		ADMS reconnoitred position for W.W.C.P. for LILLERS - STEENBECQUE Defence line. Surplus personnel of 43rd and 44th F Amb less 36 ORs of 44th F Amb proceeded by train to RAMC Base Depot	APS
"	30/5/18		ADMS inspected Sanitation of 8th KRRC and attd Composite battalion at PECQUEUR	
"	31/5/18		ADMS and DADMS attended Divisional Conference on Sanitation. ADMS First Army visited ADMS re Surplus personnel of F Ambs and medical dispositions for present requirements of Division and attached troops. 36 surplus O.Rs of 44th F Amb proceeded from TORCY by lorry to 44th F Amb at NIELLES-BLEQUIN	APS

A.P. Saint Capt RAMC
DADMS 14th Division

6

June 1918

35

140/3073.

***************** 14th DIVISION&***************

*******A.D.M.S.********

WAR DIARY FOR MONTH OF JUNE 1918

****

Instructions regarding War Diaries and Intelligence Summaries are contained in F. S. Regs., Part II. and the Staff Manual respectively. Title pages will be prepared in manuscript.

WAR DIARY
or
INTELLIGENCE SUMMARY.
(Erase heading not required.)

Army Form C. 2118.

Place	Date	Hour	Summary of Events and Information	Remarks and references to Appendices
FOULIN-LE-COMTE	1/6/18		Routine duties	APS
"	2/6/18		ADMS visited British Mission 1st Port Divn. DDMS Xth Corps visited ADMS. DADMS inspected watercarts in 41st Inf Bde Competition.	APS
"	3/6/18		ADMS visited MO. 14th Div. R.E. re suspected diptheria cases at St Quentin DADMS visited MO of 5th RIF attached from 3/6/18 to 14th Division	APS
"	4/6/18		DADMS visited No 2 RAMC Detachment (of 44th F Amb left with 14th Divn) at TORCY	APS
"	5/6/18		ADMS inspected Sanitation of 8th R.B at STEENBECQUE	APS
"	6/6/18		Routine duties	APS
"	7/6/18		ADMS visited 5th R.I.F. at MANQUEVILLE (sheet 36A)	APS
"	8/6/18		ADMS attended First Army DMS Conference at PERNES. DADMS visited M.O 68th Labour Group at TREIZENNES	APS
"	9/6/18		ADMS visited No 8 RAMC Detachment, 5th Connaught Rangers, 6th Leinster Regt and 41st Inf Bde HQ. 8 American MOs reported for duty in replacement of MOs of 43rd and 44th F Ambs detached for duty with 14th Divn.	APS
"	10/6/18		ADMS visited chateau at TREIZENNES with a view to its suitability for N.D.R.S	APS
"	11/6/18		ADMS visited American MOs with No 8 Detachment also visited No 3 Detachment	APS
"	12/6/18		Routine duties	APS
"	13/6/18		ADMS inspected billets of 61st Field Coy R.E at MOLINGHEM and visited No 20 Mobile Lab at AIRE re examination of battalions from Palestine for malaria. American MOs doing duty with 14th Division taken on the strength of No 54 C.C Stn	APS
"	14/6/18		administration of 1st Portuguese Division passed from 14th Division to Xth Corps. Orders received for Division to proceed to England	APS
"	15/6/18		MOs & ORs of 44th F Amb at TORCY rejoined their unit	
"	16/6/18		Supply personnel of 43rd F Amb at LES CISEAUX rejoined unit and Supplies personnel of 44 F Amb at ECQUEDECQUES rejoined 44th F Amb. ADMS office handed over to DADMS Xth Corps. Div. HQ proceeded to BOULOGNE	APS

Instructions regarding War Diaries and Intelligence Summaries are contained in F. S. Regs., Part II. and the Staff Manual respectively. Title pages will be prepared in manuscript.

WAR DIARY
or
INTELLIGENCE SUMMARY.
(Erase heading not required.)

Army Form C. 2118.

Place	Date	Hour	Summary of Events and Information	Remarks and references to Appendices
BOULOGNE	17/6/18		Div. H.Q. moved to Stoney Castle Camp (near BROOKWOOD). (Map sheet ALDERSHOT NORTH) via FOLKESTONE and CLAPHAM JUNCTION. 41st Bde also proceeded to Stoney Castle Camp. 42nd Bde moved to COWSHOTT Camp and 40th Bde to Bullswater Camp.	APS
STONEY CASTLE CAMP	18/6/18		ADMS visited DDMS Aldershot Command.	APS
"	19/6/18		DDMS A.C. visited ADMS.	APS
"	20/6/18		ADMS visited COWSHOTT CAMP	APS
"	21/6/18		ADMS visited BULLSWATER CAMP	APS
"	22/6/18		Dental Surgeon allotted to each Brigade Camp. Large numbers of Influenza cases occurring. All battalions now have RMO attached	APS APS APS
"	23/6/18		41st Inf Bde troops inspected by Brig. General BEATTIE. AMS	APS
"	24/6/18		Numbers of Influenza cases increasing	
"	25/6/18		42nd Inf Bde troops inspected by General BEATTIE. Special Medical Boards met to ~~examine~~ cases reported unfit for overseas.	APS
"	26/6/18		40th Inf Bde troops inspected by General BEATTIE.	APS
"	27/6/18		All battalions now complete with F.M. Equipment. DADMS A.C. visited all camps with reference to arrangements for	APS
	28/6/18		treating Influenza.	
"	29/6/18		Mobile Sprays working in Brigade camps for Influenza prophylaxis. DDMS visited Camps.	APS
"	30/6/18		Special Medical Boards met at COWSHOTT Camp to examine men of 42nd Inf Bde reported unfit for overseas.	APS

A P Saint Major RAMC
DADMS 14 Div

A7092. Wt. W12839/M1293 750,000. 1/17. D. D & L. Ltd. Forms/C2118/14.

4

14th Division.
****

W A R   D I A R Y .
****

July 1918.

Period:- From,
1st July, 1918.
To,
31st July, 1918.

For,
A.D.M.S.,
14th Division.

COMMITTEE FOR THE
MEDICAL HISTORY
Date 6 SEP.

98/36
140/3123.

Army Form C. 2118.

WAR DIARY
or
INTELLIGENCE SUMMARY.
(Erase heading not required.)

Instructions regarding War Diaries and Intelligence Summaries are contained in F. S. Regs., Part II. and the Staff Manual respectively. Title pages will be prepared in manuscript.

Place	Date	Hour	Summary of Events and Information	Remarks and references to Appendices
BROOKWOOD (England)	1/7/18		Special Medical Boards classified men of 43rd Inf Bde ~~[illegible]~~ reported unfit for GS and also similar men of 42nd Inf Bde. DADMS attended Boards.	A.P.S.
"	2/7/18		Special Medical Board met at Camp of 43rd Inf Bde to classify men reported unfit for GS. DADMS attended Boards.	A.P.S.
"	3/7/18		Div. HQ entrained at BROOKWOOD for FRANCE at 10.35 pm and arrived FOLKESTONE at 2 am (4th inst)	A.P.S.
FOLKESTONE	4/7/18		Div HQ arrived at WIERRE EFFROY (Sheet CALAIS 13)	A.P.S.
WIERRE EFFROY	5/7/18		ADMS visited DDMS BOULOGNE. One Ambulance Car sent to the Division from 44th F Amb for evacuating sick of Division.	A.P.S.
"	6/7/18		43rd F Amb rejoined Div and proceeded to FOUHEN. 44th F Amb rejoined Division and proceeded to BASSE WIOVES. ADMS visited 44th F Amb.	A.P.S.
"	7/7/18		DDMS VIIth Corps visited ADMS. ADMS visited 43rd F Amb. DADMS visited 14th MG Battn.	A.P.S.
"	8/7/18		ADMS with Chief Inspector of Drafts visited 18th York & Lancs Regt and 29th Durh. L.I. DADMS visited 14th M.T. Coy. 4 American M.Os reported for duty.	A.P.S.
"	9/7/18		DADMS visited 42nd Bde HQ. 42nd F Amb rejoined Division and proceeded to PERNES	A.P.S.
"	10/7/18		44th F Amb proceeded to LICQUES area with the 41st Inf Bde and were billeted at LA BREUIL	A.P.S.
"	11/7/18		42nd F Amb moved to FOUHEN, ~~[illegible]~~ 43rd F Amb to LA BREUIL and 44th F Amb to HELVELINGHEM (Sheet HAZEBROUCK 5.A)	A.P.S.
"	12/7/18		ADMS office moved to EPERLECQUES, 42nd F Amb to LA BREUIL, 43rd F Amb to LOUCHES and 44th F Amb to WATTEN. ADMS visited DDMS VIIth Corps	A.P.S.
EPERLECQUES	13/7/18		ADMS with DDMS visited WINNIZEELE area re medical arrangements for detachment of 14 Div proceeding shortly to work on trench lines. DADMS visited 44th F Amb re proposed site for DRS hut at WATTEN and extension of DRS at HELST.	A.P.S.
"	14/7/18		Routine duties.	A.P.S.

A7092. Wt. W12839/M1293 750,000. 1/17. D. D & L. Ltd. Forms/C2118/14.

Army Form C. 2118.

Instructions regarding War Diaries and Intelligence Summaries are contained in F. S. Regs., Part II. and the Staff Manual respectively. Title pages will be prepared in manuscript.

WAR DIARY
or
INTELLIGENCE SUMMARY.
(Erase heading not required.)

Place	Date	Hour	Summary of Events and Information	Remarks and references to Appendices
EPERLECQUES	16/7/18		ADMS visited 42nd and 43rd F Ambs	APS
"	16/7/18		DDMS VIIth Corps also O.C. 56th San Sec visited ADMS.	APS
"	17/7/18		DADMS visited ADMS. ADMS visited D.R.S.	APS
"	18/7/18		ADMS accompanied Med Inspector of Drafts to regiments of the Division where unfit men were reclassified. Capt. R THOMSON attached for instruction to ADMS office	APS
"	19/7/18		G.O.C. Division inspected all F Ambs and was accompanied by ADMS. DADMS accompanied Med Inspector of Drafts to see remainder of men paraded for reclassification	APS
"	20/7/18		ADMS visited 44th F Amb.	APS
"	21/7/18		ADMS attended Divisional Conference with GOC as President at which [illegible] [illegible] and other questions were discussed	APS
"	22/7/18		Routine duties	APS
"	23/7/18		ADMS went to CASSEL area to reconnoitre positions for Dressing Stations in connection with the WINNEZEELE line. ADMS Corps visited ADMS.	APS
"	24/7/18		ADMS visited DR Stn.	APS
"	25/7/18		DADMS visited 42nd and 43rd F Ambs	APS
"	26/7/18		Routine duties	APS
"	27/7/18		ADMS visited 42nd F Amb	APS
"	28/7/18		ADMS visited Refilling Point. DADMS visited XIth CCS	APS
"	29/7/18		Routine duties	APS
"	30/7/18		Routine duties	APS
"	31/7/18		DDMS VIIth Corps visited ADMS.	

14th DIVISION.
* * * * * * *

W A R   D I A R Y

for

A.D.M.S., 14th DIVISION,

From, 1st August, 1918.
To, 31st August, 1918.

1/9/18.

COMMITTEE FOR THE
MEDICAL HISTORY OF THE
Date 5 OCT 1918

Army Form C. 2118.

Instructions regarding War Diaries and Intelligence Summaries are contained in F. S. Regs., Part II. and the Staff Manual respectively. Title pages will be prepared in manuscript.

WAR DIARY
or
INTELLIGENCE SUMMARY.
(Erase heading not required.)

Place	Date	Hour	Summary of Events and Information	Remarks and references to Appendices
EPERLECQUES	1/8/18		ADMS visited 10th HLI at CAESTRE, 61st Coy RE at WALLEN CAPPEL and also ADsMS of 9th and 31st Divs re medical arrangements for the above named units. One officer reinforcement received	[illegible]
"	2/8/18		ADMS inspected Sanitation of 14th Signal Coy.	[illegible]
"	3/8/18		ADMS visited 44 F Amb. 20 ORs (reinforcements) received	[illegible]
"	4/8/18		DADMS visited OC 56th San Sec.	[illegible]
"	5/8/18		DDMS VII Corps visited ADMS	[illegible]
"	6/8/18		Routine duties. Capt Goodman, Edwin W. M.O.R.C. USA reported for duty and placed on strength of 44th F.A	Abel Thomson (Capt RAMC)
"	7/8/18		Routine duties. D.A.D.M.S. proceeded on Leave to England. Capt R. Thomson R.A.M.C. acting as D.A.D.M.S.	[illegible]
"	8/8/18		A.D.M.S visited Divl Rest Station (44th F.A.). The acting DAD.M.S inspected Sanitation of 89th Fd Coy RE., also water carts of No.3. and No.4 Coys Train.	[illegible]
"	9/8/18		A.D.M.S visited 42. F.A.	[illegible]
"	10/8/18		DDMS VII Corps visited A.D.M.S. The A.D.M.S inspected 43rd F.A	[illegible]
"	11/8/18		A.D.M.S Examined men for reclassification.	[illegible]
"	12/8/18		DDMS. VII Corps visited AD.M.S.	[illegible]
"	13/8/18		The 43rd F.A. moved by march route from Zudrove to LEDERZEELE, with the 43rd Brigade group. The G.O.C. and A.D.M.S. inspected D.R.S (44th F.A.) at WATTEN	[illegible]
"	14/8/18		43rd F.A. moved by march route from LEDERZEELE to BISSEZEELE.	[illegible]
"	15/8/18		43rd F.A. moved by march route from BISSEZEELE to DROGLANDT (27/K 1 C 0.0).	[illegible]
	16/8/18		Routine duties	[illegible]

A7092. Wt. W12839/M1293 750,000. 1/17. D. D & I. Ltd. Forms/C2118/14.

Instructions regarding War Diaries and Intelligence Summaries are contained in F. S. Regs., Part II. and the Staff Manual respectively. Title pages will be prepared in manuscript.

WAR DIARY
or
INTELLIGENCE SUMMARY.
(Erase heading not required.)

Army Form C. 2118.

Place	Date	Hour	Summary of Events and Information	Remarks and references to Appendices
EPERLECQUES.	17/8/18.		Routine duties	NJ.
"	18/8/18.		A.D.M.S. inspected 3rd (S.A.A.) Sect D.A.C. TOURNEHEM. 43rd F.A. ~~established~~ moved (NJ) to HARINGHEN.	NJ.
"	19/8/18		42nd F.A. moved from HELVELINGHEM to AUTINGUES by march route.	NJ
COUTHOVE (CHATEAU)	20/8/18		The A.D.M.S Office established at COUTHOVE CHATEAU. The 44th F.A. moved to 27F25 d 8·8 (Ambulance Farm).	NJ.
"	21/8/18		The A.D.M.S visited D.D.M.S. IInd Corps; 44th FA at AMBULANCE FARM; and 43rd F.A. at SOLTAU CAMP (HARINGHEN), where a Divisional Rest station has been established	NJ
"	22/8/18		D.D.M.S II Corps visited A.D.M.S.	NJ.
"	23/8/18.		42nd F.A moved from Eperlecque Area to SCOUT CAMP 27/F 28 C.7.4. The D.A.D.M.S returned from Leave. The A.D.M.S proceeded on leave to England. Lt Col. Egan acting as A.D.M.S. The A.D.M.S. visited A.D.M.S 34th Division	NJ.
"	24/8/18		ADMS visited 42nd, 43rd and 44th F.Ambs	APS
"	25/8/18		ADMS visited O.C. 104th F Amb at A.D.S. of 34th Divn, 43rd Bde HQ (in the line), 61st and 62nd Field Coys RE, ADMS 34th Divn and DDMS IInd Corps	APS
"	26/8/18		ADMS visited ADMS 34th Div. 15 reinforcements (O.Rs) reported for duty. Orders received from 14th Div. G for 14th Div to relieve 34th (British) Division in the left Divisional Sector of the IInd Corps line.	APS.

(A9175) Wt W2138/P360 600,000 12/17 D. D. & L. Sch. 52a. Forms/C2118/15.

Instructions regarding War Diaries and Intelligence Summaries are contained in F. S. Regs., Part II. and the Staff Manual respectively. Title pages will be prepared in manuscript.

WAR DIARY
or
INTELLIGENCE SUMMARY.
(Erase heading not required.)

Army Form C. 2118.

Place	Date	Hour	Summary of Events and Information	Remarks and references to Appendices
CHATEAU COUTHOVE	27/8/18		ADMS visited DDMS IInd Corps, ADMS 34th Div, 42nd 43^d and 44th F Ambs. DADMS visited RTO MENDINGHEM re conveyance of 120 ORs of 44th F Amb to BOLLEZEELE (Corps Rest Station)	
			Advance party of 42nd F Amb took over forward posts of 104th F Amb (incl. A.D.Stn at 28/A.30.central)	APS
"	28/8/18		42nd F Amb completed relief of 104th F Amb in the line. 43rd F Amb relieved the 102nd F Amb at the Main Dressing Station LEISHMAN Camp (19/W 23 a.3.8).	
			44th F Amb relieved 103rd F Amb at the IInd Corps Rest Station BOLLEZEELE (27/A 22 C&d) and detachment of 103rd F Amb at L'EBBE FARM (27/F.29.b8.2).	APS
			ADMS visited 44th F Amb.	
"	29/8/18		ADMS visited L'EBBE FARM, Corps Rest Station and DDMS IInd Corps	APS
"	30/8/18		DADMS visited 43rd F Amb.	APS
"	31/8/18		ADMS visited A.D.Stn with reference chiefly to delousing chambers	APS
			DADMS visited L'EBBE FARM (44th F Amb)	

A P Saint Major
RAMC
DADMS 14th Div^n

(A9175) Wt W2358/P363 600,000 12/17 D. D. & L. Sch. 52a. Forms/C2118/15.

4

9R 38

WAR DIARY

of

A.D.M.S., 14th Division.

****

September 1918

From:- 1/9/18.

To:- 30/9/18.

140/3262

A.D.M.S. Division 14

To,
D.A.G.,
G.H.Q., 3rd Echelon.

COMMITTEE FOR THE
MEDICAL HISTORY OF THE WAR
Date 9 NOV.1918

Records D A C

Army Form C. 2118.

Instructions regarding War Diaries and Intelligence Summaries are contained in F. S. Regs., Part II. and the Staff Manual respectively. Title pages will be prepared in manuscript.

WAR DIARY
or
INTELLIGENCE SUMMARY.
(Erase heading not required.)

Place	Date	Hour	Summary of Events and Information	Remarks and references to Appendices
CHATEAU COUTHOVE	1/9/18		A/ADMS visited No 2 Coy Train and examined men preparatory to their being reclassified by M.I.D	APS
"	2/9/18		A/ADMS visited No 3 Coy Train and also the AD Stn, Collecting Post (DEAD END) and all RAPs	APS
"	3/9/18		A/ADMS visited No 4 Coy Train	APS
"	4/9/18		A/ADMS visited 44th F Amb (C.R. Stn) with the AA & QMG 14th Div. DADMS visited Nos 29 and 12 Light Railway Operating Coys re train arrangements for AD Stn	APS
"	5/9/18		A/ADMS visited detachment of 44th F Amb at L'Ebbe Farm. DADMS visited DDMS IInd Corps	APS
"	6/9/18		DADMS visited AD Stn and also HQs of 41st, 42nd and 43rd Inf Bdes	APS
"	7/9/18		A/ADMS visited DDMS IInd Corps. DADMS visited Divisional Gas Centre (43rd F Amb) ADMS returned from leave	APS
"	8/9/18		DDMS IInd Corps visited ADMS. DADMS visited 43rd F Amb	APS
"	9/9/18		ADMS visited AD Stn, Collecting Post at DEAD END and DUHALLOW railhead	APS
"	10/9/18		ADMS visited M.D. Stn and inspected Sanitation of 20th Middlesex Regt at BRAKE CAMP 28/A.30.	APS
"	11/9/18		ADMS visited all RAPs.	APS
"	12/9/18		DADMS visited MD Stn and also PUGWASH and SIDNEY light railway Sidings	APS
"	13/9/18		ADMS visited HQ train with M.I.D. who reclassified 70 men of Div^l Train. DADMS visited R.T.O. MENDINGHEM re conveyance of 44th F Amb personnel from ~~HE~~ BOLLEZEELE to POPERINGHE	APS

(A9175) Wt W2353/P36 600,000 12/17 D. D. & L. Sch. 52a. Forms/C2118/15.

Instructions regarding War Diaries and Intelligence Summaries are contained in F. S. Regs., Part II. and the Staff Manual respectively. Title pages will be prepared in manuscript.

WAR DIARY
or
INTELLIGENCE SUMMARY.
(Erase heading not required.)

Army Form C. 2118.

Place	Date	Hour	Summary of Events and Information	Remarks and references to Appendices
COUTHOVE ~~14/9/18~~	14/9/18		ADMS visited MDStn, ADStn, L'EBBE FARM and DDMS IInd Corps.	APS
"	15/9/18		ADMS 9th Div visited ADMS. DADMS inspected Sanitation of Mobile Vet Sec.	APS
"	16/9/18		43rd F Amb move from ROUSBRUGGE and occupy BOWLBY CAMP (27/E6 d central)	
"			as a MDSn, DRS and Divisional Gas Centre. ADMS visited 10th HLI at SCHOOL CAMP (27/L3 c 9.6)	APS
"	17/9/18		ADMS visited TAVISTOCK HOUSE (28/H1 b 7.1.) re Construction of new road to the	
			WWCP there. DADMS visited XIXth Corps (DDMS)	APS.
"	18/9/18		ADMS visited Area Commandant DICKEBUSCH area re Sites for F Ambs, also visited	
			DDMS IInd Corps and ADsMS 29th and 36th Divs	APS
"	19/9/18		14th Division transferred to XIXth Corps. 44th F Amb took over part of MDStn (28/H.8. a. 9.8)	
			from 36th Div and the ADStn (28/H29. c. 3 6) from 41st Div. 9th Divn took over ADStn	
			(28/A30 central) and forward Posts from 42nd F Amb. ADMS visited 43rd F Amb (27/E6. central),	
			ADStn and DDMS IInd Corps. DADMS visited DDMS XIXth Corps & Area Commandant DICKEBUSCH	APS
"	20/9/18		43rd F Amb. moved to Trappist Farm (27/K17 b. 1. 4). 42nd F Amb moved to HILLHOEK (27/L14 d cent)	
			ADMS office moved to ORWELL FARM (28/G19. d). ADMS visited ADStn (28/H29 c. 3. 6) and RAPs at	
			(28/H24 c. 1. 2.) also 42nd F Amb at HILLHOEK. ADMS 9th Div. took over from ADMS at COUTHOVE	APS.
ORWELL FARM.	21/9/18		ADMS attended Conference of ADMSs assembled by DDMS XIXth Corps. Reconnoitred proposed MDStn at	
			LONG BARN (28/G30 d 5.7) and chose site for Div. WWCP at 28/H.23 c.5.4. Visited both these sites later with Adjutant RE. re improvements.	APS.

(A9175) Wt W2359/P360 600,000 12/17 D. D. & L. Sch. 52a. Forms/C2118/15.

Army Form C. 2118.

Instructions regarding War Diaries and Intelligence Summaries are contained in F. S. Regs., Part II. and the Staff Manual respectively. Title pages will be prepared in manuscript.

WAR DIARY
or
INTELLIGENCE SUMMARY.
(Erase heading not required.)

Place	Date	Hour	Summary of Events and Information	Remarks and references to Appendices
[illegible]RWELL FARM.	22/9/18		Visited MDStn (28/H8 a. 98) and ADStns and RAPs. 4 officer reinforcements reported for duty. Visited D. R. Stn HILLHOEK (42nd F Amb) and 43rd F. Amb at TRAPPIST FARM	APS
"	23/9/18		42nd F Amb establish a D.R. Stn at ARNEKE (27/H24 a). 43rd F Amb took over Site at WHITE FARM (27/L23.a 6.0) from 139th F Amb including the Advanced Army Dysentery Centre. 44th F Amb establish a M.D Stn at LONGBARN. Visited 42nd Bde HQ and MD Stn. also 43rd Bde HQ re proposed RAPs. DADMS visited 43rd F Amb at WHITE FARM.	APS
"	24/9/18		Visited MDStn, 15th L.N. Lancs Regt and 14th M.G. Bn. Visited MDStn with RE re improvements visited 43rd F Amb. DDMS XIX Corps visited ADMS.	APS
"	25/9/18		43rd F Amb supply tent subdiv. to Corps WWC. Stn at BRANDHOEK (28/A12 b.8.4). Visited MDStn and Corps WWC Stn.	APS
"	26/9/18		DMS II Army visited MDStn. DADMS visited 43rd F Amb	APS
"	27/9/18		Visited MDStn. ADStn and RAPs and 43rd F Amb.	APS
"	28/9/18		14th Div commenced an attack on ST ELOI CRATERS and THE BLUFF. All objectives captured within 2 hours (Zero hour 5.30 am). DADMS visited RAPs, ADStn, Div WWCP and MDStn. ADMS later visited Medical Posts. Bearer Relay Post and Car post pushed forward to VOORMEZEELE.	
"	29/9/18		Wounded of 14th Division troops admitted between Zero (5.30 am) ~~and~~ on 28th inst to 5.30 am on 30th was 191 ORs and 2 officers. 14th Div Infantry withdrawn to DICKEBUSCH area. ADMS office moved to 27/K24 C.2.3. Visited MDStn, ADStn and Div WWCP and 43rd F Amb.	APS
27/K24.C.2.3.	30/9/18		Visited ~~43rd F Amb~~ 44th F Amb concentrate at LONGBARN. ADMS office moved to 28/B15.a 5.1.	APS

A S Saint[illegible] Major DADMS. 14th Div.

(A8795) Wt W2358/P1063 500,000 12/17 D. D. & L. Sch. 52a. Forms/C2118/15.

SECRET. DIARY. Copy No. 34

R.A.M.C. OPERATION ORDER No. 14 by Colonel J. Hay Campbell, D.S.O., A.M.S., Commanding R.A.M.Corps, 14th DIVISION.

Reference Maps - Shoets 27 and 28, 1/40,000.

1. (a) The 14th (British) Division on a date and at a time to be notified later will carry out an attack, the first objectives of which are the St.ELOI Craters and The BLUFF.

(b) The 42nd Infantry Brigade will be on the right, the 43rd Infantry Brigade on the left and the 41st Infantry Brigade in Reserve.

(c) For the purpose of this attack,

J. = Day of attack.
H. = Hour of Zero.

Any particular day before the attack will be shown as,

J - 1, etc.

Any particular time before Zero

4 - 1 hour 10" etc.

Similarly days and times after will be shown as

J + 1, H + 20" etc.

2. (a) At the commencement of the attack Regimental Aid Posts will be located as follows:-

42nd Infantry Bde: 28/I.31 c 2.9. (Double)
Support Bn: 28/H.36 c 7.8.

43rd Infantry Bde: 28/H.24 c 1.2.
28/H.30.central.
Support Bn: 28/H.24 c 1.2.

(b) Should the tactical situation permit, Regimental Medical Officers, after consultation where possible with the O.C. Unit, will advance their R.A.Ps. in accordance with the progress of the attack.

Any such change will be reported immediately by the Medical Officer concerned to the O.C., 44th Field Ambulance at the Advanced Dressing Station (28/H.29 c 3.6.), particular care being taken to notify the time of despatch on all reports.

All communications from R.M.Os. with reference to progress or requirements will be similarly addressed.

(c) At H - 4 hours the O.C., 44th Field Ambulance will despatch 3 squads of 4 bearers to the 42nd Infantry Brigade R.A.P. (Double), 2 ½ squads to each of the 43rd Infantry Brigade R.A.Ps. and 1 squad to each Support Bn: R.A.P..

Bearer Officers of the 44th Field Ambulance will keep in touch with R.M.Os.

(d) As R.A.Ps. are advanced, Bearer Relay Posts will be established by the 44th Field Ambulance between R.A.Ps. and the A.D.Station.

3. (a) The O.C., 44th Field Ambulance will be responsible for the evacuation of casualties from R.A.Ps. as far as the Main Dressing Station, and the Corps W.W.C.Station, BRANDHOEK, 28/G.12 b 9.4., and for this purpose the following posts have been established.

3. (a) contd.

A.D. Station ... 28/H.29 c 3.6.

Divl: W.W.C.Post . 28/H.35 c 5.4.

M. D. Station ... LONGBARN, 28/G.30 d 5.7.

Gas Centre ... 28/G.30 b 0.9.

Directing Boards from R.A.Ps. to Divl: W.W.C.P. and A.D.Station will be erected after dark on J - 1 day.

(b) The Bearer Divisions of the 42nd and 43rd Field Ambulances will be at the disposal of O.C., 44th Field Ambulance, and in addition a party of not less than 200 strong with the usual proportion of Officers and N.C.Os. from the Battalion in Brigade Reserve will be available for employment as extra bearers in case of necessity.

O.C., 44th Field Ambulance will apply direct to Advanced Divisional H.Q. (HAGUE FARM, 28/H.31 a 6.9.), if he considers it necessary to use this party.

4. Method of evacuation of wounded.

(a) Wounded unable to walk.

To R.A.Ps.
By Regimental Stretcher Bearers.

From R.A.Ps to A.D.Station.
By Field Ambulance Bearers.

The fullest use will be made of the Monorail running from VOORMEZEELE to HEMMEL Dump (H.29 b 2.3.) O.C., 44th Field Ambulance will furnish a control post for the Monorail trucks at the corner of ENGLISH WOOD (28/H.29 d 2.2.).

Two Light Railway trucks will be handed over at VIJVERHOEK Siding to O.i/c A.D. Station on J - 1 day for conveyance of cases on the Light Railway between R.A.Ps. at 28/H.24 c 1.2. and the A.D.Station

If the situation permits Ambulance Cars will be sent as far forward as possible on the CAFE BELGE - VOORMEZEELE Road.

On receiving orders from the A.D.M.S. the O.C., 44th Field Ambulance will move forward the A.D.Station to the neighbourhood of VOORMEZEELE or SPOIL BANK. Personnel for this purpose will be earmarked in advance.

From A.D.Station to M.D.Station.
By Divisional Ambulance Cars.

From M.D.Station to C.C.Station.
By M.A.C.Cars. O.C., No. 2 M.A.C. is on the telephone through 14th Division exchange.

Certain special cases for immediate operation will be sent through in Divisional Ambulance Cars direct to C.C.Stations, in which case A.T.Serum will be given at the A.D.Station and Field Medical Cards marked accordingly, particulars of the case being sent to Main Dressing Station on A.F. W.3210 for record. With this exception A.T.Serum will not be administered in advance of M.D.Station and Corps W.W.C.Station

4. contd. .

(b) Wlaking Wounded.

To Divisional W.W.C.P. on foot or returning vehicles, thence to Corps W.W.C.Station by Lorry.

At Zero hour 8 lorries will be sent forward to the M.D.Station, and 4 to the Corps W.W.C.Station, BRANDHOEK. They will be at the disposal of the O. i/c Divisional W.W.C.P., who will control their movement between the Divisional W.W.C.P. and the Corps W.W.C.Station, BRANDHOEK.

Any Walking Wounded arriving at the Main Dressing Station will be conveyed by Light Railway from NAPIER SIDING (28/G.30 a 3.8.) to the Corps W.W.C.Station, BRANDHOEK. A train of three trucks will be stationed at NAPIER SIDING at H + 3 hours for use as required.

(c) Soldiers fit to return to duty.

These will be sent to the Straggler Posts at OUDERDOM, 28/G.30 c 6.9., and Infantry Brigade H.Q.S by arrangement with the D.A.P.M.

5. Corps W.W.C.Station.

The O.C., 43rd Field Ambulance will place one Tent Sub Division at the disposal of O.C., 105th Field Ambulance at the Corps W.W.C.Station, BRANDHOEK. This Tent Sub Division will be responsible for the dressing and recording of 14th Division casualties passing through the Corps W.W.C.Station.

6. The O.C., 43rd Field Ambulance will detail a Medical Officer as Detraining Medical Officer, REMY Light Railway Siding and an unloading party consisting of 1 N.C.O. and 8 men.

The D.M.O. will be responsible for the detraining of Walking Wounded and lying slightly wounded arriving for C.C.Stns.

7. RECORDS and REPORTS.

All wounded arriving at the Main Dressing Station will be shown as admissions to 44th Field Ambulance.

Wounded of the 14th Division passing through the Corps W.W.C.Station will be shown as admissions to 43rd Field Ambulance, and the O.C., 43rd Field Ambulance will send a D.R. to the Corps W.W.C.Station daily at 8 a.m. to collect A.Fs. W.3210 in respect of these cases.

A D.R. from the A.D.M.S. Office will call at the Corps W.W.C.Station every three hours after Zero for reports as to the number of wounded (14th Division only) admitted during the previous three hours.

The O.C., 44th Field Ambulance will send a report to this Office every three hours after Zero containing the figures for British and German wounded admitted to the M.D.Station during the previous three hours.

8. The A.D.M.S. Office will remain at ORWELL FARM, 28/G.19 d 4.2.

A.P. Saint

26/9/18.

Major,

for Colonel, A.D.M.S.,

Distribution:-

Copy No 1. O.C., 42nd Field Ambulance.
2. " 43rd " "
3. " 44th " "
4 -17. All R.M.Os.
18. E.M.O. BRANDHOEK.
19. 14th Division "G".
20. " " "A".
21. C.R.E., 14th Division.
22. O.C., 14th Signal Coy.
23. H.Q., 41st Infantry Bde.
24. " 42nd " "
25. " 43rd " "
26. O.C., 15th L.N.Lancs: Regt:.
27. " 14th Bn: M.G.C.
28. D. G. O.
29. D.D.M.S., XIX Corps.
30. A.D.M.S., 35th Division.
31. A.D.M.S., 34th "
32. A.D.M.S., 41st "
33. Diary.
34. File.

Oct 1918

14th DIVISION.
****

VR 39

140/0323

WAR DIARY of A.D.M.S., 14th DIVISION.
****

From:- 1st October, 1918.
To:- 31st October, 1918.

1/11/18.

COMMITTEE FOR THE
MEDICAL HISTORY OF THE WAR
Date 4 DEC. 1918

Army Form C. 2118.

Instructions regarding War Diaries and Intelligence Summaries are contained in F. S. Regs., Part II. and the Staff Manual respectively. Title pages will be prepared in manuscript.

WAR DIARY
or
INTELLIGENCE SUMMARY.
(*Erase heading not required.*)

Place	Date	Hour	Summary of Events and Information	Remarks and references to Appendices
WARATAH CAMP 28/G15a5.1.	1/10/18		Visited ADMS 30th Div, DDMS XV Corps and ADSto of 30th Div at MESSINES	APS
"	2/10/18		43rd F Amb moved from WHITE FARM 27/L23a60 to 28/T10 central and established a M.DSta there and	
			an A.D.Sta at MESSINES in conjunction with 97th and 98th F Ambs respectively.	app'dix. 1.
			Reconnoitred for a site for 44th F Amb on NEUVE EGLISE – DRANOUTRE ROAD	APS
"	3/10/18		Visited MDSta, ADSta, 44th F Amb at OUDERDOM and 42nd F Amb at ARNEKE (Sheet 28).	
			44th F Amb moved to 28/S 18 d 5.9.	APS
"	4/10/18		DMS and DDMS visited MDSta. Two Sections 44th F Amb moved from OUDERDOM to VLAMERTINGHE	
			to take medical charge of 42nd and 43rd Inf Bdes in the YPRES area. Reconnoitred for DRS site at BAILLEUL	app'dix 2. APS
"	5/10/18		Visited 44th F Amb at VLAMERTINGHE and 42nd and 43rd Inf Bde HQs at YPRES. 42nd F Amb	app'dix 3
			moved from ARNEKE to 'The Asylum' at BAILLEUL and established DRS there	APS
"	6/10/18		Visited DDMS XV Corps and ADMS 31st DIV. Visited DRSta. HQ and 1 Section of 44th F Amb	app'dix 3.
			rejoined remainder of unit at VLAMERTINGHE	APS
"	7/10/18		Visited 43rd F Amb at 28/T10 Central.	APS
"	8/10/18		Visited MDSta, ADSta and 41st Inf Bde HQ (Bde in the line)	APS
"	9/10/18		ADMS office moved from WARATAH CAMP to CAESTRE (Sheet 27). 42nd F Amb and	
			DRSta moved from BAILLEUL to ST JANS CAPPEL	APS

(A9175) Wt W2353/P360 600,000 12/17 D. D. & L. Sch. 52a. Forms/C2118/15.

Instructions regarding War Diaries and Intelligence Summaries are contained in F. S. Regs., Part II, and the Staff Manual respectively. Title pages will be prepared in manuscript.

WAR DIARY
or
INTELLIGENCE SUMMARY.
(Erase heading not required.)

Army Form C. 2118.

Place	Date	Hour	Summary of Events and Information	Remarks and references to Appendices
CAESTRE	10/10/18		visited M.DSn and new DRS at ST JANS CAPPEL	APS
"	11/10/18		Routine Duties.	APS
"	12/10/18		visited 43rd FAmb, 42nd Inf/Bde HQ (at YPRES) and 44th FAmb	APS
"	13/10/18		44th FAmb moved from VLAMERTINGHE to 28/M.33.c.43. visited Advanced Div. HQ at WULVERGHEM (Sheet 28) and MDSn.	app'dix 4 APS
"	14/10/18		Patrols of 14th Div crossed river LYS. RAMC Order No 15 issued reference projected operations on divisional front. DADMS remained in neighbourhood of Advanced Div HQ to maintain liaison between MDSn and Div HQ.	app'dix 5. APS
"	15/10/18		visited 43rd FAmb. 43rd FAmb established ADSn at HOUTHEM (28/P20 a 03), a Bearer Relay Post at 28/P16 d 02 and Car Relay Post at 28/P.15 c.	app'dix 6 APS
"	16/10/18		ADSn moved from MESSINES to 28/P.31 d 37. 2 (O.R) reinforcements received	app'dix 6A APS
"	17/10/18		visited 42nd FAmb. ADMS office moved from CAESTRE to CORPS FARM. (28/T10 Central) 44th FAmb established M.DSn at MESSINES at 1100.	app'dix 6A. APS
CORPS FARM	18/10/18		ADMS visited ADSns. Div HQ (Advanced) moved to WERVICQ-SUD (Sheet 28). 44th FAmb moved to 28/V12 a 9.9 and established ADSn there. ADSn at 28/P31 d 3.7. Converted into MD.Sn. 43rd FAmb in afternoon moved to 28/V12 a 99 and established MDSn there. 44th FAmb and ADSn moved to LE BLANC FOUR (28/X 19 d). 20 (O.R) reinforcements received.	appdix 7 app'dix 8 APS.

Instructions regarding War Diaries and Intelligence Summaries are contained in F. S. Regs., Part II. and the Staff Manual respectively. Title pages will be prepared in manuscript.

Army Form C. 2118.

WAR DIARY
or
INTELLIGENCE SUMMARY.
(Erase heading not required.)

Place	Date	Hour	Summary of Events and Information	Remarks and references to Appendices
CORPS FARM	19/10/18		ADMS office moved from CORPS FARM to LE BLANC FOUR (28/X19d). 44th F Amb moved to WATTRELOS (37/A22c) and established ADSn there. 43rd F Amb and M.D.Sn moved to LE BLANC FOUR. Visited 43rd F Amb. 42nd F Amb and DRSn moved to 28/P.36 b 6.3.	APS.
LE BLANC FOUR	20/10/18		Visited 44th F Amb and ADSn	APS
"	21/10/18		ADMS Office moved to MOUSCRON (29/S22 a 6 4)	APS
MOUSCRON	22/10/18		Visited 44th F Amb. Reconnoitred for site for DRSn at PETIT AUDENARDE (Sheet 37). 42nd F Amb and DRSn moved to 37/A18. b. 8 2. 44th F Amb established an ADSn at 37/B.9.a. 3.4. 43rd F Amb and MDSn moved to 37/A22. c 3.8.	app'dix 1 APS.
"	23/10/18.		DDMS XV Corps visited ADMS. ADMS recommended (to GOC Div) formation of Early Treatment Rooms for Venereal Disease.	APS
"	24/10/18.		Visited Town Commandant TOURCOING re procedure for Segregation of civilian Venereal Cases. Visited DRSn.	APS.
"	25/10/18		Bearer Relay Post establishing at 29/U21. a 9 8. and Car Relay Post at 29/U20 d. 7. 8.)	APS
"	26/10/18.		Visited Early Treatment Room at LUIGNE (Sheet 29) of 29th DLI and Baths at HERSEAUX (Sh. 37)	APS
"	27/10/18		Visited 43rd and 44th F Ambs and the DRSn (42nd F Amb)	APS
"	28/10/18		G.O.C. Div. inspected the F Ambs. Visited DDMS XV Corps.	APS
"	29/10/18		DDMS inspected 43rd F Amb.	APS
"	30/10/18		Visited 43rd and 44th F Ambs. 1 (officer) reinforcement received. 1 officer sent to 30th Div (struck off strength).	APS
"	31/10/18.		Visited 42nd and 44th F Ambs.	APS

A P Saint major RAMC
DADMS 14th Div

(A9175) Wt W2358/P360 600,000 12/17 D. D. & L. Sch. 52a. Forms/C2118/15.

SECRET.

Appendix No 1

Copy No. 31......

ADMINISTRATIVE ORDER No. 29 by Colonel J. Hay Campbell, D.S.O., A.M.S., Commanding R.A.M.Corps, 14th Division.

Reference Map - Sheet 28, 1/40,000

1. The 14th Division will move to the MESSINES - WYTSCHAETE - KEMMEL Area on 1st and 2nd October.

2. The 41st Infantry Brigade will take over the line of the WARNETON - COMINES Railway from U.12 central to P.33 d 0.4. from the 30th Division; relief to be completed by 1200 on 2nd October.

3. The 43rd Field Ambulance will take over part of the accommodation of the 30th Division A.D.Station at MESSINES from O.C., 98th Field Ambulance as an A.D.Station, and part of the accommodation of the 30th Division M.D.Station at T.10 central from O.C., 97th Field Ambulance as a M.D.Station by 1800 on 2nd October; details of accommodation to be arranged direct between Os. C. concerned.

4. The O.C., 43rd Field Ambulance will be responsible for the collection and evacuation of sick and wounded from Units of the 14th Division in the line from 1800 on 2nd October up to which time they will be evacuated through the A.D.Station of the 30th Division.

5. The O.C., 44th Field Ambulance will be responsible for the collection of sick from all Units of the Division not provided for in para: 4 from 0600 on 2nd October.

6. The 44th Field Ambulance will move on 3rd October to a site on the NEUVE EGLISE - DRANOUTRE Road, the location of which will be notified later.

7. The D.R.Station (42nd Field Ambulance) will remain for the present at ARNEKE.

8. Field Ambulances to acknowledge.

A. D. M. S.
No
Date 1/10/18.
14th DIVISION

R Saint

Major, D.A.D.M.S.,
14th Division.

Distribution:-

1 - 3, Field Ambulances.
4 -18, R. M. Os.
19, O.C., No. 14 M.A.C.
20, 14th Division "G".
21, " " "A"
22, C.R.A., 14th Division.
23, C.R.E., " "
24, 41st Inf: Brigade.
25, 42nd " "
26, O.C., 14th Div: Train.
27, D.D.M.S., XV Corps.
28, " " " " XIX "
29, A.D.M.S., 30th Division.
30, " " " " 31st "
31,32, War Diary.
33, File.

SECRET.

Copy No. 20.

ADMINISTRATIVE ORDER No. 30 by Colonel, J. Hay Campbell, D.S.O., A.M.S., Commanding R.A.M.Corps, 14th Division

****

Reference Map - Sheet 28, 1/40,000.

1. The 44th Field Ambulance will send two Sections to the YPRES Area on 4th October, 1918, from which date inclusive they will be in Medical charge of the 42nd and 43rd Infantry Brigades.

2. An advance party from 44th Field Ambulance will proceed to VLAMERTINGHE on 3rd inst: and obtain billets for above two Sections from the Area Commandant, VLAMERTINGHE.
Location of billets allotted to be notified to this Office.

3. O.C. Sections will apply to Staff Captains, 42nd Infantry Brigade, (28/I.10 d 2.1.) and 43rd Infantry Brigade, (28/I.8 a 5.4.), for locations of Units.

4. The remaining Section and H.Q., of 44th Field Ambulance will remain at 28/S.17 d 8.8. in charge of Divisional sick not provided for by 43rd Field Ambulance and above two Sections.

5. 44th Field Ambulance to acknowledge.

3/10/18.

A. R. Saint
Major,
for Colonel, A.D.M.S.,
14th Division.

Distribution:-
1. 44th Field Ambulance.
2. 43rd " "
3-8. R.M.Os of 42nd & 43rd Inf: Bdes.
9. 14th Division "G".
10. " " "A".
11. C.R.E., 14th Division.
12. H.Q., 42nd Infantry Bde.
13. " 43rd " "
14. " 14th Div: Train.
15. D.D.M.S., XV Corps.
16. " " " " II "
17. Area Commandant, VLAMERTINGHE.
18-19. Diary
20. File.

SECRET..

Appendix No 3

Copy No. 28

ADMINISTRATIVE ORDER No. 61 by Colonel J. Kay Campbell, D.S.O., A. D. M. S., Commanding R.A.M.Corps, 14th Division.

------------------- oOo -------------------

Reference Maps:- Sheets 27 and 28, 1/40,000.

1. The 42nd Field Ambulance will move on 5th instant from the HOSPICE, ARNEKE to the ASYLUM, BAILLEUL, staging night 5th/6th at CAESTRE.

2. An Advance Party will proceed to BAILLEUL on 5th instant and relieve holding party of 44th Field Ambulance.

3. On arrival at BAILLEUL, the 42nd Field Ambulance will establish a D.R.Station, and collect the sick of Units now in medical charge of H.Q. Section 44th Field Ambulance (at - 28/S.17 d 5.9.), commencing on 7th instant.

4. The H.Q. Section, 44th Field Ambulance will rejoin remaining Sections at MOATED FARM, VLAMERTINGHE, (28/H.2 d 7.2.) on 6th instant.

5. Field Ambulances to acknowledge.

A. D. M. S. No. 4/10/18. 14th DIVISION

A. Saint
Major,
for Colonel, A.D.M.S.,
14th Division.

Distribution:-
1-3. Field Ambulances.
4-18. All R.M.Os.
19. 14 M.A.C.
20. 14th Division "G".
21. " " "A".
22. " Signal Coy, R.E.
23. H.Q., 41st Infantry Bde.
24. " 42nd " "
25. " 43rd " "
26. 14th Div: Train.
27. D.D.M.S., XV Corps.
28-29. War Diary.
30. File.

SECRET.

Copy No. 21

ADMINISTRATIVE ORDER No. [illegible] by Colonel J. Hay Campbell. D.S.O.
A.D.M.S., Commanding R.A.M.Corps, 14th Division.

---------------o0o---------------

Reference maps:- Sheets 27 & 28, 1/40,000.

1. The 43rd Infantry Brigade will move on October 12th and the 42nd Infantry Brigade on October 13th from the YPRES Area to the 14th Divisional Area.

2. The 44th Field Ambulance will move on the 13th Octr: from VLAMERTINGHE to 28/H.33 c 4.5.

3. From 13th inst: inclusive the sick of the 43rd Infantry Brigade will be collected by 43rd Field Ambulance. The Units of the Brigade will be located as follows:-

Headquarters	...	T.5 b central.
"A" Battn:	...	T.8 a.
"B" & "C" Battns:.		T.5 a and T.[illegible] a.

4. From 14th inst: inclusive the 44th Field Ambulance will collect the sick of the 42nd Infantry Brigade and of all troops (less the D.R.C.) now under the medical charge of the 43rd Field Ambulance. Units of the 42nd Infantry Brigade will be located as follows:-

Headquarters	...	T.8 c 1.8.
"A" Battn: .	...	T.8 a.
"B" & "C" Battns:.		N.31 a and c.

5. Field Ambulances to ACKNOWLEDGE.

A.R. Saint
Major,
for Colonel, A.D.M.S.,
14th Division.

12/10/18.

Distribution:-

1-3. Field Ambulances.
4-18. R.M.Os.
19. 14th Division "A"
20-22. Infantry Brigades.
23. 14th Div: Train.
24. D.D.M.S., II Corps
25. " " " " XV "
26-27. War Diary.
28. File.

SECRET.

Appendix No 5

Copy No. 33

R.A.M.C. OPERATION ORDER No. 15 by Colonel J. Hay Campbell, D.S.O. A.D.M.S., Commanding R.A.M.Corps, 14th Division.

----------------- oOo -------------------

Reference Map:- Sheet, 28, 1/40,000.

1. The 14th Division may be called upon to advance at short notice in case the pressure of the X Corps attack induces the enemy to relinquish his positions on the Divisional front.

2. O.C., 43rd Field Ambulance will be prepared to move forward all Medical Posts at short notice in accordance with the progress of operations.

3. At Zero hour the medical situation will be as follows:-

R.A.Ps.:-
28/P.26 b 9.1.
28/O.36 b 3.6.
28/O.35 c 6.5.
28/O.30 b 2.3. (Artillery).

Bearer Relay Posts:-
28/O.36 b 3.6.
28/U. 4 b 2.8.
28/O.30 d 2.2. (Artillery).

A.D.Station:- MESSINES.

M.D.Station:- 28/T.10 central.

There will be no separate W.W.C.P. and Walking Wounded will proceed direct to the A.D.Station. 3 Lorries will report to O.C., 43rd Field Ambulance at 0930 on 14th October for employment in conveyance of Walking Wounded to C.C.Stations.

4. Os.C., 42nd and 44th Field Ambulances will each send all Ford Cars and one Sunbeam immediately to the Main Dressing Station.

5. O.C., 43rd Field Ambulance will apply direct to Os.C., 42nd and 44th Field Ambulances for additional Officers, Bearers and Cars if required. Personnel for this purpose will be earmarked at once by Os.C. concerned, and remain in readiness to proceed at a moments notice to the M.D.Station for duty with 43rd Field Ambulance.

6. Advanced Brigade Headquarters will be at ESPERANCE CABARET, O.36 b 3.6.

7. Either the A.D.M.S. or the D.A.D.M.S. will be at the Main Dressing Station during the 14th October. The A.D.M.S. Office will remain for the present at CAESTRE.

13/10

8. Field Ambulances to ACKNOWLEDGE.

A P Saint
Major,
for Colonel, A.D.M.S.,
14th Division.

Distribution:-
1. 42nd Field Ambulance.
2. 43rd " "
3. 44th " "
4-18. R.M.Os.
19. 14th M.A.C.
20. 14th Div: "G".
21. " " "A".
22. C.R.A., 14th Div:
23. C.R.E., " "
24. 14th Signal Coy, R.E.
25. D.A.P.M., 14th Division.
26. D.G.O., 14th Division.
27. H.Q., 41st Inf: Bde.
28. " 42nd " "
29. " 43rd " "
30. D.D.M.S., XV Corps
31. A.D.M.S., 30th Div:
32-33. War Diary.
34. File.

SECRET. Appendix No 6

Copy No. 32

R.A.M.C.OPERATION ORDER No. 16 by Colonel, A. Hay Campbell. D.S.O., A.M.S., Commanding R.A.M.Corps, 14th Division.

---------------- oOo ----------------

Reference Map:- Sheet 28, 1/40,000.

1. On the night 15th/16th October the 43rd Infantry Brigade will relieve the 21st Infantry Brigade (30th Division), on the front from the LYS at P.30 a 5.8. to the DUC DE BOURGOYNE CABARET (Q.20 d.) inclusive.

2. R.A.Ps. of Battalions in the Line will be located at:-

P.21 b 7.1.

and

P.23 b 9.8.

3. On the night 15th /16th October, the 43rd Field Ambulance will post squads of Bearers at the R.A.Ps. mentioned in para: 2, and will take over Bearer Relay Post at P.16 d 0.2. and Car Loading Post at P.15 c from the 98th Field Ambulance, (H.Q., at P.30 a 0.5.). Advance parties will proceed to those Posts before 1800 on the 15th October.

4. An A.D.Station will be established by the 43rd Field Ambulance at HOUTHEM (P.30 a 0.5.) on the night 15th/16th October. For the present the accommodation at this station will be shared with 98th Field Ambulance by arrangement ~~with~~ between Os.C. concerned.

5. Evacuation of wounded from the A.D.Station will be via OOSTAVERNE and WYTSCHAETE to the M.D.Station at T.10 central.

6. Field Ambulances to ACKNOWLEDGE.

A.E.Saint
Major,
for Colonel, A.D.M.S.,
14th Division.

15/10/18.

Distribution:-

1-3. Field Ambulances.
4-18. R.M.Os.
19. 14th M.A.C.
20. 14th Div: "A".
21. " " "G"
22. C.R.A., 14th Div:
23. C.R.E., " "
24. 14th Signal Coy, R.E.
25. D.A.P.M., 14th Div:
26. D.G.O., " "
27/29. H.Q., Inf: Bdes:.
30. D.D.M.S., XV Corps.
31. A.D.M.S., 30th Div:
32/33. War Diary.
34. File.

SECRET.

Copy No. 32

OPERATION ORDER No. 17 by Colonel J. Hay Campbell, D.S.O., A.M.S., Commanding R.A.M.Corps, 14th Division.

---------------- oOo ----------------

Reference Map:- Sheet, 28, 1/40,000.

1. The O.C., 43rd Field Ambulance will move forward the A.D.Station from MESSINES to P.31 d 3.7. by 1400 on 16th October.

2. The 44th Field Ambulance will move to MESSINES and establish a Main Dressing Station in the premises of the present A.D.Station by 1100 on October 17th up to which time the M.D. Station at T.10. central will continue to function.
An advanced party of 44th Field Ambulance will proceed at once to MESSINES.

3. Personnel of 43rd Field Ambulance remaining at T.10. central will proceed to rejoin remainder of Unit at P.31 d 3.7. at 1100 on 17th October.

4. The 2 Marquees now at T.10 central will be handed over forthwith by the 43rd Field Ambulance to the 44th Field Ambulance.

5. Field Ambulances to acknowledge.

A.D.M.S. No. 15/10/18 14th DIVISION

A.B. Saint Major
for Colonel, A.D.M.S.,
14th Division.

Distribution:-
1-3. Field Ambulances.
4-18. R.M.Os.
19. 14th M.A.C.
20. 14th Div: "G".
21. " " "A".
22. C.R.A., 14th Division.
23. C.R.E., " "
24. 14th Signal Coy, R.E.
25. D.G.O.
26-28. H.Q., Inf: Bdes.
29. 14th Div: Train.
30. D.D.M.S., XV Corps.
31. A.D.M.S., 30th Divn:
32-33. War Diary.
34. File.

SECRET.

Appendix No 7

Copy No. 34

OPERATION ORDER No. 18 by Colonel J. Hay Campbell, D.S.O., A.M.S., Commanding R.A.M.Corps, 14th Division.

------------ oOo ------------

Reference Map:- Sheet, 28, 1/40,000.

1. The 44th Field Ambulance will move from MOSSINES to 28/V.13 a 9.9. at 0830 on October 18th.

2. An A.D.Station will be established at this site on the 18th October, which will be ready for the reception of casualties by 0930, and the present A. D. Station will commence to function as a M.D.Station at the same hour.

3. Field Ambulances to acknowledge.

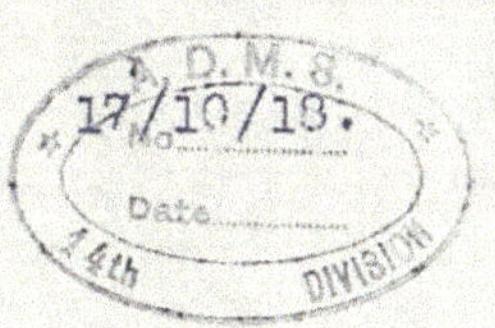

A.B.Saint
Major,
for Colonel, A.D.M.S.,
14th Division.

Distribution:-

1-3. Field Ambulances.
4-18. R.M.Os.
19. 14th M.A.C.
20. 14th Div: "G".
21. " " "A".
22. C.R.A., 14th Div:.
23. C.R.E., 14th "
24. 14th Signal Coy, R.E.
25. D.G.O.
26. 41st Inf: Bde.
27. 42nd " "
28. 43rd " "
29. 14th Div: Train.
30. D.D.M.S., XV Corps.
31. A.D.M.S., 30th Div:.
32. " " " " 31st "
33-34. War Diary.
35. File.

SECRET.

Copy No. 33

OPERATION ORDER No. 19 by Colonel J. Kay Campbell, D.S.O., A.M.S., Commanding R.A.M.Corps, 14th Division.

--------- oOo ----------

Reference Maps:- Sheets, 28, 29 and 37, 1/40,000.

1. The 43rd Infantry Brigade Group is advancing on 18th October to the Line 37/A.5 central - 29/S.30 central - 29/S.24 central - 29/S.17 central along railway to PETIT CORNIL and the 42nd Infantry Brigade is moving into Area NEUVILLE - TRIER PRETRES - BETHLEHEM - DRONCKAK.

2. The O.C., 44th Field Ambulance will move forward the A.D. Station from 28/V.12 a 9.9. to a suitable position in rear of 43rd Infantry Brigade by direct arrangement with B.G.C. 43rd Infantry Brigade, notifying new location to 14th Division "A" and to this Office.

3. When the A.D.Station has been advanced, the O.C., 43rd Field Ambulance will move forward the M.D.Station from 28/P.31 d 3.7. to 28/V.12 a 9.9., a holding party of the 44th Field Ambulance being left in charge of the site until it is taken over by 43rd Field Ambulance.

4. The O.C., 42nd Field Ambulance will move forward one Section from ST. JANS CAPPEL to 28/P.31 d 3.7. on 19th October to establish the nucleus of a new D.R.Station at this site.

5. Field Ambulances to acknowledge.

A.D.M.S. No. ___ 18/10/18.

A.P. Saint
Major,
for Colonel, A.D.M.S.
14th Division.

Distribution:-

1-3. Field Ambulances.
4-18. R.M.Os.
19. 14th M.A.C.
20. 14th Div: "G".
21. " " "A".
22. C.R.A., 14th Div:.
23. C.R.E., 14th "
24. 14th Signal Coy, R.E.
25. D.[illegible].C.
26. 41st Inf: Bde.
27. 42nd " "
28. 43rd " "
29. 14th Div: Train.
30. D.D.M.S., XV Corps.
31. A.D.M.S., 30th Div:.
32. " " " " 31st "
33-34. War Diary.
35. File.

Appendix No 9.

SECRET.

Copy No. 33

ADMINISTRATIVE ORDER No. 34 by Colonel J. May Campbell, D.S.O., A.M.S., Commanding R.A.M.Corps, 14th Division.

---------- o0o ----------

Reference Maps:- Sheets, 28 and 37, 1/40,000.

1. The 43rd Field Ambulance will move on 22nd October from LE BLANC FOUR to WATTRELOS.

2. On arrival at WATTRELOS, the O.C., 43rd Field Ambulance will establish a Main Dressing Station at 37/A.22 c 3.8

3. An Advanced Dressing Station will be established by 44th Field Ambulance at 37/B.9 a 3.4. on 22nd October. H.Q., 44th Field Ambulance will remain at present site (WATTRELOS).

4. Field Ambulances to acknowledge.

A.D.M.S. 22/10/18. Date 14th DIVISION

A B Saint
Major,
for Colonel, A.D.M.S.,
14th Division.

Distribution:-
1-3. Field Ambulances
4-18. R.M.Os.
19. 14th M.A.C.
20. 14th Div: "Q".
21. " " "A".
22. C.R.A., 14th Div:
23. C.R.E., " "
24. 14th Signal Coy, R.E.
25. D.G.O.
26. H.Q., 41st Inf: Bde.
27. " 43rd " "
28. " 43rd " "
29. 14th Div: Train.
30. D.D.M.S., XV Corps.
31. A.D.M.S., 30th Div:
32. " " " " 31st "
33-34. War Diary.
35. File.

SECRET.

Copy No. 32

14th DIVISION.

MEDICAL ARRANGEMENTS No. 17.

Reference Maps:- Sheets, 29 and 37, 1/40,000.

EVACUATION OF WOUNDED.

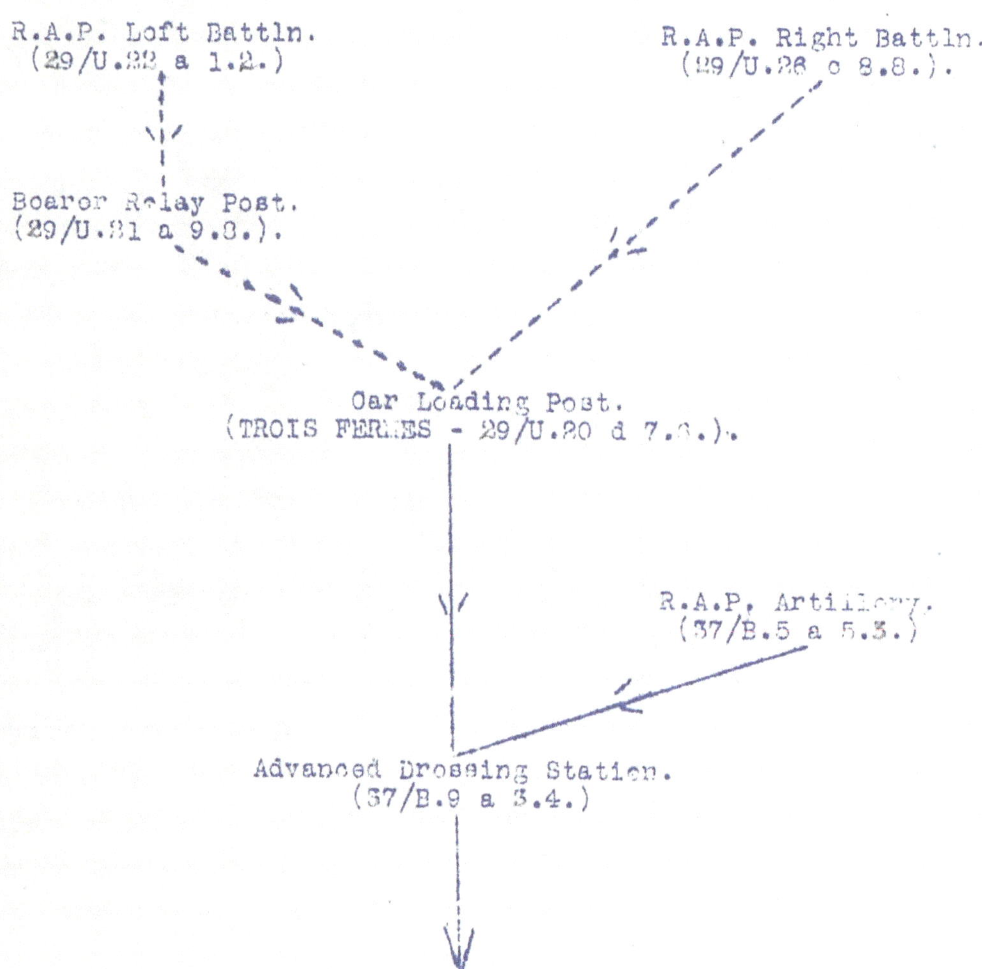

Main Dressing Station.
(37/A.22 c 9.9.).

31/10/18.

A. Saint
Major,
for Colonel, A.D.M.S.,
14th Division.

------------- Hand Carriage and Wheeled Stretcher
_____________ Motor Ambulance Car.

Distribution:-

1. 42nd Field Ambulance.
2. 43rd " "
3. 44th " "
4-18. R.M.Os.
19. 14th M.A.C.
20. 14th Division "G".
21. " " "A".
22. C.R.A., 14th Division.
23. C.R.E., " "
24. 14th Signal Coy, R.E.
25. D.G.O.
26. 41st Infantry Bde.
27. 42nd " "
28. 43rd " "
29. D.D.M.S., XV Corps.
30. A.D.M.S., 40th Division.
31. " " " " 30th "
32-33. War Diary.
34. File.

Nov 1918 4

140/3400

Vol 40

14th DIVISION.
****

W A R D I A R Y.
***** **********

of

A.D.M.S., 14th Division.

for period.

1st November, 1918.
to
30th November, 1918.

****

A.D.M.S. No. 30/11/18. 14th Division

COMMITTEE FOR THE MEDICAL HISTORY OF THE WAR
Date 10 MAR 1919

Instructions regarding War Diaries and Intelligence Summaries are contained in F. S. Regs., Part II. and the Staff Manual respectively. Title pages will be prepared in manuscript.

DAC

Army Form C. 2118.

WAR DIARY
or
INTELLIGENCE SUMMARY.
(Erase heading not required.)

Place	Date	Hour	Summary of Events and Information	Remarks and references to Appendices
MOUSCRON	1/11/18		visited 44th F Amb	APS
"	2/11/18		went to MENIN and arranged with M.O 30th Div. Reception Camp to inspect Sick from 14th Div reception camp in that town	APS
"	3/11/18		visited 43rd F Amb.	APS
"	4/11/18		ADMS office moved to 9 PLACE DE THIERS, TOURCOING. visited D.R. Stn.	APS
TOURCOING	5/11/18		visited M.O 14th DAC and inspected 14th DAC venereal early treatment Room	APS
"	6/11/18		visited MAIRE of WATTRELOS and Civilian doctor reference assistance to be given by 43rd F Amb in coping with influenza epidemic among civilians. visited 44th F Amb	APS
"	7/11/18		Routine duties	APS
"	8/11/18		DDMS XV corps visited ADMS. Visited 44th F Amb	APS
"	9/11/18		A.D.Stn. moved to ESPIERRES. Germans found to have retired from front facing 14th Divn. 14th division placed in Corps reserve. ADMS visited A.D Stn.	appdx 1. APS
"	10/11/18		visited 42nd F Amb	appdx 2 APS
"	11/11/18		Order received at 0800 that hostilities to cease at 1100.	APS
"	12/11/18		visited No 9 B.R.C. Hospital	APS

(A9175) Wt W2358/P360 600,000 12/17 D. D. & L. Sch. 52a. Forms/C2118/15.

Instructions regarding War Diaries and Intelligence Summaries are contained in F. S. Regs., Part II. and the Staff Manual respectively. Title pages will be prepared in manuscript.

WAR DIARY
or
INTELLIGENCE SUMMARY.
(Erase heading not required.)

Army Form C. 2118.

Place	Date	Hour	Summary of Events and Information	Remarks and references to Appendices
				A. Thomson Capt
TURCOING	13/11/18		The A.D.M.S visited 43rd F.A. and 42nd F.A.	
"	14/11/18		The 43rd F.A moved from WATTERLOS to BONDUES Area, and is located at 36/E 22 b 9-3. The D.D.M.S XV Corps, visited the A.D.M.S. The A.D.M.S. attended a conference on Education at Turcoing.	AT appendix 3
"	15/11/18		44th F.A moved under 43rd Bde Infantry arrangements to Turcoing.	AT appendix 4
"	16/11/18		The A.D.M.S visited 43rd and 44th F.A. at their new locations	AT
"	17/11/18		Routine duties.	AT
"	18/11/18		Major General Guise-Moore, with D.D.M.S. visited 44th F.A at TURCOING; where the officers and N.C.O's of 43rd F.A paraded also. He then proceeded to 42nd F.A to visit the D.R.S. This (visit) was a farewell on our Division leaving the 2nd Army.	AT
"	19/11/18		Routine office duties	AT
"	20-11-18		Capt. THOMSON proceeded on leave to Paris. ADMS visited 44 F.As [illegible]	
"	21-11-18		Routine duties. Instructions issued for [illegible] F.As to act as "S.M.O's" [illegible] in Infantry Brigade [illegible] groups, with special reference to supervision of sanitation	JWL
"	22-11-18		F.As asked to submit schemes for [illegible] training (to include instruction in RAMC technical subjects) & "education".	JWL
"	23-11-18		Routine duties - ADMS visited TOURCOING [illegible]	JWL

D. D. & L., London, E.C.
(A8001) Wt. W1-71/M2031 750,000 5/17 Sch. 52 Forms/C2118/14

Instructions regarding War Diaries and Intelligence Summaries are contained in F. S. Regs., Part II. and the Staff Manual respectively. Title pages will be prepared in manuscript.

WAR DIARY
or
INTELLIGENCE SUMMARY.
(Erase heading not required.)

Army Form C. 2118.

Place	Date	Hour	Summary of Events and Information	Remarks and references to Appendices
TOURCOING	24/11/18		Visited DDMS XVth Corps	APS
"	25/11/18		Visited DDMS XVth Corps. Conference of Ambulance Commanders re new influenza vaccine	APS
"	26/11/18		Visited 42nd F Amb and 14th M.T. Coy.	APS
"	27/11/18		DDMS XVth Corps visited ADMS	APS
"	28/11/18		Routine duties	APS
"	29/11/18		Visited 44th F Amb	APS
"	30/11/18.		Visited 43rd F Amb and 46th Sanitary Section	APS.

A.P. Saint Major
DADMS
14th Div.

D. D. & L., London, E.C.
(A8001) Wt. W1 71/M2031 750,000 5/17 Sch. 52 Forms/C2118/14

SECRET.

app'dix 1

Copy No.

OPERATION ORDER No. 20 by Colonel, J. Hay Campbell, D.S.O., A.M.S., Commanding R.A.M.Corps, 14th Division.

---------------------------- oOo ----------------------------

Reference Maps, Sheets, 29 and 37, 1/40,000.

1. The 14th Division will attack the enemy on "J" day on the front, C.21 b 2.7. to U.30 c. central.

2. The 43rd Infantry Brigade will be in the front line, the 42nd Infantry Brigade in Support and the 41st Infantry Brigade in Reserve.

3. On J - 1 day the O.C., 44th Field Ambulance will move forward the A.D.Station from 37/B.9 c 3.4. to DOTTIGNIES, 37/B.5 b 3.4.

4. At "H" hour on "J" day the Medical Situation will be as follows:-

R.A.Ps. at 29/U.28 a 1.2. - Left Battn:
29/U.28 c 9.7. - Right "
29/U.19 c 6.8.)
37/B. 5 a 5.3.)- Artillery.

Bearer Relay Post ... 29/U.21 a 9.8.

Car Loading Post ... 29/U.20 d 7.8.

Advanced Dressing Stn:. at DOTTIGNIES (37/B.5 b 3.4.).

Main Dressing Station " WATTRELOS, 37/A.22 c 9.9.

5. On "J" day the Advanced Dressing Station will be advanced to ESPIERRES Chateau, 37/C.2 d 8.3. as soon as the tactical situation permits.

6. As soon as the Advanced Dressing Station has been advanced as in para: 5 the O.C., 43rd Field Ambulance will establish a Main Dressing Station at DOTTIGNIES.

7. Motor Ambulance Cars will work as far forward as possible and will cross the ESCAUT by bridge at HELCHIN as soon as this is available.

8. O.C., 44th Field Ambulance will apply direct to Os.C., 42nd and 43rd Field Ambulances for any additional Officers, Bearers or Cars required.

9. Field Ambulances to acknowledge.

A.D.M.S. No. 8/11/18. Date 14th Division

A.Saint
Major,
for Colonel, A.D.M.S.,
14th Division.

PTO

Distribution:-

1-3. Field Ambulances.
4-18. R.M.Os.
19. 14 M.A.C.
20. 14th Div: "G".
21. 14th " "A".
22. C.R.A., 14th Div:
23. C.R.E., " "
24. 14th Signal Coy, R.E.
25. D.G.O., 14th Div:
26. H.Q., 41st Inf: Bde.
27. " " 42nd " "
28. " " 43rd " "
29. 14th Div: Train.
30. D.D.M.S., XV Corps.
31. A.D.M.S., 39th Div:
32. " " " " 40th "
33-34. War Diary.
35. File.

appdix 2

SECRET.

Copy No. 34

OPERATION ORDER No. 21 by Colonel J. Hay Campbell, D.S.O., A.M.S., Commanding R.A.M.Corps, 14th Division ... ...

---------------------------- oOo ----------------------------

Reference Maps:- Sheets, 29 and 37, 1/40,000.

1. O.C., 44th Field Ambulance will move the Advanced Dressing Station to ESPIERRES Chateau, 37/C.2 d 8.3. by 1230 on November 9th.

2. The Main Dressing Station will remain for the present at WATTRELOS.

3. Field Ambulances to acknowledge.

A. R. Saint
Major
for Colonel, A.D.M.S.,
14th Division.

A.D.M.S.
No.
9/11/18.

Distribution:-

1-3. Field Ambulances.
4-18. R.M.Os.
19. 14 M.A.C.
20. 14th Div: "G".
21. " " "A".
22. C.R.A., 14th Divn:
23. C.R.E., " "
24. 14th Signal Coy, R.E.
25. D.G.O., 14th Divn:
26. H.Q., 41st Inf: Bde.
27. " " 42nd " "
28. " " 43rd " "
29. 14th Div: Train.
30. D.D.M.S., XV Corps.
31. A.D.M.S., 29th Divn:
32. " " " " 40th "
33-34. War Diary.
35. File.

SECRET.

Appx 3

Copy No. 9

OPERATION ORDER No. 21 by Colonel J. Hay Campbell, D.S.O., A.M.S.
Commanding R.A.M.Corps, 14th DIVISION ... ...

-------------- oOo --------------

Reference Maps:- Sheets 36 and 37, 1/40,000.

1. The 43rd Field Ambulance will move tomorrow, 14th inst: to the BONDUES Area, under 41st Infantry Brigade orders, and will continue to collect the sick of this Brigade.

2. The 42nd Infantry Bde is moving from DOTTIGNIES to HERSEAUX tomorrow, 14th inst:, and the 42nd Field Ambulance will collect the sick of this Brigade.

3. Field Ambulances to acknowledge.

A.D.M.S. No. 13/11/18. 14th DIVISION

R. Thomson.
Captain,
for Colonel, A.D.M.S.,
14th Division.

Distribution:-

1. 42nd Field Ambulance.
2. 43rd " "
3. 44th " "
4. H.Q., 41st Infantry Bde.
5. " " 42nd " "
6. 14th Division "G".
7. " " "A".
8 D.D.M.S., XV Corps.
9-10. War Diary.
11. File.

SECRET. *appx 4*

Copy No. *11*

OPERATION ORDER No. 93 by Colonel J. Hay Campbell, D.S.O., A.M.S., Commanding R.A.M.Corps, 14th Division.

---------------- oOo ----------------

1. The 44th Field Ambulance will move under 43rd Infantry Bde arrangements tomorrow morning, 15th inst; to TOURCOING.

2. The 42nd Field Ambulance will continue to collect the sick of 42nd Infantry Brigade.

3. Field Ambulances to acknowledge.

A.D.M.S. No. 14/11/18. Date 14th DIVISION

R. Thomson
Captain,
for Colonel, A.D.M.S.,
14th Division.

Distribution:-

1-3. Field Ambulances.
4. H.Q., 41st Inf: Bde.
5. " " 42nd " "
6. " " 43rd " "
7. 14th Division "G"
8. " " "A"
9. H.Q., 14th Divl: Train.
10. D.D.M.S., XV Corps.
11-12. War Diary.
13. File.

Dec. 1918 6

WAR DIARY OF A.D.M.S. OFFICE 14th DIVISION.

1st DECEMBER 1918
to
31st DECEMBER 1918.

140/3479